TEAM DYNAMICS

Essays in the Sociology and Social Psychology
of Sport including Methodological
and Epistemological Issues

HANS LENK

ISBN 0-87563-141-X

Published by
STIPES PUBLISHING COMPANY
10 - 12 Chester Street
Champaign, Illinois 61820

TABLE OF CONTENTS

iii

Conflict and Achievement in
Top Athletic Teams

Sociometric Structures of Racing Eight Oar Crews

Introduction

Top achievement teams of amateurs have hardly ever been analyzed by means of a sociometric investigation. However, it is just
these groups which perform achievements at an impressively high
level subsequent to long, systematic preparation. Achievements of
such a level are not performed by the frequently tested ad hoc groups
solving a determination task or spontaneously established groups, i.e.
in a situation which has hitherto been analyzed by social psychologists
(44; 45; 23, p. 155ff; 22, p. 56ff). In contradistinction to school
classes (39) a sports team performs a genuine group achievement which
is only engendered in the cooperation, that is, it is not additively
summed up from single and individual performances. Quality and efficiency of cooperation play a decisive role in these teams since they
enforce top achievement requirements against their members. However, amateur teams have to be distinguished from professional
groups insofar as their members voluntarily, without existential compulsion, without direct "material benefits," take over those team tasks
besides their usual vocational jobs. This might also be detached from
most professional working groups by the fact that the members are
approximately of the same age and young adults of the same sex. Together with the external group leadership, they establish the regimen
of preparation training as well as goal and aspiration level. Besides,
the group does not "produce" material objects to be purchased, but
materializes an abstract non-paid achievement of a symbolic value.
All these mentioned factors may lead to dynamically important group
distinctions in sociograms noticeable in contradistinction to the groups
of the kinds previously mentioned.

This is especially true for teams with a movement pattern of
equal form, like rowing. In spite of the narrow cooperation, hardly
a functionally hierarchically differentiated division of role assignment
determines the kind and level of achievement. [1] Does this lead to a
lower rank gradient (23, p. 169) within the team? Do rank differences
develop less distinctively than usual? Do leadership fights occur at
all? Are only weak conflicts to be found as a result with no dynamical
group causes? Does the high level of achievement particularly result

Translated from Soziale Welt 15(1964):307-343.

from such a lack of internal conflicts ? Or is one obliged, by contrast with functionalistic adaptation theory of "the less internal conflicts the higher the actual group achievement", to assess conflict to be less dysfunctional than unavoidable (Dahrendorf 9) ? The expression "conflict", by the way, is used here in a more general sense than in common language. Every obvious contrast or discrepancy of interests within a group is conflict in this sense. Is a certain measure of internal aggression to be looked upon as a motivating factor of top achieving behavior "igniting" so to speak, or at least furnishing conditions or prerequisites for this behavior ?[2]

Sixty-one percent of a representative sample of sportsmen of all disciplines responded to a questionnaire of filter questions, that they had joined a sporting group or club because of the "human relations" and the expected "comradeship". Only eight percent answered, "because of the sporting achievement". (10) Does the sociometric structure of top rowing eight oar crews allow conclusions to the effect that, in similar strength, the motive of looking for comrades, viz. an affiliation or sociability motive, outweighs the achievement motive when a person enters a team or when a crew itself comes into existence ?

The following investigations of four different German high performance eight oar crews present their respective sociometric structures in their characteristic features with respect to a mutual comparison and provide some first contributions to answer questions about rank differentiation, internal conflict, and achievement motivation.

The Investigated Crews

Questionnaires supplemented by extensive observation were completed with the following eight oar racing crews:

		Time of Questionnairing
O	Olympic champion eight oar crew from Ratzeburg and Kiel	1960
W	World champion eight of Ratzeburg	1962 and 1963
V	"Second eight" of Ratzeburg	1963
S	Eight oar crew of the training pool of Berlin-Spandau	1964

These crews may be distinguished from each other by characteristic and typical features. O was a so-called "racing association" crew, consisting of two subgroups of four rowers each, coming from two clubs, towns of which are located at a distance of 70 miles apart. I shall use the terms "racing (or training) association", "racing (or training) group (or squad)" synonymously, referring to a permanent cooperative partnership of at least two clubs recruiting crews together. In contrast to O, in S, athletes from four clubs formed a "racing and training association", consisting of five clubs, closely located, having permanently united to row together. W and Z were "pure club crews", that is, all their rowers belonged to the same club. Whereas W performed the world's best achievements, Z, in the same year, started in the lower, so-called "secondary class" of achievement, although relatively successfully. W and Z exercised together frequently.

The implications and consequences of the sociologically different recruitment and status of these crews can be particularly well compared because almost all other factors influenced the three crews O, W and Z in the same manner. The coach, the location and kind, as well as regimen of training, the boats, the time of joint training within the week, time scheduling and even place of regatta races were almost totally the same. Also, in these "pure" club crews, several rowers came from a distance and had to stay overnight in provisional lodging at the training location, the small town of Ratzeburg, like their predecessors from O. S had in common with these crews only the method and regimen of training.

Nearly all rowers were undergoing training for their professional careers. Whereas O was a crew consisting of students only, there were four students and one pupil in W and, in Z, four students and one elementary school teacher had joined together. In S, three students and one municipal clerk rowed together. All others were employees in their vocational training. One member of W had already participated in O. Coxswains were not submitted to the questionnaire. They were boys of fourteen to sixteen years of age, who did not represent equally valued and assessed partners for sociometric choices. This is true both for reasons of age and because their achievement, being a purely administrative-technical one which, although it is deemed necessary and decisive for success, will not be assessed as a genuine top athletic achievement. Only in one case, the coxswain was selected (π) and this, to be sure, was only as a roommate, although the formulation of the questions permitted the choosing of coxswains as boatfellows, too.

The Questions, Representation and Evaluation of Answers

The rowers should nominate on questionnaire forms:

1.   with which two rowers, from the whole training association squad, would they prefer to sit in the same boat (preference choice rowing);

3

2. with whom or with which two athletes from their own crew do they row "only reluctantly or unwillingly" ("rejection" rowing);

3. which rower from their own eight appears, in their opinion, to be the best one to be captain of the crew;

4. with which two rowers from the whole training group would they prefer to live in a room during a sports journey conducted to participate in a regatta, etc. (preference choice roommate);

5. with whom or with which two athletes from their own crew would they "only reluctantly or unwillingly" live, in the same room ("rejection" of roommate).

Although in questions 2 and 5, it was asked with whom one would only reluctantly or unwillingly row or live together, this sociometric choice will be called "rejection" in the following study. This word is basically too strong, but there was no short and yet apt expression. "Rejection" is to be understood as meaning "reluctantly" or "unwillingly". However, sometimes such "rejection" increased to become genuine conflict.

Combinations of related questions (1, 2 and 4, 5) made it frequently possible to determine whether the nomination followed merely personal sympathies or technical sporting criteria of preference, as, for instance, assessed strength of achievement, psychic capacity of self-conquest, technical, as well as routine skill. The asymmetry of the questions asking for choice of rowers from the whole training squad on one hand, but for rowers from one's own eight oar crew on the other, permitted the direction of preference choices outside. This permits conclusions on the cohesiveness and consensus of the crew, although only one factor of this complex social phenomenon is met by their results. And yet the sociometric questions concerning conflicts remained restricted toward one's own crew.

In order to get informative decisions, the number of possible nominations was restricted to two. Nobody was able to simply list all members of his crew, and thus, to dispense with a real decision. The fact that this restriction was nevertheless broken by the rowers of W, then, is all the more important. It is to be mentioned, too, that in the first year of investigation, crew O was asked only questions 1, 2, and 3.

Because of the possible socio-psychic feedback on the "psychic atmosphere" of the crews and possibly on the level of achievement by a suggestive or "leading" effect of the questionnaire, or by the reaction toward the answers which could not, in spite of the anonymity in evaluation, be kept totally secret within the training squad, or by the effect of tensions and irritations in top athletic training, these questionnaires could not be repeated regularly, or even several times during the racing season. The crew W, however, was questioned in both years of its unmodified existence. There were characteristic changes of the sociometric structures and, complying with this, also of the external and observable behavior in 1963 which, to a great degree, could be predicted in 1962 on the basis of the analyzed sociograms (29). A confirmation of these predictions certainly points to the fact that the sociometric analysis comprises sufficient components of the social structure to allow micro-sociological prognoses, that is, to fulfill the chief tasks of the scientific theory or model.

As in factor analysis during rotation of data (34; 43) some information is lost and the respective survey suffers somewhat (41), the result of the questionnaires was represented in sociograms and sociomatrices. A group of only eight individuals permits a sufficiently distinctive, easily understandable and almost unique ordering within sociograms, if the individuals are symbolized by circles in different rank orderings, the individuals receiving most preference or "rejection" choices figuring at the top of the sociogram, those individuals having received none or minimum choices figuring at the bottom. Besides, the criterion of Borgatta (5; 41) has to be met in order to minimize the number of crisscrossings of lines. Up to automorphic mappings by lateral exchanges of sides of the sociogram, restricted to the internal ordering, the overall order of the sociogram then, is unique. Selected individuals not sitting in the eight oar crew are represented on the right side of the sociogram outside the bulk of circles representing the members. On the right side beside each sociogram, the proportion of choices is noted, referring to each individual with the respective rank of choice numbers.

In the matrix representation the first nominations of preferred or "rejected" co-members were, as far as possible,[3] arranged in a matrix $A=(a_{ij})$ of canonical shape (Katz 25; 14; 7) fulfilling the condition $\sum_{i=1}^{8} \sum_{j=1}^{8} a_{ij} (i-j)^2 = min$. The value +1 (preference choice) was symbolized by a plus sign (+) in the original matrices. "Rejection" was symbolized by minus (-) and the value 0 (indifference) was not symbolized at all. The respective figures, except 0, however, characterize the values in the other matrices because they are genuine numbers, that is, the respective numbers of two step connections via successive choices in a sequence or "three step choices" as well as the degree of changes of numbers of choices. In order to facilitate comparison with the first matrix of preferences of rowers, its order was preserved in the other matrices of the same crew. This was possible, since no new, not clearly distinguishable cliques were formed. So, there always resulted a very simple matrix of changes, which has only to be added to the original matrix in order to get the changed one. The clique structures within the crews are revealed by the square and cubic matrices of the respective symmetric submatrices--for which $a_{ij}=a_{ji}$--from the respective positive matrix elements (12; 33, 32,13'; 14). This means that single choices and choices directed outside are neglected in analyzing complete clique structures.

Some additional remarks regarding symbolization may be useful. The preference choice matrix for rowing (o_{ij}) belongs to the crew O, the matrix (w_{ij}) to W, respectively, etc. The choosing rower is always noted on the left input of the line concerned. $(o_{ij}+)$ is the submatrix of (o_{ij}) consisting of the positive elements of this original matrix. The symmetric submatrix of $(o_{ij}+)$ again, is (o_{ij}^{s+}). The respective exponential matrices are symbolized by

$$(o_{ij}^{s+(2)}) = (o_{ij}^{s+})^2 = (\sum_{e=1}^{8} o_{ie}^{s+} o_{ej}^{s+}) \text{ and } (o_{ij}^{s+(3)}) = (o_{ij}^{s+})^3 = (\sum_{ek=1}^{8} o_{ie}^{s+} o_{ek}^{s+} o_{kj}^{s+}).$$

By analogy, similar formulae result respectively for (w_{ij}), (s_{ij}), and (z_{ij}).

The element of the symmetrical square matrix of the original symmetric matrix represents the number of successive two step connections in a sequence of nominations between the elements of the original matrix or the members of the crew, that is the connection which can be realized in two steps of successive choices.[4] In the main diagonal the number of such two step choices is found which will lead from a respective element toward itself, thus, representing the number of mutual choices. Since every mutual choice is counted with each respective partner, half the trace of the matrix $(a_{ij}^{s+})^2$ represents the total number of mutual choices within the sociogram, $1/2\sum_{i=1}^{8} a_{ii}^{s+(2)}$.

The trace is an invariant against linear transformations, that is, it does not change, if the lines and columns of the matrix or of the original matrix are somehow exchanged. The matrix $(a_{ij}^{s+(3)})$ characterizes the number of symmetric three step connections between the elements, respectively. The three step connections of one element with itself, characterize the complete three member cliques[5] in which the element is participating. The number of those three step connections is to be found in the respective cell of the main diagonal of the cubic symmetrical matrix. Each larger complete clique consists of such three member cliques following the structure of a topological simplicial decomposition. From the number of three step back connections in each diagonal cell the number of members of a clique is calculated according to $\alpha = (n-1)(n-2)$. (12; 33)--Not quite complete cliques are revealed by the main diagonal of the non-symmetric matrix $(a_{ij}^{+})^3$ if only one choice is lacking in order to complete the three member clique.

Sociometric structures of eight oar shell crews

4.1 O--Racing association crew of two clubs.

The crew O consisted of four rowers xi and yj (i, j, =1,...4) of each of the clubs x and y, respectively.

The sociogram and the symmetric submatrix of positive elements show clearly detached groupings of choices within the respective clubs x and y. All mutual choices are directed into their own subgroup of club fellows. In each of these a clique of three persons each developed. To be sure, there are no complete cliques in which all participants are mutually choosing themselves, that is in $(o_{ij}^{s+})^3$ there are no diagonal elements, but this was already precluded by the restriction of number of choices in any case. The matrix $(o_{ij}^{s+})^2$ shows that nevertheless, three members of each club subgroup are connected with one another by four mutual choices, $1/2 \sum_{i=1}^{8} o_{ii}^{s+(2)} = 4.$

x2 and y2 are the connecting central individuals within the subcliques. The index of centrality after Bavelas (2) according to the received choices within one's own clique is, e.g. for y2, 4.0, for y1 and y3, 2.67.

According to the statistical expectation, one-directional choices should, within a set of eight selectors, each having two choices, occur five times more frequently than mutual choices. The number of expected mutual choices is $\binom{n}{2}p^2=2.3$, $p=2/n-1$ in the selection probability for two vote choices under the condition n=8. 11.4 single one-directional choices remain. The ratio of 8:4 of one-directional as compared with mutual choices in O, therefore, points to the establishment of subgroups and cliques.

O--preference choice--rowing

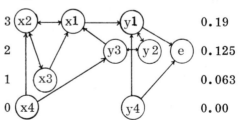

3 (x2) →(x1) →(y1)	0.19
2 (y3)(y2)(e)	0.125
1 (x3)	0.063
0 (x4) (y4)	0.00

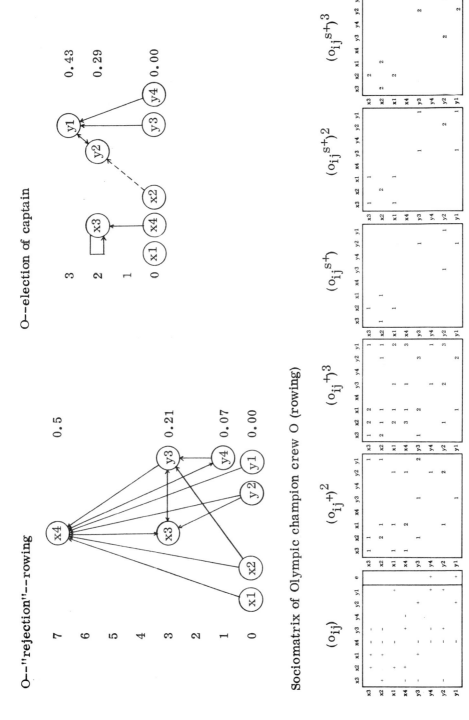

O--election of captain

O--"rejection"--rowing

Sociomatrix of Olympic champion crew O (rowing)

If one would also take into account the single selections, the same result occurs. The relative frequency[6] of the choices remaining within the respective subgroups, that is, 0.75 in x, 0.63 in y, excels the relative frequency of voices given toward the outside, being 0.25 in x and 0.38 in y.

Since the choices over-representatively remained in the subgroups, they could not accumulate toward one or two persons. Thus, the relative little rank differentiation of the crew being $R_0=0.22$ is explained.

This rank differentiation was measured by $R = \dfrac{1}{n} \sum\limits_{ij=1}^{n} (R_i - R_j)^2$
where $i \neq j$ and $i-j=$min., i, j=1, . . . =n; R_k symbolizing the rank numbers only considered once; $n \neq 8$.

In addition, the relative frequency of "rejections" directed into one's own subgroup, 0.5 in x, 0.125 in y, is less than the respective relative frequency of "rejections" of 0.6 across the borders of one's own clique. The internal social distances[7] are in the subgroups $d_{xx}=8$ and $d_{yy}=2.4$, which is much less than the total internal social distance within the crew $d_{oo}=56$ and also less than the social distances of the respective subgroups against one another, $d_{xy}=24$ and $d_{yx}=80$.

If the ratio of "rejections" directed from a group, a, into another one, b, as regards the preference choices directed into this other respective group, would be equal to the respective internal ratio, $\dfrac{Aab}{Vab} = \dfrac{Aaa}{Vaa}$, then, group a would be at a limit point. That means that with this ratio and the respective social distances and also with less distance toward those outside the group, a could no longer be detached or delimited by social distance against b. At this point, the following would be valid $\dfrac{d_{ab}}{d_{aa}} = \dfrac{|a| \cdot |b|}{|a| \; (a-1)}$. For two groups of four members, this would mean $d_{ab}/d_{aa}=1.25$, $|a|=4=|b|$. Within our crew, the distance ratios of x and y remarkably surpass the value of 1.25. Thus, they characterize how distinctively the groups are detached from one another, $d_{xy}/d_{xx}=3$; $d_{yx}/d_{yy}=33.4$, on average 18.2. The external distance is, on an average, 18.2 times as big as the internal distance. Whereas, on an average, the external distances of the subgroups with $1/2(d_{xy}+d_{yx})=52$ correspond to the total internal distance of 56, this is not the case with the ratios $\dfrac{V_{xy}}{A_{xy}}$ and $\dfrac{V_{yx}}{A_{yx}}$. In contradistinction to the total ratio of the crew $V_{oo}/A_{oo}=1$, it is 0.43 on the average, that means it is distinctively displaced in the direction of more frequent "rejections" and less frequent preference choices between x and y.

The comparisons between their respective distances show that the sub-group y more distinctively detached itself from x than vice versa. The probability of choices from y into x is 0.13, the probability in the other direction being 0.25. The relative probability of "rejections" going from y into x is 0.63, the reverse being 0.38. However, in contrast to usual group dynamical theses, the greater distance and

9

detachment does not lead to greater internal cohesion within y. The rowers of y even emit two choices toward the outsider, e. In addition, x_1, x_2, and x_3 are interconnected with themselves by a three-choice sequence revealed by the diagonal elements of $(o_{ij}{}^+)^3$. Only one single choice is lacking to form a complete clique, whereas in the subgroup consisting of y_1, y_2, and y_3 no such three-step back connections exist and only two further choices would complete the clique. The measure of cohesion is the same in both subgroups beings $K_x = K_y = 0.25$. The definition of this measure of cohesion is the following: $K_a = df \dfrac{\overrightarrow{V_{aa}}}{V_{aa}} \dfrac{1-p}{p}$, $p = 2/n-1$ being the probability of choice for two vote selections; $n=4$; V_{aa} being the number of mutual choices in a. The measure of cohesion, thus, is far below the statistically probable and expected cohesion of $K = \dfrac{(2)^n p^2 (1-p)}{n(n-1)p(1-p)p} = 0.5$. The same is true, however, for the measure of repulsion $\rho_a = df \dfrac{\overleftrightarrow{A_{aa}}}{A_{aa}} \dfrac{1-p}{p}$; $\overleftrightarrow{A_{aa}}$ being the number of mutual "rejections" in a, $\rho_x = \rho_y = 0.1$.

Chiefly because of the restriction of the number of choices impinging mainly on single selections, the total cohesion $K_o = 1.25$ is bigger than the respective cohesion of the subgroups. The measure K_o, however, does not take into account the selections directed outside which, in turn, weaken the "cohesion" of the total group in the widest sense. 0.88 of the possible choices are directed into the crew. Relatively, the probability that a member of the crew is chosen at all is still somewhat higher than the probability of being chosen within his own subgroup, these probabilities being 0.75 and 0.63, respectively. All this apparently is a decisive factor for the unity and holding together of the crew in spite of the large external distances between the subgroups.

With one exception, the selections of a crew captain, too, are directed into one's own subgroup. In this case additionally, x_2 chose y_2 only "with certain reservations". Sociometrically speaking, a "leadership dual" developed (22, p. 133ff) between the exponents x_3 and y_2 of both subgroups. It was also the group contrast which banked up strong subgroup antagonisms and leadership tensions. These could only be controlled from outside, that is, by the coach. They even reached the press headlines once.

O displays the largest relative rank differentiation $R_{o, rej} = 0.59$ of all the analyzed crews with respect to the "rejections", the highest possible value being $R_{rej} = 0.88$, as well as the largest standard deviation $o_{rej} = 2.33$ deviating from the mean value 1.75. All this and the higher probability of "rejection" within x, 0.5 as against 0.125 in y, respectively, is due to the fact that x_4, the "star of rejections", is also unanimously "rejected" by his own subgroup. He receives half of all "rejections", seven being the highest possible number. Everybody within the crew only "reluctantly and unwillingly" rowed together with him. Since both subgroups unanimously rejected him and since x_4 was one of the strongest achieving rowers, this reveals that no group dynamical antitheses are expressed here, but personal antipathies. The assessment of achievement capacity alone explains why x4 was nevertheless retained in the crew. By contrast, the second rower without any received choice, y4, is a marginal person. He agrees with the others in "rejecting" x4 and chooses the star y1 of his subgroup. Nobody except x4 rejects him. He does strive, but not uncritically so, to be accepted in the clique, for he rejects y3 and chooses an outsider.

From the structure of "rejections" in general follows the fact that the sociograms of O are split up according to the borderlines between the clubs, that the nominations in this crew were not assigned merely according to criteria of achievement. Otherwise one must have chosen x4. Also, y1 was not the strongest achieving rower, not even in the subgroup y. Personal antipathies and sympathies also superimposed themselves on the achieving motives in the preference choice of rowers. Such antipathies are thus responsible for the large rank differentiation of "rejections" and for their statistically improbable structure showing a correlation of only $r=0.05$ towards the expectation[8] (see table Annex 1). The standard deviation within the preference choices, by contrast, is only 1.2 and the structure of these correlates considerably with the statistical expectation, $r=0.71$. Preference choices within the crew O, thus, are distributed in a, statistically, in a very probable manner, whereas the negative ones are completely improbable. The preference choices concentrate less on the most successful receivers of sociometric votes--50% of the votes are directed toward a third of the crew --than would be the case in sociograms of school classes (39) in which an average of only one-fourth of the pupils received half of the votes. By contrast, however, half of the "rejections" of the crew concentrated on only one-eighth of the crew, that is, much more than in the comparable school classes in which half of the rejections would concentrate on one-fifth. Structurally speaking, the diagram of "rejections" is much more distinctive and exposed. The structure namely constitutes a supremum semi-lattice.

However, there is a certain continuity of assessment to be found within the crew. Within the whole crew there are no completely contrary nominations toward one another, for no two line vectors from matrix (o_{ij}) are fully contrary to one another. However, the choices are not statistically independent from one another. Only the pairs (x3, x4) and (x3, y2), respectively, chose independently from one another, because their line vectors are orthogonal toward each other, and that means with two line vectors that they are linearly independent from one another, (x3, x4)=(x3, y2)=0.

According to these results, the rowers themselves in some other additional questionnaires labelled the crew throughout as a pure rational association for the common purpose of success and not as a particularly special unity stressing comradeship between the two clubs, x and y. The "racing squad" however, was originally constituted by such contacts of comradeship and fellowships of the rowers without official representatives cooperating. The leading boards of both clubs, however, carried club centristic motives and aims into the crew. Eventually, the special unity, as it existed at first, began to split up into the "x-members" and the "y-members" and began to display such structural relationships as the sociograms show. The questionned athletes predominantly interpreted this split-up as being due also to club influences. The establishment of cliques under external pressure is a source of danger for the climate within the total group (23, p. 159ff). Consequently, typical group dynamical conflicts and discrepancies developed, sometimes almost leading to the dissolution of the "racing group". An advantage of such a "racing squad" from two equally strong groups being subgroups of larger associations, is, from a socio-psychological point of view, to be seen in the fact that the conflicting groups are easily visible from the very beginning. Conflicts are more easily recognized, localized, and perhaps, controlled, since, with a high probability, they would arrange themselves so as to be directed across the respective club borders (28). From the point of view of athletic achievement, however, there was no disadvantage to be found in O on grounds of those group tensions. In such case, one should have noticed a decrease in achievement from the starting state of a special unity of comradeship between the clubs; for the amount and regimen of training and the technical handling of the movements did remain on approximately the same level. The strength of achievement of the crew even increased in the two years in which the crew existed, parallel with the strength of conflict in its increase. The crew was not beaten at all and won the Olympics in 1960. Sports crews can, therefore, perform top athletic achievements in spite of strong internal conflicts. Some theses of ethologists and by Dahrendorf, thus, are confirmed by this example.

4.2 S, "Racing association" crew in a "racing group" of five clubs.

S was also representing a "racing squad" but, in contradistinction to O, with rowers from four clubs coming from a permanent "racing group" of five clubs. The rowers were I, II, . . . VIII. A totally different sociometric structure resulted than in O. Clique structures parallel to borderlines of clubs cannot be discovered at all.

Not only in the preference of boat fellows, but also in the choice of roommates the mutual choices remained, with one or two, below the expectation value of 2.3. Four choices, that is, 25% of all, were directed outside of the crew. For this reason, the measure of cohesion, $K_x = 0.18$ or 0.42 for the respective choice of roommates, was below the probability theoretical value of 0.5. The matrix $(s_{ij}+)^3$ reveals by its trace such a small transitive interlacing of the choices that only

S--preference choice--rowing

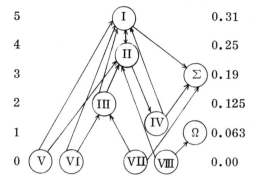

S--preference choice--roommates

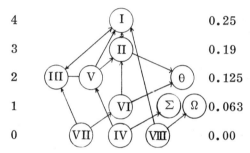

S--"rejection"--rowing

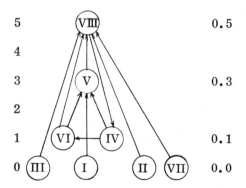

13

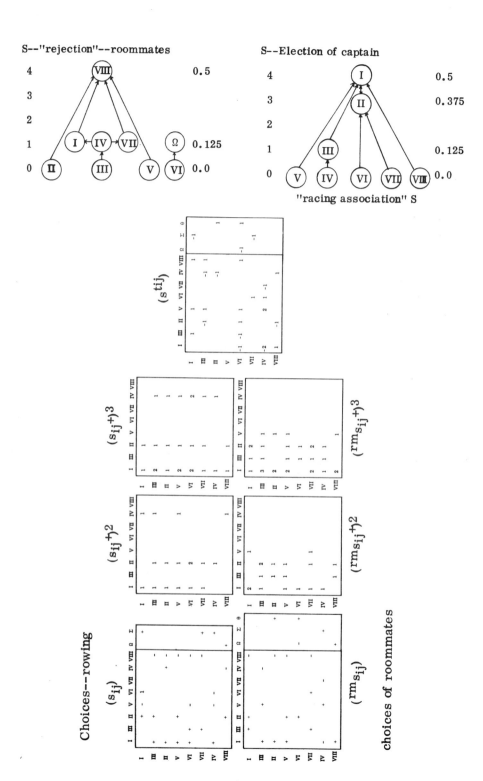

S--"rejection"--roommates

S--Election of captain

"racing association" S

(s_{tij})

$(s_{ij}^+)^3$

$(^{rm}s_{ij}^+)^3$

$(s_{ij}^+)^2$

$(^{rm}s_{ij}^+)^2$

Choices--rowing

(s_{ij})

$(^{rm}s_{ij})$

choices of roommates

14

three rowers are bound back to themselves by a three-step connection or triangular choice, namely I, II, and IV. In the preference choice--rowing, no special groupings stand out with the exception of the mutual choice between I and II. Nevertheless, these positive choices do not correspond to the statistical expectation in any greater amount than with O, the correlation being 0.04. Nine choices are concentrated toward the top representatives I and II, whereas only three are pointed into the range of those receiving one through three choices, which probability, theoretically speaking, should show up with the largest frequency. 6.42 individuals should statistically be found in this range of received choices. The distribution is dispersed with $o^2=3.5$ and the variation $\sigma=1.87$ around the mean value of 1.5. With the selection of roommates, this expected middle range still gets four chosen members from the crew. Therefore, the respective distribution curve is less dispersed around the same mean value, $^{rm}\sigma^2 = ^{rm}\sigma = 1.41$, and is somewhat more approximating the expected distribution $(r=0.45)$.

Rowers of nine pairs (as compared with three in the sociomatrix of rowing preference, where only I and II, VI and VIII, VII and VIII, respectively, distributed the nominations independently of one another) voted in statistical independence of each other in the choice of roommates, (I, III) = (I, IV) = (I, VIII) = (III, VI) = (III, VII) = (III, IV) = (V, VIII) = (VI, VII) = (VI, IV) = O. That is, the choice of roommates is less directed and led by other factors as, for example, criteria of achievement or leadership qualities. The popularity of an individual is rather distributed by chance here with the exception of the received choices by I and II. Therefore, the relative rank differentiation with $^{rm}R_S = 0.25$ is very low as compared even with the respective differentiation in the preference of boat-fellows where $R_S = 0.33$.

Neither the occurrence of several rowers choosing exactly the same way nor of some voting strictly contrary to one another took place. Furthermore, only V made his preference choice of rowers the same as his preference selection of roommates. The inner or scalar product of his respective line vectors in (s_{ij}) and $(^{rm}s_{ij})$ divided by the number of choices emitted by him respectively is a measure of conformity, $(V, V^{rm})/3 = 1$. Otherwise, however, the structure changes remarkably with the nominations of roommates. For instance, VI and IV modify their choices by seven and six degrees, respectively. VI decided both choices independently of each other, $(VI, VI^{rm}) = 0$. IV did, in fact, already choose somewhat contrary to the other selection, $(IV, IV^{rm})/4 = -0.25$.

The matrix $(_st_{ij}) = df\ (^{rm}s_{ij}) - (s_{ij})$ displays the differences in an overall view. The (square) measure of modifications between the nominations for the rowing preference and the choice of roommates may be characterized by $\sum_{i_1 j=1}^{8} (_st_{ij})^2$ This is an invariant against orthogonal transformations and independent of exchanges of lines and columns as well as of signs of single differences. The difference is 5.2 measured only within the crew; in total, that is, including the preference choices directed outside, it is 5.7. The changes toward the positive assessment in the preference of roommates are 12 times bigger than the respective changes toward a negative one. Thus, the ratio of preferences as compared with "rejections" V_{ss}/A_{ss} grows from 1.2 toward 1.73. The internal distance is smaller with the choice of roommates, that is 38.1 instead of 47.6.

The matrices $(^{rm}s_{ij}^+)^2$ and especially $(^{rm}s_{ij}^+)^3$ show a stronger concentration of two-step and three-step connections of preference choices among the rowers I, II, III, and V, that is, an "almost-clique" or a "quasi-clique" F displaying no internal distance at all, $d_{ff} = 0$, noticeably reveals itself. To be sure, five choices are lacking to constitute a complete clique of twelve choices necessary for this, but the prescription by the experimenter only to assign two choices did not allow all possibilities of choices. All except one choice by II, but no "rejections", were directed toward this very subgroup. In the preference selection of rowers as boat-fellows, however, I "rejected" V, apparently for reasons of achievement assessment. The other rowers of the subgroup E of outsiders in the crew direct an emotional preference into this quasi-clique at least once. That is, they do not detach themselves very much from this quasi-clique, $d_{EF} = 3$, whereas the quasi-clique detaches itself very distinctly from this subgroup E within the crew, $d_{FE} = 48$.

I and II, the most preferred individuals in the preference choice of rowers are also most frequently selected in the preference of roommates as well as in the nomination for a crew captain. In all cases they chose each other, too. Obviously, according to the opinion of their crew-fellows, they are the most popular and also the most proficient rowers. However, in contrast to the group dynamical theorem of divergence (Bales 22, p. 138) no leadership competition developed between them. The whole crew did not even distinguish according to the criteria "popularity" and "strength" or "capacity of achievement" between them. This would, to be sure, have been difficult, since one of them is the most experienced rower, whereas the other one is the stronger one with respect to physical strength and talent. In assessing the top positions, this crew is, more than the others, influenced by the halo-effect (23, p. 166). In a "racing group" like this, therefore, there need not exist a leadership "dual" as in O, consisting of two competing subgroups from different clubs.

Furthermore, this crew S, did not assign preferences of rowers as boat-fellows according to criteria of achievement only, for the particularly physically strong rower IV received only one choice.

Personal "rejections", being achievement oriented here, concentrated predominantly on one single person, namely VIII, as in O. This is true for both diagrams of "rejections", the relative rank differentiation being $R_{S, rej} = 0.38$ and $^{rm}R_{S, rej} = 0.4$, respectively. Hence, the structures of "rejections" resulting were also somewhat improbable here as compared with expectation, the correlation with expectation being $r = 0.09$ and $^{rm}r = 0.16$. However, the relative frequency of materialized possibilities of "rejections" is relatively small, as compared to O, in particular as regards the preference of roommates, 0.44 compared to 0.88 in O. That is, both structures of "rejections" are somewhat remarkably more weakly realized and pointed more to this statistically most important middle range than one could have expected from a theoretical point of view. Only three instead of 6.42 rowers are to be found in this range. With respect to the preference choice of roommates, nonetheless, Pearson's skewness coefficient of distribution, $\dfrac{\text{Mean value - modal values}}{\sigma}$, is relatively low (0.3). These findings are compatible only if the structure of "rejections" has only a weak weight within the sociometric structure of relationships. Indeed, the measure of repulsion ρs is zero for both diagrams, since no mutual "rejections" occur at all. Even the "star of 'rejections'", VIII, selected the most popular athletes I and II once each and refrained from every "rejection" in the preference choice of roommates. Hence, he intended to reduce the isolation. VII, a marginal person without reception of choices at all, distributed his nominations in a similar conformistic manner. He assigned his positive choices toward the middle rank positions and "rejected" VIII like the holders of these middle ranks.

The small amount of group dynamically motivated "rejections" and the lack of distinctive cliques of clubs reveal the fact that, although the rowers belonged to different clubs it did not engender tensions in this crew, contrary to the situation in O. Two out of three mutual preferences crossed the border between clubs. Twenty-three out of thirty-two preference choices are directed toward a member of another club. On the other hand, only ten "rejections" crossed club borderlines; eight remained within the respective clubs' subgroups.

Therefore, club centristic conflicts as they governed the whole social structure within O as a result of a competitive relationship between two equally strong subgroups from two clubs, cannot develop and impact the social structure of a "racing group" from four clubs or even five clubs. The club memberships and assignments to clubs are too multiple, too obscure and the representations of club interests are too weak in the concert of all these interclub relationships to allow competitive club centrism to develop, to get an effective auto-stereotype, or to impinge itself on the overall social structure of the crew. The potential group antagonism is prohibited by the lack of a distinct polarity of a dichotomic contrast which could have formed a condensation core around which mutual hetero-stereotypes of scape-goating could be established. Followers of the quasi-clique F, for

₆₂W--preference choice--rowing

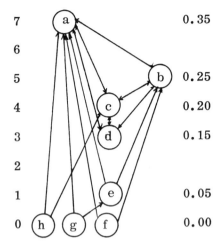

₆₃W--preference choice--rowing

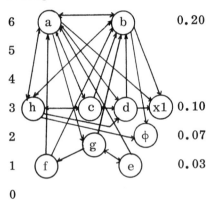

₆₃W--preference choice--roommates

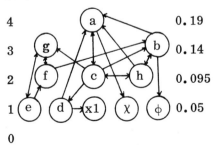

18

$_{62}$W--"rejection"--rowing

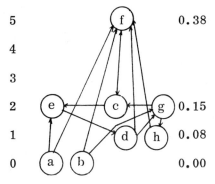

$_{63}$W--"rejection"--rowing

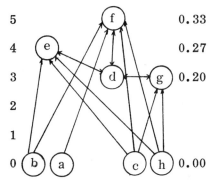

$_{63}$W--"rejection"--roommates

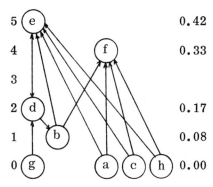

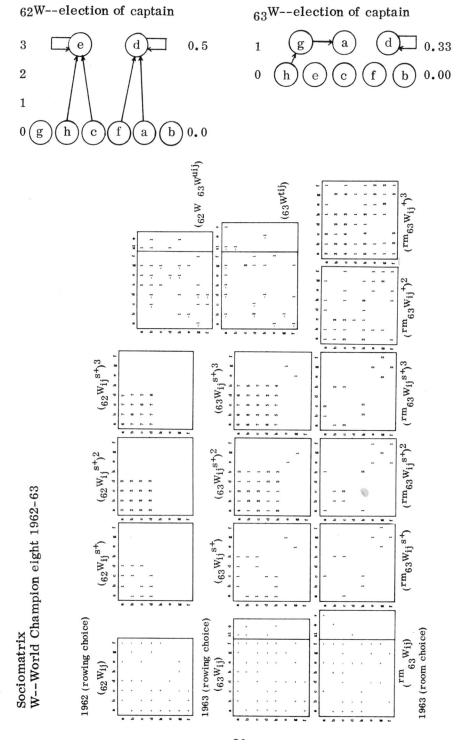

62W--election of captain

63W--election of captain

Sociomatrix
W--World Champion eight 1962-63

20

instance, belong to three different clubs. There was no auto-stereotype for subgroups, but clearly for the whole crew concentrating on a we-group image and frequently occurring in statements referring to "we training athletes." This we-group auto-stereotype turned out to be somewhat directed against the older generation of all participating clubs in general.

In sum, therefore, the crew S, in sharp contrast to the dualism of two cliques in O, shows a relative harmonic, although not very strongly integrated sociometric structure. The reason that this structure does not strongly correspond to statistical expectation may be that the members are relatively unanimous about the distribution of proficiency predicates and because group dynamical discrepancies and conflicts were practically non-existent.

To avoid group tensions and dualisms within "racing squad" crews, therefore, it is useful and recommendable to gather rowers from more than two or three clubs in a "racing association." This measure, however, does not necessarily have a remarkable impact on the strength and level of achievement. From the point of view of achievement, the crew S was much less proficient and less strong than the respective champion crews O and W, although S was coached according to the same methods and the same intensity and regimen of training. However, the rowers in S were, on the average, less physically talented than those in O and W. In addition, the crew S had not such a convenient and favorable place of training.

4.3   W--Pure Club Crew
4.3--1. $_{62}$W--Questionnaire of 1962.

The crew W with the rowers a, b, ...h was a mere club eight oar crew. At first, it is obvious with respect to the preference sociogram regarding the choice of boat-fellows that four rowers did not stick to the prescription only to select two of their fellows.[10] Therefore, the distribution of sociometric preferences here could not be exactly compared with statistical expectation of such a distribution of twenty --or in 1963, thirty--choices; for the calculation of expectation values was usually based upon the presupposition that all athletes made an equal number of choices, i.e., two. Since such a distribution of sixteen choices was expected, the correlation here is not only a measure of compliance between the real distribution and statistical expectation, but also with the "expectation" of the experimenter. The premises could not be separated from one another. Nevertheless, it is most significant that this case occurred, that there was a deviation from expectation to such a remarkable degree, just in such a way (r = -0.18). (The exact measure of correlation and the tentative assessment of its reliability is, in any case, somewhat dubious in such a low value range: see the note attached to the table of correlations (Annex 1).

21

The fact that the four rowers did not stick to the prescribed number of choices had the effect that the individual preferences were widely dispersed ($\sigma^2 = 6.25$, $\sigma = 2.5$) around the mean value of received votes (2.5).[11] Apparently, one got into difficulties in selecting amongst several fellows. Does this, as well as the fact that no choices were directed outside, reveal a strong emotional integration of the crew? On the other hand, the highest number of preference choices are, on the whole, concentrated toward very few upper position individuals. Half the number of preferences are directed toward a portion of 0.2 of all members (in 1963 toward 0.38). This is to say that the relative rank differentiation $_{62}R_W = 0.42$ seems to be much more explicit than with O revealing only $R_O = 0.22$. The square rank difference in W is the biggest occurring among all positive preference choices of all eight oar crews.[12] On the other hand, the social internal distance $(_{62}d_{WW}) = 36.1)$ is smaller and the measure of cohesion $к_{62}W = 1.88$ higher than in the other crews. Both measures, however, as well as the relatively low repulsion of $\rho = 0.23$ are also influenced by the fact that the rowers emitted 1.25 times too many choices. If one would expect four choices by each subject, the cohesion would have been 0.56, that is average. The number of mutual choices would even then come out to be under average, that is, 6 against 9.95, according to the expectation, although the expectation value for two vote choices being 2.3 is considerably surpassed here. The chief diagonal of the matrix $(_{62}W_{ij}^{s+})^2$ shows that each of four persons are reached by three mutual choices and that these vice-versa choices contribute the only amount toward half the trace: $\frac{1}{2}\sum_{i=1}^{8} {}_{62}W^{s+(2)}{}_{ii} = 6$. The matrix elements $_{62}W^{s+(3)}{}_{ii}$ in addition, show that four rowers are participating in complete cliques. The criterion of cliques after Festinger (12) and Luce-Perry (33, 13) reveals that there is one single large complete clique C of those four rowers, $_{62}W^{s+(3)}{}_{ii} = 6 = (n-1)(n-2) \rightarrow n = 4$.

In the sociogram, this clique is distinctively prominent. All members chose each other. No mutual choices occurred otherwise. Each clique member is connected with each other individual in the clique on seven ways in three step choice sequences, but none of the crew members outside the clique, A, can reach another outsider using such a se sequence at all. The narrow interlacedness, closedness, and integration of C cannot be demonstrated more clearly. The establishment of C also explains the improbability of choice distribution. The prescription to make only two choices was broken only by the clique members, also indicating the strong integration of C. The internal distance d_{CC}

= O, the cohesion $K_C = \infty$, the repulsion ρ_C O/O, that is undetermin-ed--all these magnitudes represent the most extreme values possible.

The choices remain within the clique with a relative frequency of one, that is with certainty. In the whole crew, positive choices are directed into the clique with the relative frequency of 0.95. It is also somewhat surprising that the probability that outsiders directed their preference choices into the clique is relatively high, namely 0.88. Although the clique, as far as possible, detaches itself from them, $d_{CA} = \infty$, they in turn detach themselves in practice very little from the clique, $d_{AC} = 6.85$. Since the outsiders do "reject" themselves with the probability of 0.25 and only choose themselves at 0.125, since the internal distance is remarkable, $d_{AA} = 24$, and their cohesion vanishes, they do not establish a counterclique. In contrast to the crew O, where two equally strong closed subgroups were pitched against one another, here the complete clique C alone governs the whole social field of relationships without a real polarity developing.

Since the emotional integration and closedness of a subgroup al-ways causes great social distances toward the outside (24, p. 27) and even rejections and hostility with outsiders, it can here be inferred with certainty that the extremely strong establishment and detachment of the clique cannot have come about by assessments of characters and sympathies. In fact, the clique consisted, according to the judgment of the coach and others, of only the strongest achieving rowers in the crew. The clique, however, did not row together in another four, that is, it did not crystallize around another special institutional criterion or because of necessarily involved frequency of interaction. The achievement capacity in rowing, or to be more precise, the image of achieving capacity of the individual according to the assessment of the fellows, was the criterion of preference in this crew explicitly orient-ing themselves toward top performance; the crew won the world cham-pionship in this year. This fact clearly reflects itself in the socio-metric structures. Otherwise, presumably the only member who was a newcomer to the club would not have gotten the most but one number of choices. Maybe some personal quality has contributed to that as well. Besides, other emotional assessments also superimposed them-selves onto the achievement oriented preference choice. The rower being the most strongly achieving in the judgment of others did not re-ceive any positive choice from outsiders and did not get the most pre-erences.

If one orders the set of all members in the sociogram, that is, of chosen members in a rank order according to the number of received choices including zero, the quasi-order relation $\leqq_r$ between the individ-ual obtains a reflexive and transitive relation; for all persons or

23

elements of the set: α, β, γ the following is valid $\alpha \underset{r}{\overset{\leq}{=}} \alpha$; $\alpha \underset{r}{\overset{\leq}{=}} \beta$ and
$\beta \underset{r}{\overset{\leq}{=}} \gamma \rightarrow \alpha \underset{r}{\overset{\leq}{=}} \gamma$. With respect to $\underset{r}{=}$ also $\underset{r}{\overset{\leq}{=}}$ is antisymmetric; $\alpha \underset{r}{\overset{\leq}{=}} \beta$ and
$\beta \underset{r}{\overset{\leq}{=}} \alpha \rightarrow \alpha \underset{r}{\overset{\leq}{=}} \beta$. Therefore, each sociogram constitutes a partially order-
ed set (15, 16) with respect to $\underset{r}{=}$ as an abstract equality relation. This
shows only that the set of sociometric choices can be described alge-
braically and structured theoretically.

Some sociograms, however, additionally meet the conditions of
further axioms of a stricter mathematical structure. Thus, the preference choices of rowing fellows in the crew $_{62}W$ also fulfill the condition that for each two elements there is exactly one least common
supremum, sometimes called the upper limit or union, with respect to
$\underset{r}{\overset{\leq}{=}}$. Thus, this set of sociometric choices constitutes a supremum
semi-lattice (15).

It must be mentioned, however, that with some sociograms including mutual connections between individual elements, that is, mutual
choices or mutual "rejections" obtaining, one has to take into consideration special provisions that the antisymmetry or identity of the respective semi-lattice is retained. Thus, one may analyze all partial
sociograms having the same elements and relations, but only counting
each mutual connection as one single relation. This preservation of
antisymmetry or identity has especially to be taken into account for
semi-lattice structures with mutual connections in them. If, in each
respective case, only one direction of choices is taken into consideration, then semi-lattices always occur having the same number of elements, but displaying a slightly different structure of relational connectedness, that is, the same structure obtaining only up to mere sense
direction. This restriction has no influence on the closedness of the
social structure. On the contrary, the mutual connections naturally
increase the closedness of a partial or substructure. This is especially valid for the integration and closedness of cliques, quasi-cliques,
etc. However, one can also deal with these sociograms as multigraphs,
that is, as diagrams with different relations. Finally, one may separately analyze the so-called "induced indifference relation," "δ chooses
β and β chooses δ" which is engendered by mutual choices.

The fact that the supremum semi-lattice structure obtains in the
sociogram of preference choices--rowing in $_{62}W$, has a sociological
functional significance within the communication structure displaying
rank differentiation. Two members of the hierarchical social structure
clearly know to whom, as the immediate higher rank holder, a petition
or an information is then to be conveyed. In sociograms of preference
choices a semi-lattice structure uniquely establishes a rank order in

this sense without precluding occasional rank equality. To each two
elements there is exactly one least common supremum. It may be
hypothetically inferred that such a structure has a sociometrically
stabilizing effect, rendering more clear rank relationships. The elements representing "nodal" points which necessarily must occur in a
semi-lattice structure between the rank layers consisting of two or
more elements may represent orienting and coordinating instances in
systems of alternating alliances (21, p. 419 ff). In fact, in the crew
$_{62}$W, the rowers e and d representing the leading individuals according
to the election of captain are to be found in such rank coordinating positions. This is especially obvious with e. If rank differentiation is
high, as in the case of $_{62}$W, all this turns out to be of more relative
significance because such a great rank differentiation endangers stability. Besides, the structure is seldom to be encountered statistically, the correlation values regarding expectation are, in these examples
with semi-lattice structures, very low, 0.05; 0.04; -0.18, respectively (see Annex 1). Such a structure represents a specific high
structural closedness. This is particularly highlighted by the following
example. In our eight oar crew, W, the closed clique structure, (and
at the same time the semi-lattice structure) were lost in the following
year (see 4.3.2, Crew $_{63}$W). Emotionally charged and motivated conflicts broke out in the crew $_{63}$W and, parallel to this, characteristically, the structure of "rejections" of roommates displayed the property
of being a semi-lattice; being structurally prominent and hypothetically
stabilizing the respective feature, namely, the conflict causing "rejections." In the Olympic champion crew, O, only the striking structure
of "rejections" displayed semi-lattier character. Only the crew S
showed a similar character in the uniquely clear and distinctive structure of captain's election. If one did not take into consideration the
preference choices directed outside, both sociograms of preferences in
S would constitute semi-lattices. Hence, they lost this character of
mathematical structural integration by the fact that preferences were
directed outside. Again, the mathematical structural integration
exactly corresponds to the sociologically particularly stressed structural closedness. It can hardly be expected that this parallelism is by
chance and does not display sociological significance. The somewhat
disorganized crew, Z, did not show up with such a structural closedness.

The diagram of "rejections" in the crew $_{62}$W was somewhat mass-
ed in the middle ranks and corresponds, therefore, much more with
expectations, r = 0.65, than did the respective preference selections.
The materialized portion of possible "rejections" is, to be sure, with
0.81 a little less than in O (0.88), but remarkably stronger than in S
(0.63 and 0.44). It is somewhat peculiar, however, that the outsiders
rejected the clique members with a lower probability than vice-versa
(0.39 as against 1). The members of C realized all the possibilities

25

of "rejections," of course, directing them all outside. Envy of achievement or jealously of positions, hence, was not to be found with the rowers outside the clique in the crew. On the other hand, the clique very distinctively detached itself, less from the total group of outsiders in the crew than from f. Objectively assessed, f is not the weakest performing rower. But, in the respective year of investigation he rowed together with others and against them in smaller boats, in which most of the training took place--on fewer occasions than did the others with one another. Thus, the members of the crew could not get a real image about his achieving capacity. In addition, he also used to have relatively little social interaction with the team-fellows outside training time. Therefore, it could not be decided in 1962 and 1963, how far a wrong image of achievement capacity or lack of interaction or personal character traits of f determined the motive of "rejections." One year later, however, in the systematically performed qualification test in the skiff he placed fourth among all crew members, somewhat surprising his co-fellows who then began to obviously emotionally integrate him into the group. The rower h is a marginal person striving at at reception within the governing clique. He preferred the stars of the clique and "rejected" f as they did in a conformistic way.

In spite of the strong interlacedness of choices within the clique, and the high probability with which outsiders selected clique members, nine pairs--as in S--emitted statistically independent votes, $(e, a) = (e, b) = (g, h) = (g, b) = (c, g) = (d, g) = (f, b) = (f, a) = (f, h) = 0$. The rower g chose in the most independent manner. Contrary combinations of choices did not occur. However, the pairs (a, c and b, d) chose, positively and negatively, in complete conformity with one another, if one takes into consideration that they could not choose themselves, $(a, c)/4 = (b, d)/4 = 1$. This dependency, too, underlines the unity of the clique.

A particularly significant specialty was displaced by the sociogram of election of captain, namely a completely symmetric structure with respect to e and d. Both rowers are selected by two others and also choose themselves. C and f, thereby emit their preference choice across the clique borderline. This is also a sign for the non-emotional motives of clique establishments. Here, as in the "racing association" crew O, two equally strong leadership poles had developed. It can also be here inferred that the leadership structure is labile. Disagreement and discord, for instance, in technical and administrative problems would be expected to occur if the crews should decide by themselves, and the proposals of the leading figures would differ from one another. Like O, W was also unable to develop and act independently. Only an external authority like the coach could lead and hold the crew together as a unity. On grounds of the prominent leadership "dual" and the extremely strong detachment of the clique from the ousiders, one had to predict in 1962 (29) that the crew would nevertheless split into counter cliques and that the "rejections" would become emotionally aggravated

--this would especially obtain between leading figures--and that the crew in general would be exposed to serious leadership conflicts and competition which might even endanger its existence.

4.3.2 $_{63}$W--Investigation of 1963

It was possible for the crew W to be analyzed and investigated one year later, in 1963, with the same membership still obtaining ($_{63}$W). Which characteristic changes were to be stated?

The rowers made even more choices, thirty in the preference choice--rowing, and twenty-one in the selection of roommates, re spectively, that is each one 3.75 in the mean. The emission of prefer- ences, was widely dispersed around this value, $\sigma = 1.88$, $\sigma^2 = 1.37$, the skewness of distribution according to Pearson being 0.55. The ex- pectation with which this distribution is compared is not only a statis- tical one but also a methodological one. With this restriction, how- ever, the distribution almost completely corresponds to the statistical expectations of a two choice election, $r = 0.96$. The ranks, according to received nominations are further concentrated in the middle range, $\sigma = 1.83$, in the preference election of roommates $^{rm}\sigma = 0.97$. The mean value of received nominations in the crew, however, was higher than in 1962, now displaying 3.13. The rank sum had been displaced upward by 5. Fifty percent of the nominations were no longer directed toward the portion of 0.2, but toward 0.38 of the numbers of rowers or toward 0.41 in the selection of roommates.

Despite the greater number of mutual choices ($\frac{1}{2} \sum\limits_{i=1}^{8} {}_{63}W^{s+(2)}{}_{ii} = 8$; in the selection of roommates, 5) the cohesion decreased from 1.88 to 1.43, or 1.14 in the election of roommates, respectively. The re- pulsion was almost quadrupled toward 0.83.

The concentration of "rejections" remained practically unchanged (1962, 50% of choices toward 0.22, 1963 toward 0.20, or 0.16 in the election of roommates). The social internal distance also changed relatively little--from 36.1 toward 33.4, or 37.5 in the election of roommates, respectively.

Five choices, that is 0.17 of all, are now directed toward outsid- ers (in 1962 none did). Now, predominantly members of the clique C directed their preferences outside precisely four times as much as the outsiders in the crew. According to the specifically high achievement motivation, expectation, and image the clique chose the relatively strongly achieving rower XI, an Olympic champion, and ϕ, who became a European champion in another boat the same year. Both of these also received a sympathy preference in the choice of roommates.

The matrix $({}_{63}W_{ij}^{s+})^3$ displays in its diagonal elements that three complete cliques existed, for three different numbers occur. The following decomposition according to the clique criterion (12, 33, 32, 13) indicates that these are three complete cliques of three members each --triples, (3-1)(3-2) = 2; 2 (3-1)(3-2) = 4; 3 (3-1)(3-2) = 6. Hence, the cliques must overlap. A is member in all of them; c and h are members in two partial cliques respectively; and b as well as d in one. Following (w_{ij}) however, c and d chose b, and h chose d; thus, d and b are nevertheless narrowly attached to the other partial cliques. The big complete clique C, therefore, is split up into three smaller complete cliques, formally speaking, establishing another clique C' for the completion of which only three choices, that is, 0.15 of all, lack. This new "almost clique" did accept h as a new member. This rower had had a great leap of achievement capacity in the year before, and one year later he placed first of the whole crew in the qualification test. In addition, he had worked to gain the acceptance by and reception in the clique already in 1962 (see 4.3.1). He also got the highest increment in choices with four positively directed changes. In 1962 he got no positive preference nominations at all, now there were three.

The positive nominations now fall into the corresponding clique with a much smaller relative frequency of 0.7 than in 1962 when the respective frequency was 0.95. The repulsion within the clique, of course, remains unnoticeable, no mutual "rejections" obtaining and no unisensory "rejections". The value of repulsion is therefore undetermined, O/O. But the cohesion has decreased from infinite toward $\kappa_{C'} = 0.78$. Even more distinctively, the elections of roommates reveal how little the clique was held together by personal sympathies but, instead, by the achievement motive. The clique cohesion $^{rm}\kappa_{C'} = 0.33$ is far below the probable measure of 0.5. In the election of roommates only 0.55 of the possible internal preference choices within the clique were performed. Five choices are lacking for completeness, they are directed outside. Furthermore, the preferences from all over the crew only now fall into the clique C' with a relative frequency of 0.57. Whereas there was no internal distance within the clique C' with respect to the election of boat-fellows, in the election of roommates the members are distanced with the measure of $^{rm}d_{C'C'} = 1.82$ against one another. C' no longer contains any complete triple with respect to elections of roommates. Thus, the clique does not close itself up with such strong emotionality as in 1962 and it is not so closed as with respect to the election of rowers. This corresponds to the fact that the clique C' was socially approximating toward the outsiders A' somewhat more, without giving up the distinctive detachment from them. Instead of the infinite social distance in 1962, now there is a distance of $d_{C'A'} = 180$, or of $^{rm}d_{C'A'} = 135$ in the election of roommates, respectively. The differences of assessment, however, remain great. This is revealed in the fact that e and g emit their preference choices according to both criteria (rowing and roommates) slightly on the contrary. The internal or scalar products of their line vectors with that from the members of the clique C' are all below zero, except $(a, e) = (d, e) = (^{rm}d, ^{rm}e) = 0$.

On the other hand, the outsiders A' now noticeably detach themselves from the clique, which was not the case in 1962. Instead of 6.85, their external distance toward C' is now 11.25 or even 30 in the election of roommates. Their internal distance, being 24 in 1962, has now disappeared, $d_{A'A'} = ^{rm}d_{A'A'} = 0$. To be sure, in the achievement election their preferences are more frequently directed into the clique C' than not, by four against three, but emotionally it is the other way around being 1:5. 0.83 of the possibilities of choosing amongst the outsiders are materialized, only one preference choice is lacking for the establishment of a complete clique consisting of e, g, and f. The cohesion of this new clique vanishes only because in a two vote choice within a three member group the probability for being not chosen is 0 from theoretical reasons, $1-p = 1-2/2 = 0$. In three member groups the cohesion for two vote choices is always zero. That is, this measure is not applicable here.

The asymmetric matrix $(_{63}{}^{rm}W^+{}_{ij})^3$ reveals how much both of these 'almost-cliques' are now emotionally standing against one another. Within the cliques, in C' only two pairs and in A' only one pair is not connected by three step connections. Between the cliques, however, eleven ordered pairs are not thus connected; and with respect to the others, the number of three step connections--that is, the transitive interlacedness between the cliques--is much less than within C' or A' respectively. Since the positive choices predominantly remained in both cliques the confrontation of nominations (and therefore the relative rank differentiation) is much less in the election of roommates; $rm_{R63w} = 0.22$, than the respective measure in the election of boat-fellows--which did not change since 1962, being the same for preferences and "rejections", namely 0.42. The rank differentiation with respect to the "rejection" of roommates is according to expectation larger than with the preference elections, $^{rm}R_{63}W$, rej = 0.38.

All "rejections" according to the preference of rowers now cross the clique borders. With the exception of one, the same is true for the election of roommates. Three "rejection" nominations more were emitted than in 1962, three mutual "rejections" occurred (in 1962 only one). Since four rowers are topping the hierarchy of "rejections" now, the distribution is contrary to expectation, $r = -0.79$. However, the rejection of roommates displays a statistically completely different distribution, $r = 0.4$--the difference being an indication that different motives of "rejections" impinged on the sociograms. Interestingly, with respect to the "rejections", the rowers generally stuck to the two vote prescription.

In fact, in contrast to 1962, two cliques were now emotionally pitched against each other, just as was predicted on grounds of the sociometric structure and the leadership dualism before (see 4.3.1, 29). The semi-lattice structure stabilizing the positive rank structure in 1962 now occurred again, but in the diagram of "rejections" of roommates. This sociogram appears now to be structurally stressed and stabilized.

Whereas in going over from the election of boat-fellows from 1962 to 1963 the relation between the changes from positive to negative assessments remained nearly unchanged:

$$\sqrt{\sum_{i,j}(u^+_{ij})^2} \Big/ \sqrt{\sum_{l,k}(u^-_{lk})^2} \quad = 1.09 \text{ --in particular since,}$$

over-proportionally, many positive assessments were newly emitted-- their respective ratio of differences between the election of boat-fellows in 1963 and the election of roommates in 1963 uniquely tended toward the negative part, 0.84, that is, the change toward the "rejections" obviously increased. The total change in the election of rowers from 1962 to 1963 amounted to:

$$\sqrt{\sum_{i,j}(u_{ij})^2} \quad = \quad 4.9 \text{ within the crew, to 5.38 including the nomi-}$$

nations directed outside. The difference between election of rowers and election of roommates was again that much in 1963 amounting to 4.9, or to 5.29 with the nominations directed outside. This difference corresponds to that between the respective elections of rowers and roommates in S.

As (u_{ij}) and $(_{63}t_{ij})$ show, g is most differently judged by his co-fellows; compared to 1962, five subjects judged him differently according to the preference election of boat-fellows. Again, five athletes attributed another nomination to him in the election of roommates than in the corresponding rowing preference questionnaire. Almost all of these latter changes are in a positive direction, that is, he is assessed as being relatively weak in performance, but one does not "reject" him as a roommate. The objective qualification test of the next year confirmed this assessment of achievement. He changed his preference of rowing fellows by five choices, as against 1962, just as h did. The biggest change in judgment from one year to another was performed by b; he distributed his preferences and rejections completely differently from seven other rowers. On the other hand, together with g, he least distinguishes between the respective elections of boat-fellows and roommates. By contrast, the rower a separates most distinctively in this regard; in seven positions he changed his choice. Even single nominations reveal how differently both elections were assessed. C "rejects" g as a boat-fellow but prefers him as a roommate. D, on the other hand, does not like to live together in one room with b, but prefers him as a rowing fellow.

The leadership struggles and conflicts led to the consequence that e as well as d were remarkably more "rejected" than in 1962. Even in the preference choice of boat-fellows each of them experienced three down-gradings. With the exception of a, the total clique C' "rejected" the leadership candidate, e, who remained outside the clique. All outsiders, in turn, unanimously "rejected" d, the leader within the clique C'. He, again, "rejected" all outsiders. With respect to the questionnaire for roommates, both leadership poles "reject" one another. The members of C' do not like to live in one room with e. The outsiders, with the exception of f, do not like to have d as a roommate. E now surpasses f as the most "rejected" member of the crew. The crew has totally lost confidence and fidelity toward their leaders from 1962, after the conflict had broken out. Later, these conflicts increased to such a degree that they were reported in the press. Five rowers now refrained from electing one another as candidate for captain. One of them, d, assigns an isolated choice to himself. E refrains from any nomination. Obviously, the crew no longer has internal leadership. It is disorganized as to leadership hierarchy and could only be held together by the external authority of the coach. Nevertheless, the crew won the European championship in this year again beating the strongest opponent from the world championship regatta of the previous year. Objectively, measured by the regular training achievements in terms of the so-called "Einstellzeit", that is, the average time over eight successive training heats on the interval distance, the crew had grown stronger in achievement. This is to say that the level of achievement did not suffer from the rank conflicts and tensions between the leaders.

In the following year (1964), a qualifications test in the skiff was performed in order to rule the rank conflicts and to increase the individual achievement motivation. Hereby, a unique rank succession crystallized, no longer being dependent on the establishment of subjective images. Everybody in this qualification test for the membership in the crew had to stand out against any other competitive candidate. The objective rank order as to achievement capacity will presumably not have changed very much in three quarters of the year, mostly off-season time. Thus, one may assume that the objective rank order, on the statistical average, already existed in 1963. The rank correlation coefficient after Spearman

$$\rho = 1 - \frac{\sum_{j=1}^{n} (R_{(im)j} - R_{(obj)j})^2}{n(n^2 - 1)} = 0.46;$$

n=8, however, did not reveal a strong correlation between the rank order of images and the objective order of achievement. The correlation was not even significant, since the 95% reliability limit lies at P = 0.64. Compared to 1962, the corresponding correlation coefficient of the 1963 image rank order in comparison to the objective one is now even less, amounting only to 0.35. Again, with the mentioned assumption, it may be inferred that the rank order of images of achievement capacity of each individual rower was not reliable. The

31

rowers misassessed their own and their fellows' rank position to a re-markable degree. The problems occurring with this subjective assess-ment of achievement rank orders and achievement capacity are dealt with elsewhere. In any case, however, if a rank order with respect to achievement capacity is to be undoubtedly established in a top level athletic team--and this may be useful because of the presumable con-flict decreasing function, as was confirmed by W--this can best be ac-complished by an objective qualification test.

One of the two leadership poles, e, was eliminated from the crew on the grounds of this qualification test. Did this and the unique estab-lishment of a rank order lead to the consequence that all conflicts dis-appeared? No, they were merely displaced to another location, inter-estingly enough, no longer within the crew. Since there seemed to be no apt scapegoat within the crew--f had proved to be relatively strong in achievement--the little coxswain now had to play the scapegoat. He was in somewhat unjustifiable degree assigned the responsibility for all mistakes of the crew by the leader and other members. He was even reproached for mistakes which he could not have caused, etc. Obviously, a top athletic team of such a structure and tradition cannot suddenly do away with a certain remarkable amount of internal aggres-sion. Apparently, this crew could not exist without a certain amount of internal aggression. It must be taken into account here, however, that the extremely strenuous physical load of exhausting athletic training leads to a typical nervous irrascibility and irritability during the sea-son and in the state of high achievement training. Therefore, conflicts in top level athletic teams are highly likely to break out during the sea-son. The sociometric structures, therefore, can be more easily tested and confirmed with regard to external behavior here than in other kinds of groups. Top level athletic teams are especially suitable, therefore, for sociometric analyses of groups in extreme stress and load situations.

4.4. Z--A Club Crew of Less Achievement Capacity

In 1963, when the world champion eight crew $_{63}$W was question-naired, a so-called "second eight oar crew" Z, consisting of the rowers J, K, L . . ., Q was coached in the same training center. This crew started in the next lower, less achieving class, and was investigated at the same time. However, it showed a completely different socio-metric structure as compared with all hitherto analyzed crews.

In deviation from the value of expectation of 2.3 in the preference selection of boat-fellows, no mutual nomination occurred. There is no clique to be pointed to or even to loom up, for the symmetric submatrix of preference choices is the zero matrix $(z_{ij}{}^{s+}) = 0$. Also, the non-symmetrical one is almost equal to the symmetric one only displaying two nominations. No mutual or three step connections developed in this crew Z. The social interlacedness and interconnection is conceiv-ably low. The cohesion is 0, $K_Z = 0$. Only two out of all seventeen

Z--preference choice--rowing

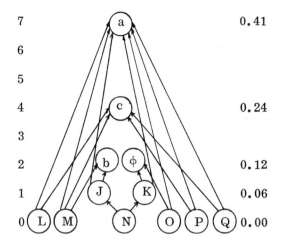

Z--preference choices--roommates

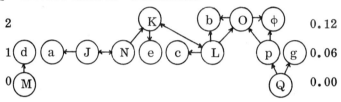

Z--"rejection"--rowing

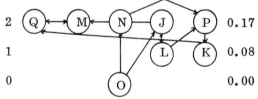

Z--"rejection"--roommates

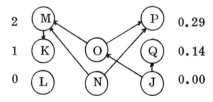

Z--election of captain

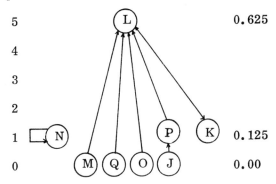

<!-- scale: 5, 4, 3, 2, 1, 0 with values 0.625, 0.125, 0.00 -->

Sociomatrix

"Second Eight" crew Z of Ratzeburg

Z--preference choice--rowing

(Z_{ij})

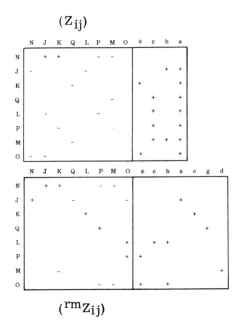

$(^{rm}Z_{ij})$

(Z^{tij})

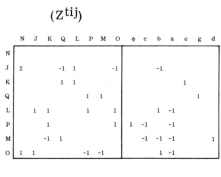

	N	J	K	Q	L	P	M	O	φ	c	b	a	e	g	d
N															
J	2		-1	1			-1			-1					
K			1	1							1				
Q					1	1						1			
L	1	1			1	1					1	-1			
P		1						1	1	-1		-1			
M			-1	1							-1	-1	-1		1
O	1	1			-1	-1					1	-1			

34

choices were directed into one's own crew. Six rowers are isolated; according to the statistical expectation it should only be one, or more precisely 0.7. 88.4% of the nominations, thus, are directed outside, nearly all of them into the "first eight oar crew" $_{63}$W and the rest of them toward the already mentioned rower, ϕ, who was assessed to be a very strongly achieving one, later winning a European championship in another boat class.

This crew Z is socially disintegrated and disorganized. Its internal distance d_{ZZ} is 300. The ratio between positive and negative nominations in preference and "rejection" questionnaires nearly disappeared, $V_{ZZ}/A_{ZZ} = 0.017$, for no rower of the crew received more than one choice and only two are elected even once--statistically speaking, a completely improbable distribution, the correlation as to expectation being r = 0.03. This distribution, however, can be uniquely explained. Every rower prefers to row with the stronger achieving members of the world champion eight crew. Characteristically, only members of the 'achievement clique' C' are nominated.

The "star" of W, a, is also the "star" of Z. All of the top ranking rowers of $_{62}$W with respect to the preference of boat-fellows are also nominated here--a, b, and c. The achievement motive and the corresponding assessment, therefore, is the obvious reason for these abnormal preference choices. Some confirming evidence for the contention that no other reasons were decisive may be found in the fact that the sociograms of "rejections" here more closely approximate the random distribution than with all other crews, the respective correlations being 0.79 to the "rejection" of boat-fellows and 0.56 to the "rejection" of roommates. Also, the election of roommates may point to this conclusion since it, too, rather corresponds with the expected distribution more than any other sociogram, $^{rm}r = 0.65.$ [13] In this choice, there are only two isolated rowers. Moreover, the rowers also elected e and g from the counter clique A' within the crew W as roommates whom they do not count as strongly achieving rowers and whom they, consequently, did not choose in the preference questionnaire for boat-fellows. By contrast, a and c being assessed as the most strongly achieving rowers of W and being preferred eleven times in the concerning preference of boat-fellows, here get only one choice apiece. The square difference only regarding the external choices of boat-fellows and roommates is 3.74; and the ratio of changes in positive and negative directions tends to the negative side by 0.87. The outsiders are less frequently chosen as roommates. Also, the square total difference between nominations as boat-fellows and as roommates, including the choices directed outside, is relatively high, amounting to 6.08. All this provides distinctive evidence for the achievement orientation of the preference choice of rowing-fellows.

However, the achievement oriented election leads to the consequence that strongly achieving outsiders, namely a, b, and c get six further choices. In sum, thus, nine (corresponding to 53%) of the choices were directed outside. Therefore, the rank differentiation amounting to only 0.18, hardly surpasses that of the preference choice of boat-fellows, where $R = 0.125$. The internal distance of the room-mate election is still $^{rm}d_{ZZ} = 50$, remarkably higher than with the other crews S or W. Thus, it follows, although the square difference within the crew between roommate and boat-fellow elections amounts to a normal height of 4.8 (0.6 relatively) and tends toward a positive election:

$$\sqrt{\sum_{i,j=1}^{8-} t^{+2'}{}_{ij}} \Big/ \sqrt{\sum_{1,k=1}^{8} (t^{-}{}_{kl})^2} = 1.9 \; ;$$

although the cohesion increased toward $^{rm}\kappa_Z = 0.38$ (two mutual choices) and the repulsion vanishes (no mutual "rejection"; $^{rm}\rho_Z = 0$ as against $\rho_Z = 0.63$), the crew is emotionally only weakly integrated.

On the grounds of these pathological conditions, the measure of dispersion with respect to received choices within the eight is very low, $\sigma = 0.43$ ($^{rm}\sigma = 0.7$). However, if one would take into account all receivers of choices, then, $\sigma' = 1.83$ would be nearly similar to all other crews.

The "rejections" are similarly weakly differentiated, $\sigma_{rej} = 0.68$, $^{rm}\sigma_{rej} = 0.78$, $R_{rej} = {}^{rm}R_{rej} = 0.18$. The "rejections" concentrated less than in all other crews with respect to the preference choice -- rowing, that is, 50% of the "rejecting" voices fell into half of the crew. However, the "rejection of roommates amounted to a "normal" proportion of 0.21. It is not possible to state a corresponding proportion with respect to the preference choices, since only 12% of the choices fell into the crew itself, or 47% in the election of roommates. 50% of the choices would, linearly extrapolated, be directed toward the proportion 3.64 or 1.06 of the crew (= 1.0), respectively.

The social disintegration is also expressed in the votings if one is to individually compare them. In the $\binom{n}{2} = 28$ comparisons between two corresponding sets of nominations 22 inner or scalar products vanish, if one takes into consideration only the distribution of choices within the crew, but "rejections" included. With respect to the pure achievement election toward outside, of course, one does not choose statistically independently from one another, with the exception of N as regards most of his fellows. In addition, two choices turned out to be slightly contrary to each other, their scalar product being negative. The same is also revealed by the preference choice of roommates in general, that is including the consideration of choices directed outside. Seventeen sets of choices are independent from one another, six tend to contrary directions. K decided statistically independent from all other roles. J, Q, and M only in two cases each nominate dependently on another one, but tending into opposite directions. The only positive dependencies are $(N, L) = (L, P) = (P, O) = 1$; $(N, O) = 2$.

36

It is true however, that the crew voted with great unanimity for one captain, L. A leadership dual does not exist. Probably L was the only personality in the crew with leadership qualities, so the lack of proper candidates engendered the unanimity of choices.

In sum, this eight oar crew Z is nearly alone held together by the fact that the rowers could only participate in eight oar crew rowing contests if they partook in "second class" races and if they joined forces. Every single one except N strived to get into a crew with more strongly achieving rowers. With respect to their sporting aim as a crew, the sociometric structures of preferences and "rejections" of this crew are completely disorganized.

Summarizing Survey--Top Performances Despite Internal Conflicts

The significant sociological differences of the investigated eight oar crews with respect to recruitment according to club membership, to their different levels of achievement and of achievement motivation, to their being influenced by the larger "training associations", etc., very distinctively reflect in the sociometric choices, especially in the preferences or "rejections" of boat-fellows.

The sociometric structure of the "racing association" crew O was uniquely ruled by the group dualism between the two club subgroups. This is true with respect to the preferences--rowing as well as to the election of captain. To retain positive assessments within the respective club cliques was evidently a factor outweighing all other kinds of distribution which might be otherwise explained, as for example, by referring to achievement motivation. Group antagonism caused strong conflicts within the crew.

In contrast, in the "racing association" eight oar crew S consisting of members from four clubs, the club memberships could not detach and pronounce themselves in distinctive polarity in relief against each other. No club centrism developed. Leadership conflicts did not exist --a "racing community" crew, therefore, need not have a leadership "dual". The predicates for proficiency in achievement and popularity crystalized around the same top representatives of the crew. Thus, the assessment according to achievement strength, routine and popularity could not be separated as motivating factors for preference choices, as, e.g., the divergence theorem of group dynamics would suggest.

Distinctively and predominantly the achievement motive determined the preference choices--rowing within both club crews. In W the clique of rowers being assessed to be the most strongly achieving ones detached itself so distinctively and articulately that eventually an emotional counter-reaction of the outsiders within the crew was engendered

37

and the crew split up into two counter-cliques. Leadership conflicts between both exponents of the cliques broke out and the internal leadership structure of the crew was destroyed.

In the club crew Z, pure achievement choices were directed so predominantly outside, that is into W, that a closed sociometric structure did not develop at all. This disintegration was transmitted to the emotional social structure of the crew, too, although to a weaker degree. Z was essentially a pure ad hoc crew held together only for the time being because no better opportunity for joining a stronger team or starting in rowing contests was available for the members.

In sum, surveying all crews, the "preference choices--rowing" of boat-fellows prevailingly tended to be based on the criterion of assessing achievement levels.[14] However, distinctively pronounced group antagonisms or strong personal antipathies, if existant (as in O), superimposed themselves onto the achievement choices. The three crews O, W, and Z were teams oriented at and held together only by the common purpose of top athletic achievement. They developed, beyond this sporting coherence, only a relatively weak emotional integration. Instead, they displayed distinctive and sometimes fierce internal conflicts which could only be ruled and controlled by an external authority, that is the coach. The crew S did not display a high internal integration either, but it did not develop leadership and subgroup conflicts. Besides, in this crew not only achievement motivation on the one hand or sympathy on the other hand determined the sociomatric choices, but both often did in comparable conformity.

However, the crews most burdened and split by conflicts displayed a much higher level of achievement capacity. Even Z was somewhat stronger than S because it beat S. The difference of achievement between Z and S, however, was not very large. Z, again, displayed only minor internal conflicts because of its disintegrated internal social structure. O and W, the crews with by far the strongest conflicts and tensions endangering the cohesion of both crews considerably and also displaying the highest rank differentiation according to "rejections" each at the time of their existence were by far the best achieving crews in the world.[15] All that was recorded and analyzed now evidently leads to the following conclusion. Even fierce social internal conflicts in top performance rowing crews need not noticeably weaken their achievement strength and capacity if these conflicts do not really blow up the crew.[16] To maintain the crew and the level of achievement, however, was a main point of interest to each member because his individual success exclusively depended on the crew's success. When in W a system of organized internal competition was engendered and openly displayed by staging the mentioned qualification tests in skiffs, the level of achievement capacity of the individual rowers was, on the

average, increased and by that, the performance strength of the whole
crew, too. It was replaced on two positions on grounds of the test.

Although a distinctive organizational technical role differentiation
is lacking or only weakly developed in rowing crews, the crews developed clear rank divisions with, in part, relatively high rank differentiations according to achievement points of view or sympathies or
antipathies, respectively. However, one has to except the disintegrated
crew Z, again.

In summary, then, one has to give up the functionalistic thesis
that only groups displaying no or only very weak conflicts can perform
at top achievement level. This thesis turns out to be a prejudice.
Internal conflicts need not noticeably weaken the strength of achievement of specialized top athletic groups, if these groups do not display
a complex role division in regard to role interaction and if these groups
survive in such a conflict situation which might be possible sometimes
only by means of an external authority. This external authority, however, need not even possess real compulsive power.

Moreover, the results of this investigation confirm that it is very
probable that in athletic teams under top performance stress, strong
internal conflicts and competition relationships may develop, if all
members really ask for top achievement with regard to their fellows
and themselves. Top achieving groups have to learn to live with conflicts, to rule and control them,[16] or even to use them for the further-
ance of achievement if possible, as in the engendered system of an
organized internal competition mentioned above. Dahrendorf provided
some evidence for the thesis that conflicts cannot be "solved" by sup-
pression or abolishment of their causes. One can only "rule" conflicts
in a meaningful way. They might be ruled by institutionalization or
compulsory chanelling, by open display and organization of the concerned groups or subgroups and by establishing fixed rules of the
game and comparison of the rank order, etc. It would be useful if all
participants would acknowledge conflicts as meaningful or, sometimes,
even unavoidable. Then, they would be able to use the "fruitful and
creative principle" (Dahrendorf [9]) of conflict and use this principle
as in the democratic procedure of qualification.

ANNEX 1: Correlation With Statistical Expectation

	Preference Choice Rowing	Preference Choice Roomates	"Rejection" Rowing	"Rejection" Roomates
Olympic Champion O	.71	--	.05	--
Spandauer RG S	.04	.45	.09	.16
World Champion $_{62}$W	-.18	--	.65	--
World Champion $_{63}$W	.48	.96	-.79	.04
'Second eight oar crew' Z	.03	.65	.79	.56
	.24	.65	.16	.25
ϕ	(ϕ_3 = .22)		(ϕ_3 = .03)	

Because of the small number of elements, n = 8, the limits of significance are relatively wide. Examples given, with 95% reliability, dependence is only to be defended with $r > 0.706$, that is, by the underlined coefficients of correlation in the table. Also the average coefficients are not different from another at a significant rate. However, the test coefficient of 0.85 leads to the expectation that a statistical difference between the preferences-rowing and the preferences-roommates is probable. According to the expectation, then, the preferences of roommates correspond rather to a random distribution than the preferences-rowing where certain motives, as for instance in principle achievement values, tend to lead and direct the choices in a more unisensory way.

ANNEX 2: Statistical Distribution Data With a Respect to Preference Choices and "Rejections"

A. Preference Choices	Olympic Champion O	Spandauer RG:S		World Champion 1962/62/W	World Champion 1963/63/W		Lower Class Crew Z	
		row-ing	room-mates		row-ing	room-mates	row-ing	room-mates
Executed Choices	16	16	16	20	30	21	17	17
Directed into the crew	14	12	12	20	25	18	2	8
Relative frequency with which the choices fell into the crew	0,88	0,75	0,75	1	0,84	0,86	0,12	0,47
Respective probability	0,88	0,75	0,75	(1,25)	(1,56)	(1,13)	0,13	0,5
Mean value number of received choices ϕ	1,75	1,5	1,5	2,5	3,13	2,25	0,25	1
Dispersion around ϕ	1,44	3,5	2,0	6,25	3,36	0,94	0,19	0,5
Standard deviation (variance)	1,2	1,87	1,41	2,5	1,83	0,97	0,43	0,71
Pearson's skewness	-1,04	0,8	1,06	1	0,07	0,26	0,58	0,0
Number of isolated members	2	4	3	3	0	0	6	2
Relative square rank differentiation	0,22	0,33	0,25	0,42	0,42	0,22	0,13	0,18
Portion of the crew to which 50% of the choices is directed	0,33	0,19	0,31	0,20	0,38	0,41	(3,64)	(1,06)
Number of mutual choices	4	1	2	6	8	5	0	2
Cohesion Coefficient $\varkappa$	1,25	0,18	0,42	1,88	1,43	1,14	0	0,38

ANNEX 2: (Con't)
B. "Rejections"

	14	10	8	13	15	12	12	7
Perform nominations	14	10	8	13	15	12	12	7
Portion of the realized "rejections" directed into the crew out of 16 possible ones ("rejection" probability)	0,88	0,63	0,44	0,81	0,94	0,75	0,75	0,44
Mean value of received "rejections"	1,75	1,25	0,88	0,63	1,88	1,5	1,5	0,88
Dispersion around this mean	5,44	2,94	1,61	1,87	3,92	3,5	0,46	0,61
Standard deviation	2,33	1,71	1,27	1,37	1,98	1,87	0,68	0,78
Pearson's skewness	0,75	0,73	0,3	-0,27	0,95	0,8	-0,74	0,49
Number of non-"rejected" rowers	4	4	4	2	4	4	1	3
Relative square rank differentiation	0,59	0,38	0,4	0,42	0,42	0,33	0,18	0,18
Portion of crew to which 50% of the choices is directed	0,125	0,125	0,125	0,22	0,20	0,16	0,5	0,21
Number of mutual "rejections"	3	0	0	1	3	1	1	0
Repulsion Coefficient ρ	0,94	0	0	0,23	0,83	0,25	0,63	0
C. Internal Social Distance	56	47,6	38,1	36,1	33,4	37,5	300	50
Preference--"rejection"-- ratio V_{aa}/A_{aa}		1,2	1,73	1,54	1,67	1,5	0,017	1,114

FOOTNOTES

[1] The special role the "stroke" had in earlier times loses its importance increasingly. In modern training in small boats, mostly in skiffs, each rower performs the respective tasks which were hitherto reserved to the strokesman. A race is technically planned to such a precise degree that only in unforseen special cases the "stroke" or the coxswain has to decide spontaneously. This is reflected in the sociometric choices insofar as only in two of five cases the "stroke" got the most preference choices.

[2] Ethologists like Lorenz (31), p. 397 ff. and elsewhere, see also (42) tend to defend such theses on grounds of a species historical comparison and their investigation about animal intra-specific aggression. But the problem of aggression and alleged inherited components seems to be unsolved and very complex. Although there may be some inherited components or dispositional factors for aggressiveness, certainly it is also dependent on situations and education. The problem cannot be dealt with here.

[3] Only with respect to the eight oar crew itself we find square matrices here. If there are choices directed outside, the matrices become rectangular ones. Predominantly, attention was paid here to a formulation that the square matrix of the eight oar crew displayed canonical form; only here one main diagonal and, thereby, the canonical form is uniquely determined. The choices directed outside, therefore, were mostly neglected with respect to the ordering of the lines and columns and marked outside on the right side in special columns. This is justified, since they do not display clique structures, etc.

[4] In cell i,k of the square of the positive matrix, a 1 is only contributed, if at the same time a 1 in column 1 of line i and in line 1 of column k there is a certain number 1, that is if i chooses 1 and 1 chooses k. This is true also for nonsymmetrical matrices. If i=k, then a mutual choice is given in which the individual i is involved. An analogous statement is valid for the three step connections in cubic matrices and, of course, for higher powered matrices.

[5] The concept "clique" is also applied here even if, strictly speaking, only an "almost-clique" is at hand (33, 32), that is, when not all persons are choosing one another but when one or two direct connections are missing. A genuine clique with complete mutual choices is called a "complete clique."

[6] The expression "relative frequency" in what follows refers always to a portion amongst the really emitted nominations. The term "probability," by contradistinction, refers to a portion of realized emitted nominations amongst all possible ones, the restriction to two nominations for each person being taken into consideration. Logically speaking, these "probabilities" also are relative frequencies in a finite set.

[7] A concept of social distance is defined here somewhat differently than in Hofstaetter (22, p. 154). Beside the populations of emitter and receiver groups the frequencies of interaction (here displayed by the number of choices) also the frequency of "rejections" is taken account of in the definition. The higher the frequency of rejection, the larger the distance:

$$d_{xx} = Df \frac{|x| (|x| - 1)}{V_{xx}} A_{xx} \; ; \; d_{xy} = Df \frac{|x| \cdot |y|}{V_{xy}} A_{xy} \quad ;$$

$|x|$ being the number of members of x; A_{xx} the number of "rejections" within x; V_{xy} the number of preference choices directed from the group x into the group y; etc.

[8] The expected numbers n_i of the individuals chosen--or "rejected" ones, respectively--by i nominations each is calculated as the respective sum terms:

$$n_i = 8 \binom{7}{i} \left(\frac{2}{7}\right)^{7-i} \left(\frac{5}{7}\right)^i \; ; \; i = 0, 1, \ldots, 7$$

of the binominal probability distribution:

$$n = \sum_{i=0}^{n-1} n_i = \sum_{i=0}^{n-1} n \binom{n-1}{i} p^{n-1-i} (1-p)^i$$

where $p = 2/n-1$ and $n = 8$.

[9] The inner or scalar product: $\sum_{i=1}^{8} a_{ki} a_{li}$ of the line vectors

$(a_{k1}, a_{k2}, \ldots, a_{k8})$ and $(a_{11}, \ldots, a_{18})$ out of (o_{ij}) is labelled by (a_k, a_l).

[10] One rower chose with considerable reservation even a fourth fellow. This not clearly decided case was not taken into consideration here.

[11] The standard deviation is as large as the mean value itself. Since the modal value is 0, the rare case occurred that the skewness of the distribution after Pearson is 1.

[12] By the way, for W the measures of rank differentiation in all four questionnaires for nomination of rowing-fellows in 1962 were equal. The rank differentiation is therefore always equal and unchangedly

strong. Only with respect to "rejections" is it less than in crew 0, where $R_0 = 0.59$.

[13]The nominations of preferred roommates here even lead to a relatively rare statistical-theoretical case of expectation with Pearson's skewness of distribution being zero because the mean and modal value are equal.

[14]This also corresponds to the fact that the number of isolated individuals in the preference choice of boat-fellows amounting to three is higher than the number of isolated rowers in the preference choice of roommates which is 2.6 and that is just vice versa concerning the "rejections" the numbers being 3 and 3.67, respectively. In all cases the number of isolated ones is considerably higher than the statistical expectation of 0.7. Furthermore, the preference choices rowing concentrate more nearly on the top representatives than the preference choices of roommates, since, on average, 50% in the preference-rowing fall into the portion 0.28 of the numbers of rowers, the respective number in the preference of roommates being 0.36. (Hereby, the pathological case of Z could not be taken into account where the concerned measures can only be fictitiously based on an extrapolation.) With respect to "rejections" the emotional nomination (of roommates) shows a slightly higher concentration of 0.14 as against 0.17. All preference choices, however, are dispersed farther than those in analygous sociograms of school classes (39) where a portion of 1/4 resulted. In contradistinction, the "rejections" concentrate more narrowly in the crew sociograms than in analogous school classes where the portion was 1/5. Therefore, the relative rank differentiation according to sociograms of "rejection" is higher with the eight oar crews.

[15]In all cases the intensity and regimen of training remained equal. The training was organized as effective as the most modern methods of training allowed; since the program of training was to a large amount given from outside by the coach the resulting total load and intensity would have been equal, even if the crews would not have shown any conflicts. The physical reserves would have been exploited and exhausted just as much.

[16]The vocabulary and the mathematical methods of cybernetics seem to be recommendable here as a working instrument.

REFERENCES

[1]Apostel, L.: "Equilibre logique et theorie des graphes." In: Logique et equilibre. Paris 1957, p. 119.

[1a]Bastin, G.: Les techniques sociometriques. Paris 1961.

[2]Bavelas, A.: "A Mathematical Model for Group Structures." In Appl. Anthrop. 1948, VII, p. 16.

[3]Beum, C. O., Brundage, E. G.: "A Method for Analyzing the Sociomatrix." In: Sociometry 1950, p. 141.

[4]Berge, C.: Théorie des graphes et ses applications. Paris 1958.

[5]Borgatta, E.F.: "A Diagnostic Note on the Construction of Sociograms and Action Diagrams." In: Group Psychotherapy 1951, p. 300.

[6]Coleman, J.S., MacRae, D.J.: "Electronic Processing of Sociometric Data for Groups up to a Thousand in Size." In: Amer. Soc. Rev. 1960, p. 722.

[7]Coombs, C.H.: "Theory and Methods of Social Measurement." In: Festinger, L., Katz, D. (eds.): Research Methods in the Behavioral Sciences. New York 1953, p. 471.

[8]Cartwright, D., Zander, A.: Group Dynamics, Evanston N.Y. 2 1960.

[9]Dahrendorf, R.: "Elemente einer Theorie des sozialen Konflikts." In: Dahrendorf, R.: Gesellschaft and Freiheit--Zur Sociologischen Analyse der Gegenwart. Munichen 1961.

[10]Daume, W.: "Der Verein als Träger der deutschen Turn-und Sportbewegung." In: Berliner Sport 1962, XI--XII, p. 7.

[11]Dodd, S.C.: "The Interrelation Matrix." In: Sociometry 1940, p. 91.

[12]Festinger, L.: "The Analysis of Sociograms using Matrix Algebra." In: Human Relations 1949, p. 153.

[13]Fischer, H.: Gruppenstruktur and Gruppenleistung. Bern-- Stuttgart 1962.

[14]Forsyth, E., Katz, L.: "A Matrix Approach to the Analysis of Sociometric Data. Preliminary Report." In: Sociometry 1946, p. 340.

[15] Gericke, H.: Theorie der Verbände. Mannheim 1963.

[16] Gericke, H., Martens, H.: "Verbände." In: Behnke-Fladt-Süß: Grundzüge der Mathematik. Band I. Göttingen 1958, p. 227.

[17] Harary, F., Norman, R. Z.: Graph-Theory as a Mathematical Model in Social Science. Ann Arbor 1953.

[18] Hare, P., Bales, R. F., Borgatta, E. F.: Small Groups. New York 1955.

[19] Hermes, H.: Einführung in die Verbandstheorie. Berlin-Gottingen-Heidelberg 1955.

[20] Höhn, E., Schick, C. P.: Das Sociogramm. Die Erfassung von Gruppen-Strukturen. Eine Einführung in die psychologische and padagogische Praxis. Stuttgart ^{2}1959.

[21] Hofstätter, P. R.: Einführung in die Sozialpsychologie. Stuttgart ^{2}1959.

[22] _____, Gruppendynamik. Kritik der Massenpsychologie. Hamburg 1957.

[23] _____, Sozialpsychologie. Berlin 1956.

[24] Homans, G. C.: The Human Group. New York 1951.

[25] Katz, L.: "On the Matrix Analysis of Sociometric Data." In: Sociometry 1947, p. 233.

[26] König, D.: Theorie der endlichen and unendlichen Graphen. Leipzig 1936.

[27] Leavitt, J. H.: "Some Effects of Certain Communication Patterns on Group Performance": In: Journ. Am. Soc. Psych. 1951, I., p. 38.

[28] Lenk, H.: "Renngemeinschaft und Gruppendynamik." In: Rudersport, Lehrbeilage 1962, I, p. 5.

[29] _____, "Sociogramm eines Vereinsachters." In: Rudersport, Lehrbeilage, 1962, II, p. 5.

[30] Lippitt, R., White, R. K.: "An Experimental Study of Leadership and Group Life." In: Newcomb, T., Hartley, E., Swanson, G. (ed.) Readings in Social Psychology. New York 1947, 1952.

[31] Lorenz, K.: Das sogenannte Böse. Zur Naturgeschichte der Aggression. Wien ^{2}1964.

(32)Luce, R.D.: "Connectivity and Generalized Cliques in Sociometric Group Structure." In: Psychometrika 1950, p. 169.

(33)Luce, R.D.; Perry, A.D.: "A Method of Matrix Analysis of Group Structure." In: Psychometrika 1949, p. 95.

(34)MacRae, D.J.: "Direct Factor Analysis of Sociometric Data." In: Sociometry 1960, p. 360.

(35)Moreno, J.L.: Die Grundlagen der Soziometrie, Wege zur Neuordnung der Gessellschaft, Köln-Opladen 1954.

(36)_____,"Soziogram and Sociomatrix. A Note to the Paper by Forsyth and Katz." In: Sociometry 1946, p. 348.

(37)_____, Sociometry, Experimental Method and the Science of Society. An Approach to a New Political Orientation. Beacon, N.Y. 1951.

(38)_____, Who Shall Survive? Foundations of Sociometry, Group Psychotherapy and Sociodrama. Beacon, N.Y. 1953.

(39)Muldoon, J.F.: "The Concentration of Liked and Disliked Members in Groups and the Relationship of Concentrations to Group Cohesiveness." In: Sociometry 1955.

(40)Northway, M.L.: "A Method for Depicting Social Relationship Obtained by Sociometric Testing." In: Sociometry 1940, p. 144.

(41)Nosanchuk, T.A.: "A Comparison of Several Sociometric Partitioning Techniques." In: Sociometry 1963, p. 112.

(41a)Pesquie, P.: "La cohésion de l'équipe sportive." In: Revue Education Physique et Sport 1964, pp. 67-68.

(42)Remane, A.: "Die biologischen Grundlagen des Handelns." Abh. der math-naturwiss. Klasse der Akademie der Wiss. and der Lit. in Mainz. 1950, No.18, Wiesbaden 1951.

(43)Saunders, D.R.: Practical Methods in the Direct Factor Analysis of Psychological Score Matrices. Diss. U. of Illinois 1950.

(44)Sherif, M.; Sherif, C.W.: Groups in Harmony and Tension. New York 1953.

(45)Simon, H.A.: Models of Man-Social and Rational. Mathematical Essays on Rational Human Behavior in a Social Setting. New York-London 1961.

[46] Wright, G.; Evitts, M. S.: "Direct Factor Analysis in Socio-metry." In: Sociometry, 1961, p. 82.

[47] Zurmühl, R.: Matrizen. Berlin-Göttingen-Heidelberg 1950.

ADDITIONAL LITERATURE

[48] Eitzen, D. S.: "The Effect of Group Structure on the Success of Athletic Teams." International Review of Sport Sociology. VII (1973): 7-17.

[49] Fiedler, F. E., "The psychological distance dimension in interpersonal relations," Journal of Personality, 22(1953): 142-150.

[50] Fiedler, F. E., "Assumed similarity measures as predictors of team effectiveness," Journal of Abnormal and Social Psychology, 49(1954):381-388.

[51] Gross, N. and Martin, W. E., "On group cohesiveness," American Journal of Sociology, 57(1952)546-554.

[52] Heber, R. F., and Heber, M. E. "The effect of group failure and success on social status." Journal of Educational Psychology 48(1957): 120-134.

[53] Immig, F. and W.: "Gruppendynamische Aspecte in Training and Weffkampf der männβichen Fugendnationalmannschaft im Kun-stturnen der BRD." In LeistungSport II(1972):452-457.

[54] Klein, M. and Christiansen, G., "Group composition, group structure, and group effectiveness of basketball teams," in Loy, J. W. and Kenyon, G. S. (eds.) Sport, Culture and Society, London, 1969, pp. 397-408.

[55] Lenk, H.: Leistungsmotivation and Mannschaftsdynamik. Schorndorf/Germany (Hofmann) 1970.

[56] Lott, A. J. and Lott, B. E., "Group cohesiveness as inter-personal attraction: A review of relationships with antecedent and consequent variables", Psychological Bulletin, 64, (1965), 259-309.

[57] Lüschen, G. (ed.): "Kleingruppenforschung and Gruppe im Sport". Special issue 10/1966 of Kölner Zeitschumft fur Soziologie and Sozialpsychologie. Köln-Opladen (Westdentscher Verlag) 1966.

[58] Kleiner, R. J. "The effects of threat reduction upon interper-sonal attraction," Journal of Personality 28(1960): 145-155.

[59] Martens, R., Peterson, F.A.: "Group cohesiveness as a determinant of success and member satisfaction in team performance." International Review of Sport Sociology VI(1971):49-59.

[60] McGrath, J.E.: "The influence of positive interpersonal relations on adjustment and effectiveness in rifle teams." Journal of Abnormal and Social Psychology 65(1962):365-375.

[61] Myers, A.: "Team competition, success, and the adjustment of group members." Journal of Abnormal and Social Psychology 65(1962):325-332.

[61a] Naul, R., Voigt, H.: "Zur Problematik des Divergenztheorems für leistungsorientierte Ballspielmannschaften." In: Sportwissenschaft (1972) S. 300-306.

[62] Peterson, F. A., Martens, R.: "Success and residential affiliation as determinants of team cohesiveness." Research Quarterly XLIII (1961), 62-76.

[62a] Valentinova, N. G., Myedvyedyev, V. V.: "Selected problems of small groups in sports teams." International Review of Sport Sociology I (8) (1873), 69-77.

[63] Veit, H.: Untersuchungen zur Gruppendynamik von Ballspielmanschaften. Schorndorf/Germany, Hofmann, 1971.

[63a] Veit, H.: "Die Bedeutung sozialpsychologischer Untersuchungen von Sportmannschaften fur die Praxis." In: Die Liebeserziehung 1968 S. 80-87.

[64] Vosj, K., Brinkmann, W.: "Erfolg und Zusammenhalt in Sportgruppen." In Leistungssport II(1972), 128-134.

[65] Zander, A., Stotland, E., and Wolff, D.: "Unity of group, identification with group, and self-esteem of members." Journal of Personality 28(1960), 463-78.

Kohl, K.: "Motivationsbeeinflussende Faktoren bei Basketball - und Hallenhandballspitzenspielere." In: Ausschuß Deutscher Leibeserzieher (ed.): Motivation im Sport. Schorndorf 1971, p. 299-307.

Kohl, K.: Untersuchungen zur Mannschaftsdynamik. Ergebnisse von Befragungen bei Basket-Ball - und Hallenhandballspitzen-sportlern zum Thema "Motivation im Sport." Unpublished Manuscript PH Berlin, September 1972.

Kohl, K.: "Über Bedautungsgehalte des Sportspiels." In:
Bundesinstitut für Sportwissenschaft (ed.): Bericht
über den III Europäischen Kongress fur Sportpsycholo-
gie (red. Feige, K. - Hahn, E., Rieder, H. -
Stabenow, G. Schorndorf 1973, p. 52-55.

Mutafowa, J.: "Die sozialpsychologische Struktur von Basketballmannschaften." Ibid. p. 55-59.

Veit, H.: "Untersuchungen zur Betreuung von Ballspielmannschaften." Ibid. p. 59-61.

Essing, W., Houben, H.: "Möglichkeiten und Grenzen der
Anwendung der Soziometrie als Führungshilfe in
Sportmannschaften." Ibid. p. 24-27.

Top Performance Despite Internal Conflict

An Antithesis to a Hypothesis Widely Held
in Sociological Functioning

The purpose of this paper is to refute the strict general validity of a hypothesis that seems to have been taken for granted in structural-functional micro-sociology and which is also held to be valid in various forms by other sociologists, namely, the proposition: Only small groups, which are low in conflict, or highly integrated, can accomplish at a particularly high level of performance. It is asserted that a cohesive group is more productive of record achievements (1). "With generally increasing performances there would be a corresponding increase in orientation to one's partner or fellow group members." "For group achievement, internal competition" would be "inhibitory." "The stronger the intra-group relationships" and group integration, "the greater would be the performance and vice versa" (2).

"Of course, personal tensions and conflicts, in each case, have an achievement decreasing effect. Under circumstances, a group may dissolve because of such difficulties ... in any case, however, a disharmonic, conflictuous, and tensional group is only minimally capable of achievement in the long run" (3a).

"An organization" - hence also the cooperative characteristic arrangement of a small group - would be "the more successful, the more the informal structure echoes the formal one" (3), i.e., the stronger the officially planned cohesiveness manifests itself in the formal structure of relationships.

The antithesis to be advanced here may be surprising, and thus shall be brought out for discussion. The argument is as follows: even violent internal social conflicts in highly performing teams of a certain kind need not noticeably weaken their performance capacity, if the team

Translation from "Maximale Leistung trotz innerer Konflikte" in Lüschen, G. (ed.), Kleingruppenforschung and Gruppe im Sport. Special issue of Kölner Zeitschrift für Soziologie und Sozialpsychologie 10/1966, p. 168-172. The author has to thank D.E. Kenyon for providing a first draft of the translation.

Although this short contribution to the First International Seminar of the International Committee for the Sociology of Sport is, as regards empirical data, exclusively based on the evidence of the preceding article "Conflict and Competition in Top Athletic Teams," it has, nonetheless, been integrated in this volume for two reasons. First, an argument regarding functional analysis in sociology of sport which has meanwhile been discussed to considerable extent is particularly elaborated here. Second, this paper dispensing with mathematical formulations might be more easily understood by readers without mathematical background.

continues to exist despite the conflicts. Indeed, as the conflict develops and becomes more pronounced, concomitantly, even an improved performance can result.

A discussion of the antithesis seems to be especially important. In a previous publication (4), the precise sociometric data and the corresponding matrix and vector analysis have appeared; thus the technical details can be dispensed with here.

An unconditional axiom which is characterized by "only" or "all" "every," "always," "necessarily," etc., like the thesis to be refuted here, can be denied through the presentation of only one contrary instance. Its negation, being a proposition logically equivalent to the refuting statement, can already be instantiated by one single example. The referred-to antithesis can be derived easily. If there would be a team that performs at its best despite most massive internal conflicts, or whose performance, despite the development of conflict, improves as far as possible, then the antithesis would be confirmed and, therefore, the original thesis would be clearly refuted, as the latter one and its negation are incompatible with each other. As a first counterexample the victorious German Olympic Rowing Eight of 1960, the first crew analyzed by sociometrical questionairing and participant observation, displayed sharp subgroup conflicts and leadership conflicts which were even commented in the press. This was a racing crew consisting of athletes of two clubs, four of each club.

However, this crew was originally constituted by the rowers themselves relying on a sort of comradeship, without the cooperation of any official club representative. At that time, all the rowers considered the squad as a "we group" - extra-unit between the two clubs. Conflicts did not occur. During the two years in which the team existed, the managing boards of the clubs x and y increasingly introduced club-centered motives into the crew. The member of the combined squad subsequently split into club cliques, due to which conflicts emerged distinctly. By the vast majority of the questionnaire answers the division into the two contrary cliques was traced back to the club-centered influence. The joint crew was now almost unanimously considered to be a mere instrumental exclusively success-oriented one. Several times conflict almost led to the destruction of the team. According to all available knowledge of coaching and sport science, within this eight, no noticeable decrease in athletic performance occurred as a result of the tensions within the group. Otherwise, a performance decrement would have occurred in comparison with the initial situation (of "we group"-attitude and relative conflictlessness among the members of two different clubs), for the regimen of training and the technical control of the work-outs remained on the same level. Without conflicts, at best there could have been only a small performance increase. Actually, the performance did increase and paralleled the intensity of the conflict during the two years in which the eight oar crew existed. Performance was systematically controlled and measured by frequent

53

training matches - eight times a quarter mile (560 meters exactly) - at racing speed. The crew remained unbeaten and won the Olympic championship in 1960. An athletic crew, therefore, is capable of achieving, in spite of strong internal conflicts, at the highest perceivable level of performance. The conflicts did not noticeably cause **any** decrease in performance.

The second example, the world champion eight of 1962, was not a racing squad combined out of members of different clubs, but rather a club crew. In this crew, however, there developed a complete clique of four rowers in which each man was sociometrically chosen by each other, thus setting themselves apart from the other rowers. The latter, however, chose members of the clique also. Performance envy or position jealousy apparently did not determine their choice. They did not, at the outset, form an anticlique.

As the closedness and, consequently, the emotional unity of a partial group of a social system always creates strong social tensions, indeed: even rejections and animosities from those which are excluded, it could positively be concluded here: the extremely strong formation of the clique could not have occurred as a result of personality evaluations and sympathies. As a matter of fact, the clique consisted of, according to the judgment of the coach and others, precisely the strongest rowers of the eight. The image of performance capacity of the single rower, as judged by the others formed the sociometric priority criterion in this top level crew.

A significant and remarkable feature is revealed by the sociogram of the election of the crew's captain: a completely symmetrical structure with regard to the two highest-ranking rowers, i.e., those chosen most frequently by their fellows. Both were chosen by two others and, in addition, they chose themselves. Due to the equally strong leadership polarity, the sociometric structure revealed a latent leadership conflict. Disagreements - concerning technical and tactical questions - would arise if the crew was to come up with independent decisions and the suggestions of the leading athletes would differ from each other. Like the first crew, this second squad also was not able to develop independently and to guide themselves. Here, too, only an external authority (such as the coach) could have led the team and kept them together as a unit of action and self-interpretation.

Because of the distinctive leadership dualism and the extremely strong tendency of the dominating clique, to separate from the others, one had to predict in 1962 (5) that the crew would split into two opposing groups. The aversions would have to be intensified emotionally particularly among the holders of the leadership roles due to their polarity, and the squad could be expected to become exposed to harsh leadership fights.

The eight oar crew was questionnaired and interviewed again a year later (1963) when they were still consisting of the same members. For the non-members of the dominating clique, now noticeably disengaged from the clique of the strongest athletes, the aversion towards the clique was twice as great as in 1962, based upon both the sociometric data and their observed behavior. This was true particularly in terms of roommate selections, the aversion here being five times as emphatical as a year before. The non-members of the clique now developed greater unity and an internal "we group" attitude directed against the dominating clique. The antipathy among these "outsiders" had now disappeared in comparison to 1962. They were now only one vote short of forming a complete clique themselves.

For structural and mathematical reasons, the emotional rejection at this time, no doubt stood out as being particularly stressed. The diagram of the rejections forms a supremum sublattice. In comparison to 1962, actually two cliques now faced each other emotionally as had been predicted before on grounds of the sociometric structure and the the leadership duality(5). The leadership fights, which now had erupted vehemently, resulted in a considerably more distinct mutual rejection of the two leading persons than in 1962. The team had lost confidence in the 1962 leaders after the conflict had openly erupted. As the leadership sociogram shows, the team had no internal leadership any longer. It was hierarchically disorganized and was only held together by by the outside authority of the coach. Nevertheless, the crew won the European championship during the year of the observation - once more against the strongest opponents of the world championship regatta of the preceding year. The eight had even become somewhat better in performance measured in terms of the average of eight quarter mile training times as explained above. Thus, the level of performance had not been diminished from leadership as well as status conflicts and the tension between the confronting cliques and leaders. As the regimen and dose of training and the technical control of the boat had remained at the same level and only little increase in muscular strength due winter training might have been achieved, the level of performance itself could, at best, have improved only insignificantly. And this occurred indeed, despite the conflicts.

During the following year (1964), trial meets covering the quarter mile eight times in the 'skiff' (single sculls) were held for qualification regarding membership in the eight oar crew, resulting in an internal competition now being openly generated. In consequence of these qualifying tests, two rowers were replaced by two others. However, the competition again in no way inhibited the overall level of the crew's performance. Indeed, the individual performance of five of the remaining athletes (as measured by their quarter mile times in single sculls) increased, because they had been obliged to exercise even harder before the trial. During that year the team proved to be slightly stronger than in the previous year and won the Olympic Silver Medal in Tokyo. Thus, internal competition within rowing crews by no means necessarily has a noticeable inhibiting effect upon performance as is implied by the initial thesis which this paper is going to criticize.

In comparison to other crews studied at that time (that is in 1960, 1962, 1963, and 1964), it is these two squads analyzed above, i.e., the eighth with the harshest tensions always threatening the unity of team, which achieved the highest possible top level performances in the world.

This result, as well as the fact that the development of conflict went parallel with an optimal improvement of performance, which was the highest attainable as to the best knowledge of coaching, confirm that the antithesis is correct: even vehement social internal conflicts within top level performing rowing crews need not noticeably weaken the strength of the performance at all, if altogether the team continues to exist in spite of conflict (everyone of the ambitious members was personally interested in the continuation of the team - and in his own membership - as well as in the strength of its performance). Parallel to the development or intensification of an internal conflict even an increase in performance can occur.

Summary

The initial statement analyzed in this paper, namely the universal hypothesis that only low-conflict groups can achieve at high levels of performance, is not generally valid. Its strict general validity proves to be a prejudice. * Actually, this thesis is refuted by counter-examples of two top level eight oar crews at the same time displaying intense internal conflicts and achieving world best performances.

---

*Moreover, further supporting data based on 26 American high-school basketball teams, which obviously do not achieve at top levels of performance, led to the rejection of the hypothesis that close relationships among team members would be conducive to winning many games (Fiedler, F.E., Leader Attitudes and Group Effectiveness, Urbana, Ill. 1958, p. 24). For some different findings see the articles by Martens-Peterson, Peterson - Martens, and Eitzen mentioned in the bibliography of the preceding article in this volume.

REFERENCES

[1] Hare, P., Handbook of Small Group Research, Glencoe, Ill. 1962.

[2] Lüschen, G., "Die gesellschaftliche Funktion des modernen Sports" in Krankengymnastik, 1964, p. 2.

[3] König, R. (ed.), Soziologie, Frankfurt 1958, p. 219.

[3a] Anger, H., "Kleingruppenforschung heute," in Lüschen, G. (ed.), Kleingruppenforschung und Gruppe in Sport. Kölner Zeitschrift fur Soziologie und Sozial-psychologie. Speical issue 10/1966, p. 36 f.

[4] Lenk, H., "Renngemeinschaft und Gruppendynamik," in Rudersport, Lehrbeilage 1/1962, pp. 5-7, id., Conflict and Competition in Top Athletic Teams.

[5] Lenk, H., "Soziogramm eines Vereinsachters," in Rudersport, Lehrbeilage 11/1963, pp. 5-7.

Subjective Assessments of Achievement and Sociometric Choices in World Champion Eight Crews

Images of Achievement and Rank Assignment

Generally speaking, top eight oar crews distributed their sociometric choices, with positive preferences as well as negative "rejections," according to how they assessed their co-fellows as to their level of achievement. This was found to be true in many crews. Even in crews in which other factors played an important role (as, for instance, loyalty towards the larger sporting organization, towards a club, towards friendships, etc. may impinge on the choices), the assessments as to achievement level exerted a decisive influence on the distribution of preferences and "rejections." It has to be emphasized that it is the subjective image of achievement playing the role of a selection criterion; that is, the assessment of achievement capacity the respective athlete gets or enjoys according to the opinion of his team fellows. This assessment need not reflect the actual capacity and strength of achievement and, consequently, the actual objective order of ranks as to achievement capacity in the crew. In fact, this deviation from the actual rank order is frequently found in rowing crews.

An especially revealing example was conveyed by the eight oar crew winning the world championship in 1962 and the European championship in 1963--representing a crew which was especially achievement-oriented. In order to mitigate or rule the fierce leadership conflicts and ranking struggles amongst the leading figures competing for a decision-making position in this crew, action was taken to establish a rank order as to achievement, in the crew, approximating the objective one as near as possible; to increase the individual ambition for training and thus to enlarge the overall strength of the crew; and finally, to guarantee a relatively just basis and criterion of selection for the Olympic eight in 1964 among about a dozen candidates. At the beginning of the season of 1964, qualification races in the skiff were arranged for the first time. All candidates had to compete against one another over the usual distance of interval training (approximately one-third of a mile or, more precisely, 560 meters) for several times, somehow corresponding to a normal dose of training, viz., eight times. This test was administered under fair conditions--such as, no wind obtaining. It was not possible to match all participants against each other at the same time because of the lack of equally good boats. So, the respective time was also considered. Everyone had to perform at his very best to qualify for the Olympic eight--a fact that was especially demonstrated when two very routined and strong former world champions did not qualify in the test and, accordingly, were eliminated from the team (one of these two former champions displayed a certain lack of training in the res-

pective year of the test races for he had passed some University exams
just before . The statistically overall correlation between both rank
orders--see below--could, however, only be very slightly influenced
by this fact). With the exception of certain, almost unavoidable and
objectively uncontrollable conditions--such as minor variations of wind
conditions during different qualification races or a possible obtaining
but uncontrollable inequality of different boats--this qualification test
preferred a relatively objective grading and led to a rank order of
achievement among crew members.

How did this relatively objective rank order of achievement cor-
relate with the respective subjective one within the crew? This latter
had been established by questionnaire some months before the test.
One can assume that the objective rank order did not significantly
change meanwhile. At least this was true on the statistical average
because the respective rowers were in an equal state of training and
had belonged to the top class for several years. So, a certain continuity and comparability might be assumed here; but it is only the statistical figures and overall results which we find of interest here.

A somewhat surprising result followed. Both rank orders did
not show a significant statistical correlation following a conventional
significance test--even if one is establishing weaker requirements for
significance in social sciences than in the natural sciences. The result is more surprising since most of the rowers were used to rowing
against one another in training and should have been expected, then,
to be able to reliably judge one another with respect to achievement
capacity. The rank correlation between the two rank orders was found
to be only 0.46. A statistical significant correlation as to a 95% reliability limit would only be guaranteed with a correlation of 0.64 and
higher, regarding the number of the eight candidates who were finally
elected for the crew. Only then it would have been possible to state
that the rank orders would show the statistic, significant correlation
according to the usual statistical requests. Under the above mentioned
assumptions, it follows that the rank order according to the subjective
assessments of achievements by one crew member for any other one
was not reliable. The rowers misjudged one another to a remarkable
degree although they had been expected to more expertly judge the
level and strength of their fellows and to be able to realistically compare these assessments. So, subjective assessments of achievement
capacity--that is, achievement images and spproximately objective
ranks of achievement according to the skiff qualification test results
with rowers--are not the same. As shown by this example they can
deviate from one another so far that there is no significantly proven
correlation between both rank orders. Therefore, it is not possible
or advisable to take the rank position according to the subjective assessment of achievement as a reliable measure of achievement capacity for the rowers in relationship to the respective assessments
of their fellow rowers.

A questionnaire investigating the world champion eight crew of 1966 led to a similar result, on somewhat comparable lines, although there were no qualification tests in skiff for the recruitment of this crew. Here it also turned out that the rowers were incapable of relatively objectively assessing and comparing the achievement capacity of their fellow teammates and themselves, respectively. Just prior to the world championship regatta, each rower was instructed to give a rank order listing up how he would assess the achieving capacity of the individual crew members when compared against one another. It was permissible to assign a specific rank position to more than one crew member but no more than half the crew in one position (this in order to guarantee the character of a certain, although not strict, rank order), for without rank differences there would be no rank order at all. In evaluating the results, the strongest achieving rower--by this overall achievement image within the crew--was assigned eight points. The weakest was assigned one point and the others inserted at a point distance of one point each, respectively, between those extreme ranks. Finally, rank positions being seized more than once were assigned their respective mean values. The analysis led to the following rank assessments:

TABLE I: Mutually Assessed Rank Orders of Achievement, World Champion Eight 1966.

Assessed Rowers		G	A	E	B	C	H	D	F
Assessing Rowers:	G	7	7	7	5	1	4	2,5	2,5
	A	7,5	4,5	7,5	4,5	4,5	4,5	1,5	1,5
	E	4,5	7	7	4,5	7	2	2	2
	B	7,5	7,5	6	4,5	4,5	3	1,5	1,5
	C	6	8	7	5	4	3	2	1
	H	7	3	8	5,5	2	5,5	4	1
	D	4,5	8	1	4,5	4,5	4,5	4,5	4,5
	F	8	5,5	2,5	1	5,5	2,5	5,5	5,5
Assigned Ranks		52	50,5	46	34,5	33	29	23,5	19,5
Average		6,5	6,3	5,75	4,3	4,1	3,6	2,9	2,4
Sum According to an Evaluation from +4 to -4 (0 excluded)		19	16,3	12,5	-0,5	-4,5	-9	-15,7	-19,7
Largest Rank Difference		3,5	5	7	4,5	6	3,5	4	4,5
Coach		5,5	8	2,5	1	2,5	5,5	5,5	5,5
Co-Coach		7,5	7,5	4,5	4,5	4,5	4,5	1,5	1,5
Sum of all Assessments, Crew and Coaches		65	66	53	40	40	39	30,5	26,5
Average		6,5	6,6	5,3	4	4	3,9	3,1	2,7

Looking to these rank orders of achievement images it is striking that individual assessments greatly deviate from one another. Thus, for instance, rowers E and C were appointed to be both the weakest as to achievement and the strongest! Since the rower E got high rank numbers with the exception of two assignments, he must have been too much devaluated by two fellows and the chief coach in an irrational and subjective manner--or he must have been overrated by the rest of the crew. Besides these strong differences there are also large differences of assigned rank positions to be found with the other rowers. The largest, according to single rower assessment, were on a 4.75 average; thus saying that on the average each rower is differently assessed by more than half the scale of possibilities of assignment.

Accordingly, the stated assessments of the individual rank orders deviate remarkably from one another. The highest rank correlation leading to almost exactly the same assessment is, to be sure, 0.95, but only eleven of the twenty-eight rank correlations do result at the 95% reliability level in a guaranteed statistical significant connection between the two respective rank orders. On average with 0.47, the rank correlations are to be found positive, but this average is far below the reliability limit of 0.64 for a significant positive correlation. The rowers C and F, as well as A and D, respectively stated rank orders being totally independent from one another and displaying only a correlation of 0.03. Although most rank orderings are pointing in the same direction, that is displaying positive correlation with each other--to be sure, insignificant ones--there are even some contrary assignments leading to correlation of the respective rank orders of minus 0.2 between the rowers H and D, as well as minus 0.21 between H and F.

However, a great unaniminity of almost all members is to be found in the assessment of the rowers D and F representing, according to the opinion of the crew, the weakest ones. Only they assessed themselves higher.

With the exception of the rower E, who assessed himself at the uppermost position along with others, none deemed himself to be the strongest. But, on the other hand, nobody assigned to himself a position in the lower third of the scale. Those being generally assessed to be the strongest did tend to underrate themselves--whereas, those generally looked upon as being the weakest were more apt to overrate themselves. The self-assessment therefore led to certain leveling is due to the aim not to appear too striking or to avoid showing off, or to over-compensate a hidden consciousness of one's own weakness.

Thus, one is led to the result that the general statement which was established with the eight oar crew from 1963-64 was definitely confirmed by another analysis with the world championship eight crew of 1966. The team itself was not able to unanimously assess one rank order of achievement or a fortiori, the objective rank order as to achievement comparisons. In particular, the weakest members' average assessments contained a remarkable number of wrong assessments with respect to their own level of achievement as judged by themselves and compared with those received assessments in general. Individual rowers were not able to objectively assess their fellows and themselves according to achievement strength and levels. For within strongly differing rank orders at least some must be wrongly assessed.

However, according to the overall sum of received assignments, three obviously detached achievement groups can be distinguished from one another. The strongest, according to the averaged opinion of the crew, rowers G, A, and E, clearly stand out against the middle group of the rowers B and C and perhaps also H, with respect to the received number of points. In turn, the weakest ones, D and F, as regards the general assessment of the team, are clearly detached again from this middle group. Obviously, this detachment is especially brought out if one assigns in part positive numbers as rank assessments and in part negative ones (see Table 1). In spite of the large differences in individual grading, achievement levels differentiated according to performance capacity are nevertheless relatively distinctively detached from one another with respect to the received rank position in the average. This fact, with higher probability, points towards the assumption that the sum rank order of the whole crew could be deemed approximately a more correct assessment of the "objective rank order" than the individual assessment by the individual rower. But assuming this, a very surprising statement turns out to be true; remarkably, the chief coach has wrongly assessed the achievement rank order. The rank correlation between his assignment and that of the crew is, to be sure, positive by 0.43, but both respective rank orders do not display a statistically significant dependency with one another. This would, again, only be true with the correlation of at least 0.64. Even less is his rank ordering found in statistical compliance with the assessment of the co-coach. Both rank orders only show a rank correlation of 0.32 towards one another. The co-coach, however, nearly assessed the same rank order as the whole crew--both orders being correlated with one another at rank correlation 0.91. The coaches, therefore, differ from one another strongly in their assessment of achievement, achievement capacities, and performance levels of the respective rowers. The reason might be, in part, due to the fact that each of the coaches apparently deemed the rowers which he had brought into the crew to be relatively strong. Regrettably, regarding this crew there was no approximately objective rank order of achievement established by systematic qualification or comparison in the skiff. Therefore, the actual rank order of achievement remains hidden. Nevertheless, it can be inferred clearly that preferences, obviously not objectively reflecting achievement assessments, also determined the coaches' judgments. This is to say, the assessment of achievement by the coaches is not totally reliable either.

Sociograms

Comparing these subjectively assessed achievement rank orders amongst rowers with sociometric choices led to an interesting result. To be sure, with almost all top performance crews the most rowers getting the highest numbers of choices in the respective sociometric voting--indicating which two comrades from the whole training camp one would preferably row with in the same boat--were also deemed to be very strong in their rowing achievement. Thus, five members of the world champion eight from 1966 chose the rower A (who had received the most preference votes in the sociogram of rowing preferability) to be one of the two most strongly achieving crew members. Although in this single case the assessment of achievment may be a determinant factor for the distribution for preference choices within the sociogram, in general the total structure of sociometric choices of rowers is not a pure assessment as to achieving capacity. For rower G, deemed to be the strongest one, did not receive any choice! The diagram of subjectively assessed rank orders of achievement (see Table 1) is very much different from the following sociogram of the rowing preference choices.[1]

DIAGRAM 1: Sociogram of Rowing Preference Choices in World
            Champion Eight 1966

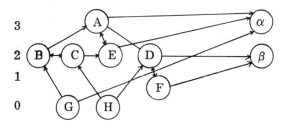

A, B, ..., H symbolize the
rowers of the eight, α and β
outsiders, respectively.

Considering the two allegedly strongest rowers, only four--that is only one-third--of the choices comply with this preference sociogram. Negatively however, such a connection is very distinctively displayed. The sociometric "rejections" resulting from the question with whom or with which two rowers did one only reluctantly or willingly row in the same boat,[2] appear, with few exceptions, to be "rejections" on the basis of an assessment of lack of achievement.

Within twelve sssignments of the weakest achieving fellows in the crew no less than nine--three quarters of the nominations--just exactly comply with the sociometric "rejections" of rowers. The following sociograms clearly reveal this, for they are very much similar to one another.

DIAGRAM 2: Sociogram of "Rejections" of Rowers in World Champion Eight: 1966

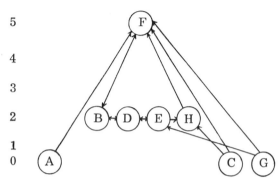

DIAGRAM 3: Assignment of the--or the Two--Weakest Rower(s) in World Champion Eight 1966

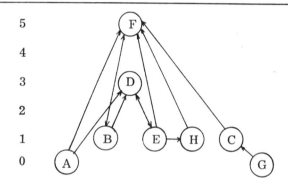

Discussion

The obvious connection between sociometric "rejections" and the appointments of the weakest rowers and similarly the lack of such a connection in the sociometric preference choice of rowers is in need of an explanatory interpretation. The crew was explicitly established as a top performance team, combined for the common purpose of athletic success, a national eight oar crew which was from the very beginning designed with the aim to win the world championship. The members took into account disadvantages in their vocational career, such as loss of time and University courses, as well as long journeys to the respective locations of training and contests--for instance, four hours air and car to travel from Southern Germany to participate in the scheduled common training camps and opportunities in Ratzeburg which is in Northern Germany. The four rowers from Berlin had already represented a very successful fourwidth coxswain, namely the silver medal winner in the European championship of the year before. Three other rowers had already won silver and bronze medals in European championships and Olympic Games, respectively. But only one of these had really won a championship of Europe and one world championship. All the others were lacking the highest athletic success although all except one had silver medals. It took years of training and exercise to reach the highest athletic goal. Everybody, with the one exception, had won a silver medal and had been--at least once--within very near reach of the highest title of world champion. The motivation to finally reach the long yearned for gold medal was apparently very stimulating to all team members. Runners-up are always more highly motivated than former champions. After having trained for almost a decade, everybody wanted to crown the hard top performance with winning the world championship, and for these reasons the expectations of each member in the team were very high. Thus, the high individual effort and endeavor as well as the sporting record of each rower, led to the considerably heightened sensitivity of each member toward every potential threat to the longed-for championship, toward which the highest motivation was directed without exception. Therefore, weaker performing rowers and weaknesses in capacity to achieve would carry a special weight within the mutual judgments and assessments. If one was estimated as being weak in achievement, he probably would be "rejected" or only be tolerated reluctantly or unwillingly as a boat fellow. Of course, those negative assessments also indirectly determine the sociogram of preferences of rowing fellows. Those who got a "rejecting" vote in the respective sociogram of "rejections" would never, of course, get a preference. vote from the same voter in the sociogram of rowing preferences. This fact is compatible throughout in that the rowers estimated on an average to be the strongest ones were not also elected automatically to be the top figures of the sociogram of rowing preferences. Perhaps the reason for the latter phenomenon is that the actual differences of achievement levels did not remarkably differ in principle and in gross classification; otherwise, the subjectively assessed rank orders of achievements could not have been so different. So, the inessential difference (according to objective achievement "classes") amongst the majority of the crew members did not lead to a decisive criterion of selection and did not induce large differences in the sociogram of preferences of rowing fellows; although these differences, later on, were subjectively stressed--maybe in part by the leading question asking for assessments of achievement capacities. The preference sociogram of rowing fellows, therefore, could only be negatively influenced and determined by the overall ruling achievement orientation, i.e., by the fact that the "rejected" members did not receive preference choices from the fellows "rejecting" them at the same time.

Thus, in spite of the prevailing achievement orientation, within the internal socio-psychological group relationships group loyalty could play a decisive role. This group loyalty, however, may to be sure only secondarily serve the aim of increasing achievement. One subordinates oneself to the achievement interests of the whole crew because this is the way--and the only way--to serve one's own best interest for success. At least, on the average, this is valid. Even those classed among the weaker ones stick to and stress group loyalty in order to be able to remain within the crew. Even when subjectively the final orientation of the individual member is egocentrically directed towards one's own success and towards one's own sporting fame and enhancement of self-experience, still that same member of the crew will abide by the expectations of the other crew to a high degree. The ruling group standardization, group norms, and even group commands require an orientation to the highest possible crew achievement to such a degree that the egocentric success motivation is concealed behind this uniting pledge of group loyalty. Stressing group loyalty in this case is ideological and, in fact, guides and determines the socio-psychic relationship of the crew members toward one another. This is all the more true since the crews were coached in the "democratic" style making up their psychic and group dynamic internal social "climate" by themselves to a considerable degree.

This group loyalty is in effect, so to speak, the group resultant of the egoistic interests of success of the individual crew members. It will therefore be pretended to be the final and upper motivation useful for justifications, or at least pretendedly used that way, and also be related as an undisputable sporting norm towards the crew of which one is, for the time being, a member. Entering a new crew, a member will easily and quickly redirect his allegiance to group loyalty toward this new crew. Just this group loyalty, however, also leads to the effect that the "rejection" of rowers assessed to be the weakest performing ones distinctively impresses itself upon sociograms of "rejections" in the social structure of relations. Structurally speaking, this is reflected in the fact that the sociometric "rejections" correlating to the assignments of a weak rower (except the one by G) are arranged--mathematically speaking--in a supremum semi-lattice, if one counts mutual assignments only once. This sociometric structural crystallization of "rejectings" according to achievement perspectives can be interpreted as an attempt of a sociopsychic reaction of the crew toward the low assessment in terms of achievement; if the rowers with images of lower achievement are to remain in the crew they are punished and distanced by a certain kind of sociopsychic "rejection."

Summary

Subjective assessments regarding achievement capacity in rowing crews, on the average, differ from one another to a remarkable degree. They may also significantly differ from the objective rank order of achievement as long as no relatively objectified internal comparison of achievement has taken place. The mere assessment or judgment according to achievement images is not objective and not reliable. This applies to the judgments of the athletes themselves and as well to the assessments by the coaches. Self-assessments tend to a compensatory leveling in the middle of the scale meticulously avoiding self-overrating as well as self-underrating. The assessments of the strongest achieving ones did not strikingly influence the sociometric preferences of rowers. However, there was an extraordinarily distinctive connection between the assessments of the weakest performing rowers and the sociogram of "rejections." The "rejection" sociogram by far consists of "rejections" stemming from achievement ratings and, consequently, gradings. High achievement motivation and the group loyalty stemming from achievement ratings and, consequently, gradings. High achievement motivation and the group loyalty stemming from and impinging on strict achievement motivation, in fact, explain this especially sensitive and distinctive "rejection" of the weakest performing members--as well as their detachment and the redirection of negative achievement assessments toward socio-psychic "rejections."

FOOTNOTES

[1] The sociograms of emotional judgments, that is choice or "rejection" of comrades as roommates on a regatta journey, do not display a remarkable connection with the assessed rank orders of achievement and also not with the positive or negative choices of rowing fellows. The sociometric preferences of roommates in this eight from 1966 did not show a very elaborate structuring, but a relatively widely branches internal interlacing. Thus, C and B each got four voices at the top; E and G were isolated, whereas three sympathy choices for β as well as one achievement and sympathy-orientated choice for α were directly towards outside. The "rejection" of roommates was predominantly ruled by five emotional "rejections" against one person, namely E. Besides, E and D made up a leadership duo in the sociometric choice of captain.

[2] The expression "rejection" actually is too strong and was not used in the proper sociometric questionnaires in order not to increase the effect of suggestiveness or leading character. But there was no very apt short nominal term. So, "rejection" here refers to what was termed in the question "only reluctantly or unwillingly." This does not deny nor exclude that occasionally in an eight oar crew, real emotional rejections and discrepancies as well as conflicts did materialize.

Surrender of Defensive and Value Layers in the Case of Top-Class Oarsmen Under Socio-Dramatic Simulated Stress

In a socio-psychological study regarding American combative groups, Sobel[1] established that personalities that had previously been well-integrated and who, after long-lasting stress situations, during competitions which put too high demands on their mental resistance, revealed psycho-normative signs of disintegration. Sobel mentioned five, clearly distinctive, psychological defensive layers or hierarchies of values in the following order, depending on the intensification of stress:

abstract ideals	hatred of the adversary	short-range military aims	self-esteem	loyalty to the group
	→	→	→	→

Thus we see, that abstract ideals were the first to be given up under the stress of battle. Loyalty to the group turned out to be the most stable value, which was broken only at the end (under heaviest stress).

Charnofsky[2] turned this result into a hypothesis regarding relations existing among a high-school baseball team (5 players). With the help of a socio-drama[1a] according to Moreno[3] he examined the succession in which values were given up in simulated stress situations. Such stress was created, by the instructor in the socio-dramatic situations, in such a way that he excluded the given player irrevocably from the team. This exclusion (occurring in a random succession regarding time) was in each case motivated by means of pointing to the five typical values or aims and by emphasizing that the team should put them into practice, which it could do only without the given player. (The terminology was in an obvious manner adapted to aims and values typical of sport.)

The player placed under stress in such a way, defended himself in the socio-drama against such exclusion, by either expressing doubt in the value which had been given as a reason for the exclusion, or by refusing to accept it, trying to provide proof of the fact that his participation was necessary to achieve the coveted aim, or by giving arguments against the reason for his exclusion based on another value, that was of decisive importance to him. Finally, some among the players referred to justice in sport and asked that procedures should be adopted which would permit an objective comparison of achievements, emphasizing the duty of the instructor to furnish proof for his accusations, that just he and not another one should leave the team.

Reprinted and adapted from International Review of Sport Sociology III(1968) 137-148.

In all these cases the sociodrama revealed an unequivocal hierarchy in the surrender of specific values and of the defensive layers. By the way, they were not chronologically surrendered, but arranged in order based on subjective evaluation of the importance of the given value attached to certain concepts. The value that is given up last, is the fundamental one. It turned out that there was a quite marked conformity in the hierarchy given by the group members, though this conformity due to a small "n" was statistically not very significant. Of the $\binom{5}{2} = 10$ possible rank correlations (according to Spearman's formula) there were five where $P = 0.7$ each and one 1.0. The average of the rank correlation coefficients was, of course, only 0.585.

After evaluating and summing up Charnofsky established the following order in the surrender of defensive layers:

Victory over the rival	School traditions	Pride in one's own abilities	Winning the championship	Loyalty to the group
1·4	2·2	3·0	3·6	4·8

Only in one case was loyalty to the group not the fundamental value, but also in one case "victory over the rival" was not the most liable aim.

This similarity to the final results of Sobel is shown by the fact that only twice was there a transposition in hierarchy and above all that loyalty to the group turned out, in both investigations, to be unequivocally the fundamental value. The rank correlations of $P = 0.80$ between the two rows is significant with a probability of over 85 percent.

The more confirmation found in further investigations for the thesis of Charnofsky and Sobel, regarding the fundamental position occupied by loyalty to the group in connection with value conceptions, the better are the opportunities for a generalization of the final result. It should be established above all, whether the central position occupied by loyalty to the group is not a special feature of the American teams, because, above all, in the United States the aim of cooperative and loyal group behavior as well as rapid social adaptation without conflicts, is one of the main components of group ideologies, with their tendencies to lay stress on other-directedness. [4] For sports sociology it is also important to check Charnofsky's hypothesis in other branches of sport with other forms of cooperation and also under different conditions, for instance in case of psycho-physical demands for top-class performances.

Such socio-dramatic experiments were conducted also with a German top-class racing-four with coxswain the oarsmen having won the silver medal in the 1965 European championship. Besides, half of the crew later on also belonged to the world champion racing-eight of 1966. Due to several sociometric surveys these oarsmen were already accustomed to social and psychological tests. [5]

The stress situation, as in the case of Charnofsky, was simulated, but had here a special weight of credibility, because the experimenter and instructor playing in the sociodrama actually was the crew's coach.

In this case the "abstract ideals" were, in contradistinction to Charnofsky's investigations, defined as aims to bring about success to the club or association, combined with the factor of "national prestige interests."

Rank Results of the Socio-dramas as Regards Giving Up of Value Layers

Oarsmen	Abstract ideals	Pride with one's own ability	Victory over rival	Winning the championship	Loyalty to the group
A	1	2	3	4	5
B	1	4	2	3	5
C	1	2	3	4	5
D	1	2	3	4	5
Mean rank attached to a given value	1	2·5	2·75	3·75	5

Rank correlation (Spearman's formula):

$$P = \frac{1 - 6 \sum_i (x_i - y_i)^2}{n(n^2 - 1)}$$

$$P_{AB} = P_{BD} = P_{BC} = 0 \cdot 7$$
$$P_{AB} = P_{AD} = P_{CD} = 1 \cdot 0$$

The average of the rank correlation is 0·85; and this is in accordance with the significance limits with a reliability of an average of about 90%.

Thus, we find a very strong conformity between these series of measurements and ranks: the oarsmen A, C and D have exactly the same order of rank, as revealed by the total results:

Abstract ideals → Pride with one's own ability → Victory over rival → Winning the championships → Loyalty to the group

Overall, there is only once among the 20 positions a shifting of two rank orders; otherwise there can be noticed only two simple interchanges of rank order. All the other 17 rank positions are arranged in the same order of magnitude.

This conformity is especially evident in the following cases:

1. The "abstract club and association ideals" and "national prestige interests" according to unanimous responses belong to the most liable values. The theoretical minimum for the relative measurements is thus really being achieved. Club-centered ideals could not win the upper hand in this team, since it was not a club team but a racing crew of oarsmen, whose members were from three different clubs. Club and national interests seemed to be not of any significance for them. This is in accordance with the result of another investigation of the author[6], according to which only 5.69% of the 88 questionnaired people, some oarsmen with international success, declared that they competed "for" their club or their native town and only 2.27% "for" their country. As regards the team of the racing-four, among the oarsmen, not one maintained to row "for" his club or his native town, while nevertheless two of them felt to be the representatives of their nation, though their formulation was rather weak, of the type: "I would at this moment not oppose a suggestion" (directly before the 1966 world championships) "to be considered a representative of the Germans".

2. "Pride with one's own ability" and "victory over the rival" were, with the exception of one dissident placed in a middle position between 2 and 3. The almost equal relative figures, regarding values, point to the only quite insignificant difference regarding importance of the two values, although 3 of the 4 oarsmen unanimously gave the same preference to these two values.

3. It was obvious that winning of the championship title constituted a highly desired goal. The oarsmen had to do hard training for years, before finally a genuine chance presented itself to win the championship title (national as well as international). Thus, we notice a dominant position of a goal for which one has to wait a very long time and has to fight very hard.

4. There was again absolute unanimity as regards the place occupied in the rank order by the value loyalty to the group. Here, the relative evaluation achieves its theoretical maximum. Group loyalty in regard to the team fellows was unanimously defended as the fundamental value, which outdistanced all the others, to which all other aims were subordinated and even were sacrificed for its sake.

To some extent this result is surprising, because in sociometric surveys and mutual evaluations of achievements of the members of the entire racing-eight that won the world championship title in 1966, this part of the team did not at all reveal itself as an obvious subclique.

Group loyalty was thus not related to this specific group, made up exclusively of those specific individuals and no others. It was easily transferred to the larger group. Thus, loyalty to the group is obviously depending only on the existence of the group and on the extent to which the members identify themselves with the aims of the group, the group ideology, and the values accepted by the group. It seems that group loyalty is a matter of course in sport, a norm, that is not a question of choice in regard to certain individuals, but something that is generally binding and automatically related to the given team to which one belongs, whose aims one accepts and desires to achieve.

Besides this, there existed leader conflicts among the entire crew of the racing-eight, based on a classically clear, almost symmetric "dual" in leadership[8]. In addition to this, many mutual dislikes in the various sociograms could be noticed (ibid). The racing-four also was divided up into two pair crews that were competing with each other during training. Could the fact that group loyalty occupies the first place in the hierarchy of values be compatible with strong inner-group conflicts? Or is the fact of group loyalty, being defended in the socio-drama as the final motivation only the result of ideological influence, of the way how norms and expectations are enforced within the group? Is it only a question of some sort of a norm, openly propagated in the manner of the questionnairing, but latently opposed by another kind of motivation? The great differentiation of groups and methods (direct observations by Sobel as against other data by Stouffer[8a]) confirm to some extent that most probably motivations based on loyalty to the group really are the most fundamental values and are not only pretended ones--at least not consciously pretended ones. If one takes into consideration the predominance of "fellowship" ideas and ideals, expressed during speeches at special festive occasions and attempts by officials to exert influence, then this seems quite probable. The genuine motivation in cases of defense of value concepts is most probably partly determined by the deepening of such values as fellowship, which is being propagated by the club in its efforts to exert its influence and by the coach.

In that case it seems that inner conflicts, such as personal ones and those connected with specific roles, can quite easily be reconciled with the final motivation of group loyalty (regarding, e.g., defense against external pressure). Of course, these problems are by no means clarified. They require more accurate examination.

There can be noticed an obvious conformity in the hierarchy of values established here and the rank order found by Charnofsky and Sobel. The rank correlation between the two series is 0·7 (significant with an almost 80% reliability). However, the comparison with Sobel's result is, methodologically speaking, more questionable. The rank differentiation is in this research on oarsmen even broader and more clearly defined than in the case of Charnofsky, since both the theoretical minimum and the theoretical maximum have been achieved in the relative measurements of value here.

In the case of the two fundamental goals and values; "Winning of championship" and "Group loyalty" one finds here absolute conformity with Charnofsky's final result. Even relative measurements are alike, almost up to two tenths.

"Victory over the rival" seems in this survey of greater significance than in that of Charnofsky, because this goal constitutes here an especially prominent value, since in 1964 there really existed a sharp situation of rivalry with the racing-four with coxswain, that won the Olympics in Tokyo. In addition to this, it was a question of season tournaments with the baseball players and as a rule not a single decisive event as in rowing where it was a matter of all-or-nothing, namely of one single contest at the championships. Even a victory before the championships is of great significance in the regatta season in the case of the crews, since there is a relatively small number of races and because such a victory is already quite a good indication who will probably be the winner at the championships; and this exerts a strong psychological influence, strongly impinging on future races, including the championships. That is why "victory over the rival" is of much greater significance for the oarsmen than a victory over a rival baseball team.

The deeply-rooted school traditions at American universities may provide the explanation for greater importance of abstract ideals in terms of school tradition in baseball contrary to the above-mentioned weak ties of the oarsmen with their club, association or to the small significance attached to national prestige and even less to "abstract ideals" in general. In Sobel's survey, abstract values and national ideals also rank with those values that are surrendered most easily.

The fundamental role of group loyalty is of course quite obvious in all the three surveys. In all three quite different strata group loyalty is mentioned as the last value surrendered. The motive for the giving up of the other four kinds of aims or values--if mentioned at all-- is loyalty to the group.

The conclusions drawn by Charnofsky for the baseball teams are true also for the German representative rowing crew[9]: One may predict with quite substantial probability that a coach who succeeds in convincing an oarsman "to agree" to leave the group, "would be much more successful, if he would appeal to group loyalty than if he mentioned any other value." It turned out that the least successful was an appeal to abstract club ideals or national interests.

Approached from the positive aspect, one could assume, together with Charnofsky, that encouragement - on the part of the coach, for instance - would be especially effective if he did not appeal to abstract ideals, but to the idea of group loyalty. However, there is a completely different social situation there, and it is problematical whether the final results following a completely different way of questioning, could be transferred mechanically. Besides, such a generalizing statement does not take into account the mutually supporting or inhibiting relationships between the various values and the effectiveness of a manipulation in this regard. Thus, any encouragement of an aggressive attitude, aimed outward, might be most effective and may, at the same time, strengthen group loyalty. Evidence can also be provided for opposite influences.[10] However, these social patterns of behavior control have not yet been examined in detail.

Nevertheless, one may draw the conclusion that a coach should not underestimate the importance of the value "loyalty to the group" even in cases where there exist conflicts inside the team and that the behavior expectations, connected with this value, exert a strong influence on the discussions inside the team and on the oarsmen's conception of the most important motives. In such a way, it may at least indirectly substantially contribute to the shaping of the psycho-social situation, even if the real and most important motives should be rather egocentric ones. Finally, one should also differentiate between subjective final evaluations, the opinion voiced demonstratively regarding such an evaluation and the actual behavior. Even if the subjective final evaluation should be egocentric (such as "pride with one's own ability") and the goal would be confirmation of one's own self-confirmation and self-advancement, the athlete will nevertheless to a considerable extent bow in his behavior to the expectations of the others, especially if the other lay special empahsis on group loyalty. At least, he will pretend to behave like this. As a rule he will not be able to assert himself against such opposition, with the exception of cases, where he takes recourse to tactics and emphasizes in advance his loyalty to the group. This tendency to hide egocentric motivations behind conformable behavior openly displayed by means of a uniform adherence to group loyalty, is especially striking in small sports groups, because group loyalty is most closely connected with the goal of accomplishing top achievements, the implementation of which can be quite easily measured more or less accurately by objective comparisons of achievements in sports. The objectivity of the measurements of achievements has to be accepted even by those guided by egocentric motives, for the simple reason that the "group comment" (the so-called public opinion inside the group based on group loyalty) demands it. "Group loyalty" or rather the expectation that is predominant in the group (which from the socio-dramatic point of view cannot be separated from group loyalty), namely that members adhere to group loyalty and act accordingly, thus serves the aims of advancing objective comparisons of achievements and improvement of the level of achievements. The coach may cleverly make use of this to guide the team or to re-arrange its ranks. Besides this, group loyalty and "group comment," of the expectation of group loyalty inside the group, intensifies the image-forming detachment of the team from those outside, promotes under certain circumstances psychological aggression against the rival teams or officials who like to order others around, and also consolidates the internal cohesion of the team. Most probably the coach can count on these processes and can utilize them.

The description of these psycho-social mechanisms in top athletic teams is, of course, still to a considerable extent hypothetical. For the sake of clarification further research will be necessary.

Summary

In the same way that Sobel in the case of American combative groups and Charnofsky in the case of high-school baseball players, established the hierarchy of values, given up as defensive layers in increasing stress situations, so this investigation, too, examined an international successful crew of oarsman with the help of simulated socio-dramatic stress, trying to find out which values are the most fundamental ones and therefore are the latest to be given up.

Result: While abstract ideals (club ideals, those of the sports association or national prestige interests) were in all cases given up most easily, the goal winning the championship" and above all the value "group loyalty" belonged to the most stable values. "Group loyalty" could even serve as a motivating factor for giving up other aims in a socio-dramatic discussion and is itself given up only at the very end or not at all. The fact that group loyalty is the last motivating factor to be given up seems automatically to be attached to the given team to which the investigated person belongs at the time and with which he identifies himself. Even inner conflicts (personal ones or divergencies regarding roles) do not seem to disturb this exceptional position. The motivation by referring to group loyalty--or at least the voiced appeal to adhere to it--is self-evident in sport, an obvious norm, to which one adheres or pretends to adhere, even if there are conflicts inside the group or when the subjective final motivation of the individual is egocentric. "Group comment" demands adherence to group loyalty. To what extent in this case, a uniform attitude is achieved, as the result of ideological influence, or even only the admission is made in the presence of the other fellows and the coach as a mere pretense, or how far group loyalty is really the most important and basic value, given up at the very end, is not yet clarified. So far, these factors could not be separated from one another, they even support one another. It would, in this case, have been necessary to separate the subjective fundamental value from pretended motivated behavior in face of social opposition. In any case, one finds a confirmation in this investigation for the final results established by Sobel and Charnofsky, testifying to the fact that these results are true not only for the competitive teams and high-school baseball players, but also for German representative groups of top athletic oarsmen. These results also yielded some practical hypotheses and rules for the work of the coach.[11]

FOOTNOTES

[1]R. Sobel, "Anxiety-Depressive Reactions after Prolonged Combat Experience: The Old Sergeant Syndrome." In Bulletin of the U.S. Army Medical Department, Combat Psychiatry Supplement, 1949. pp. 137-146.

[1a]Methodological problems and shortcomings of the method of sociodrama will not be discussed here. However, it should be taken into account that the following results are supplemented and interpreted by adding group ideological factors to the analysis compensating for some of these methodological difficulties (see below).

[2]H. Charnofsky, "Die Aufgabe von Verteidigungschichten in Drucksituationen. Eib sozio-dramatisches Experiment." In G. Lüschen (ed.), Kleingruppenforschung und Gruppe im Sport. "Kölner Zeitschrift für Sociologie und Sozial-psychologie", No. 10/1966, pp. 237-250.

[3]J. L. Moreno, "Sociometry, Experimental Method and the Science of Society." New York 1951; Id., "Who Shall Survive? Washington 1934; J. L. Moreno, L. D. Zelesny, "Role Theory and Sociodrama." In J. S Roucek (ed.), Contemporary Sociology. New York 1958, pp. 642-654.

[4]D. Riseman, R. Denney, N. Glazer, The Lonely Crowd. A Study of the Changing American Character. New Haven 1950.

[5]They were members of the eight oar crew.

[6]H. Lenk, "Zur Soziologie des Sportvereins." In Der Verein-- Standort, Aufgabe, Funktion in Sport and Gesellschaft (ed. Hamburger Turnerschaft von 1816), Stuttgart 1966, pp. 253-314 (cf. p. 306) and more extensively in H. Lenk, Materialien Zur Soziologie des Sportvereins. Ahrensburg/Germany, 1972.

[7]According to Lüschen, in his research with active members of German Sports clubs, "fellowship" was also mentioned as the foremost expectation regarding behavior: by 39% of the young active athletes in the German Federal Republic (sample n = 1880) and by 27% of the adult club members in Nordrhien-Westfalen (N = 404). For reference, see previous note.

[8]P. R. Hofstätter; Gruppendynamik. Kritik der Massenpsychologie. Hamburg 1957, p. 133 ff; Hofstätter, Einfuhrung in die Sozialpsychologie. Stuttgart 1959, p. 346 ff; Hofstätter, Sozialpsychologie. Berlin, 1956, p. 165 ff, 169 ff.

Clearly outlined "duals" of leadership in the case of crews are described in H. Lenk, "Renngemeinschaft und Gruppendynamik." In Rudersport, Lehrbeilage 1962, I. p. 5f and in H. Lenk, "Soziogramm eines Vereinsachters." In Rudersport, Lehrbeilage 1963, II, p. 5f.

[8a]Stouffer, S. A. (ed.), The American Soldier. Princeton 1949-50.

[9]In as far as such a small sample could confirm this. The complete unanimity inside the group and the complete agreement in this regard with other groups is, of course, a much stronger confirmation than statistical data alone.

[10]G. C. Homans, The Human Group. New York 1950, P. R. Hofstätter, Einführung in die Sozialpsychologie, loc. cit., p. 306, 311-322.

[11]Lately, Kohl questionnaired German student top athletes in basketball (N = 29) and German handball (m = 25) with respect to such value orientations. These ball game athletes, by deviation from the attitudes of oarsmen and American baseball players, evaluated "winning the championship" somewhat higher. This was found to be true in equal rank successions for both types of sports. Besides this, the results complied with the finding above relatively well.

BASKETBALL AND GERMAN HANDBALL PLAYERS (n = 54)

	Prestige	Pride with one's own success	Victory over the rival	Group loyalty	Winning the championship
	1	2	3	4	5
Mean rank	1.6	2.5	3.2	3.4	4.2

The rank positions according to relative weights have moved nearer to each other than in the case of the oarsmen and even more than in the analysis of baseball players' attitudes. Moreover, basketball players with real chances for winning the championship characteristically assessed "winning the championship" and "victory over the rival" higher than players without such chances did, the latter ranking pride with their own ability and success highest.

"Authoritarian" or "Democratic" Style of Coaching?

Imagine a scene on a summer evening at a lake where a man can be seen in a motorboat, following the waves of a four-oared shell as if it were attached to it. A marked bass voice shouts orders, commands without a pause to the crew by a big speaking-trumpet. Every day, at each training, the crew gets orders, against which there can be no objection. "Thirty strokes! Number three, drag higher at the end, otherwise the boat keeps going to port. Balance! Number one, don't throw water. If the next spurt doesn't work, for punishment you do two more of them!" The voice changes from soft to loud between coaxing and threatening. The four has already vanished in the twilight, but still the demanding voice can be heard slowly fading in the distance. Not only the training program, but also the racing starts and the combination of the crew is dictated to the rowers by the coach or club staff without recourse. From the beginning of the season, the athletes must resign any independency and the right of discussion.

Imagine another scene, in which a coxswainless four rows in a channel alone. The crew systematically increases the number of strokes, ending in a powerful spurt of 30-40 long strokes. In between, the rowers work slowly, relaxed, until the next spurt follows. Afterward the athletes meet a grey-haired man with broad shoulders, and they talk-- discussing, questioning, and doubting. "Why does the boat always roll to port? Is your row lock malfunctioning, Peter?" "May the level of work be different on both sides?" "No, Claus, I think you pull the oar too deeply to the stomach at the end of the pull." The grey-haired man listens patiently and then gets into the discussion, "How do we best find the cause?" All agree on a suggestion from one of the group. "We change the level of work on place two and row once again." The group dissolves, and the boys try again. The man goes off toward the boathouse. Later he returns with field glasses and watches the crew, which by now is back in the water, and he murmurs something to himself. It is not too often that he is seen at the training area. Quite often the crew works by itself. They meet only on weekends at the training place. During the week, the rowers do their training alone, in pairs, or in a skiff and work out their own training program. Often the crew attends races without the coach, but, of course, he accompanies them to the most important ones. The tactical preparation for a great race is done by discussion on the evening before the start. Observations and suggestions from the athletes and experiences and hints from the coach together make up the strategy, without which top competition cannot be won today.

These two scenes demonstrate how rowing training may be guided. They have a touch of caricature. In reality, we find only a mixture of these two extremes; usually, the stress is more or less on the side of one of these two ideal types.

The first form of coaching--let us call it the "order style" or "authoritarian" style--is the most widespread. Many coaches and many older club leaders swear by this method, which proved effective when they attended races. The second style, which includes a helpful guidance toward self-control--let us call it the "democratic" style is not so often used, although it became known thirty years ago through the slogan of coach Fairbairn: "Train the man to train himself." "The art of the coach is to make himself superfluous, " is the way Karl Adam, by now the most successful rowing coach, expressed it.

Sports training attempts to train the athletes by exercising them to the highest capacity possible. Which style of coaching is more efficient and useful, the "authoritarian" or the "democratic" style? (The expressions "authoritarian" and "democratic" should not be understood here as normative expressions of evaluation. They serve only to describe the two styles of guidance.) Which of the two methods is the better one?

American social-psychological studies of groups[1] differentiated between three styles of leading: the "authoritarian," the "democratic," and the "laissez-faire" types. (In the last category, only the task was given; the solution had to be found by the group independently.) The result was as follows. "Authoritarian" coaches characteristically turned out to be more task and achievement-oriented than "democratic" ones, the latter rather being person and personality oriented and preferring a "good climate" within the group as against the highest possible improvement of achievement. "Authoritarian" coaches, furthermore, would assess the "least preferred co-worker" in the group much lower than the "democratic" ones.[2] The atmosphere in the group was more friendly in the democratically led group. The performance of the democratic and authoritarian groups was approximately the same. Only the somewhat more refined difference occurred that, under extremely precise direct control as well as in the case of extraordinary little direct control, the task-oriented and "authoritarian" style would, on average, render a higher team success whereas, by contrast, in cases of medium direct control rather a person-oriented or "democratic" style rendered probably a top group achievement.[2] The social "climate" was friendlier in groups guided in a "democratic" style. The members were dissatisfied with the authoritarian leading; they reacted either aggressively against the leader and toward each other or with apathetic submission. In case of strong control the performance was a little higher than with the "democratic" leading style. Then soon a decrease followed. The member who reacted apathetically did not show any motivation for performance and soon the decrease of motivation began. The laissez-faire type had the poorest performance. Those with no guidance did not achieve cooperative planning or a common decision. Since the laissez-faire style does, in practice, not occur in training of teams, in particular not with regard to larger crews, it will suffice here to distinguish and discuss only the two types of the "authoritarian" (or "autocratic") and the "democratic" style of coaching. The first is characterized by a complete strategy of orders and commands; whereas, the latter stresses self-control and participatory decision-making. Groups with high integration seem to appreciate control from the group itself, but fight any domination of individuals; a German study of groups confirms this also. Dictatorship probably destroys the integration of the group. We must also mention another (American) study with the following result: The best integration was found in groups under authoritarian leadership where combination and tasks had been set up by force (this was in the military service). Fortunately, however, sports have nothing to do with enforced recruiting. In our example, the sport of rowing, the results are verified. In recent years both "authoritarianly" and "democratically" led crews won the highest international athletic successes. Top achievements, therefore, can be reached by both methods. Only with respect to the level of achievement, there is no unquestionable proof for one or the other style being decisively more successful. At least, it has to be taken into account as an essential factor, too, how strong a direct control is or can be exerted at all by the coach.

However, it was not confirmed at all in considerably many experiences with athletes and training in rowing that "democratic" coaches would be more person and personality-oriented and, consequently, neglect task and achievement orientation. [The "natural" task and achievement orientation, the requirements of strict cooperation, and precise measurability and comparability of individual achievements, particularly in conditions of internal competition might provide sufficient reasons for the difference from volunatry problem-solving groups preferred by psychologists and from ball teams.] On the contrary, the coach's achievement orientation is very compatible with a "democratic" style of coaching. To be sure, with many a "democratically" guided athlete achievement orientation and motivation was even found to be stronger than with crews under authoritarian guidance. Members of the latter groups were often observed to start reserving their forces whenever the coach only did not look. They did not really exhaust themselves, if the coach was absent, they were not able to conduct a really full-scale training by themselves, without immediate guidance and control. The "authoritarian" coach cannot afford to dispense with permanent control. Since he cannot, however, always be present like the "Big Brother" watching, it is assumed that the case of medium control often applies and that, therefore, in the long run, the "authoritarian" style of coaching might turn out to be less effective than the "democratic" one. This is particularly true since the psychic stress in top athletic training of such a strenuous sport as rowing is thus high and demanding nowadays that the complete identification, voluntary participation and engagement on the side of the athlete is necessary to stand out at all and best perform in training and racing. Such an agreement and voluntary commitment is more easily achieved under the "democratic" style of coaching than under an "authoritarian" coach representing a remorseless father figure and super-I. If the athlete actively and influentially participates in discussions and decision-making about strategies, tactics, and problems of training, races, and entries, he will more strongly identify with the eventual solution of the crew than in cases of merely obeying coaches' commands. The athlete will in part experience the eventual solution as a deicision of his own-- at least potentially. This assumption stimulated the hypothesis of some top athletic coaches as, e.g., Adam that crews coached in a "democratic" style will rather and more frequently and easily be able to mobilize reserves of motivations usually inaccessible by conscious attempts of retrieval. These reserves, however, often prove to be decisive in a contest amongst equally talented and well-trained athletes or crews. Although this hypothesis has not been, thus far, tested in a systematic manner, it is well apt to sufficiently describe many experiences of some of the best coaches with considerable reliability.

A conflict between athletes and formal authoritarian leadership always involves the danger that the will to achieve will be weakened by apathetic reaction. Many teams led in a "democratic" way develop strong tensions, but seldom a serious conflict of authority with the training leader and coach. The competition in the group increases the motivation for achievement. The danger that the team may become apathetic or relax its motivation for achievement is less apparent. Because the top crews today are nearly equal in talent and conditioning, the psychological preparedness for achievement and questions of motivation more and more become the decisive factors.

All rowers who were questioned by the present author preferred the "democratic" style, even when they were used to the "authoritarian" style and had been very successful with it. They did not want to carry out arbitrary orders, but preferred to understand why this or that method was necessary for the training. In the "authoritarian" groups there is an attitude of opposition against the leadership. The rowers feel oppressed; they obey in a grumbling fashion and only to avoid being thrown out of the group. Incidentally, in some of the authoritarian groups, there is an inner, secret "democratic" opposition (not planned and not wanted by the training staff). To the outsider, the rowers present an appearance of obedience, but nevertheless they decide independently in a democratic way on questions of racing and training tactics.

Without doubt, it is easier to direct training in an "authoritarian" manner, and this kind of organization may save time. But the "democratic" method is better for coordinating experimentation with different possibilities. It corresponds with an objective experimental attitude. Probably one finds a correct solution for an open question of a training problem much easier by discussing it, than if one single interpretation is dictated to all. This can be proven mathematically in group dynamics. Training in isolation (when rowers train during the week independently in different cities) is only possible under "democratic" guidance. Often, this kind of training was the only way to keep a crew together in spite of job responsibilities.

"Democratic" guidance educates toward independence and prepares the athlete better to overcome by himself any mishaps or emergencies in competition, when there can be no help from a coach.

A German Olympic track coach at the Olympic Games in Tokyo revealed the differences made by the kind of coaching. He saw many American athletes who casually entered the bus to the stadium by themselves, their bag swung over the shoulder. This coach complained that he had to look after the German athletes like a hen cares for her chickens. He had to bring them to the stadium up to the gate through which only athletes may pass and had to tell them: "You must turn left to get to the start, remove your training suit a minute before the start, etc., etc." At the last minute, he stopped one of his protegees with the best prospect from taking two left shoes with him. (This example should not be constructed as a judgment on national peculiarities showing up symptomatically in the training. The American university eight-oar crews have been trained in a more "authoritarian" way than the German top eights of the last decade.) Besides, the "democratic" style of coaching, if procured in combination with an objective procedure of qualifications, may somehow mitigate the principal role conflict of the coach consisting in the fact that he, at the same time, has to be an advisor, guide, and judge, asking for confidence and trust on the one hand and strictly assessing with respect to achievement criteria on the other.

By the way, the problems to guarantee a sufficient supply of younger experienced and skillful coaches could be brought nearer to solution, if the "democratic" style of coaching would have been widely spread. If athletes are trained and accustomed to cooperate and contribute in discussion, planning, decision-making and taking of responsibility, this exercise in cooperative activity certainly provides a good school of coaching--far better than if a young coach-to-be only after beginning his athletic career starts thinking, discovering and solving problems of training. The athlete formerly coached in the "democratic" style need not learn all this anew.

Without doubt, the "democratic" method is more difficult for coaches and athletes. Therefore, it cannot be recommended as the general recipe. It is not the best way for all crews. Coaching styles depend, or at least should depend, on the age group, motivation level, intelligence development, and the athletes' personality types prevailing in the team. Also, the level of performance and the type of sport call for specific modifications and adaptations in reality. In addition, the mentioned factors may accumulate and overlap. For intelligent college student crews of top level between the "authoritarian" and "democratic" styles for each crew or team combination. Preferably, however, even this way of coaching very young athletes should and can be oriented somewhat at the goal state of a "democratic" guidance to be achieved on a later stage of development. Youngsters react particularly sensitively, if they are treated as mere objects of commands or only as raw material for ambitious coaches' interests of success. Naturally, this problem of accentuation is more difficult to solve in team sports like rowing than in track and field. A crew always has to be guided to guarantee a successful, uniform action. The laissez-faire style, a kind of "abolute" democratic type is never suitable, because it does not get top results in team athletics. The "democratic" coach uses psychological skill to lead the crew by judicious discussion in the direction he wants it to go and at the same time allows the sportsmen to act as they feel right and as they have decided themselves.

This is not just a problem of training; it is an important basic problem of sports in our society. Many reports of successful top athletes reveal that they attribute a pedagogical value to their own sports experiences that is broader than for sport alone. Some who have published their opinion on this are the Olympic middle-distance runners Bannister, Chataway and Martin; rowing coach Adam, formerly himself a student world champion in boxing; the Olympic rower Rulffs, and especially, Neumann, a silver medalist of the Olympic 4 x 400 relay in 1928. Neumann gave this opinion a basis by extensive scientific studies.[3] Niels Bohr thought that his training in the Danish national soccer team had a beneficial effect on his mental ability, in the atomic physics field. The athlete indeed cannot acquire talents through competition and performance which automatically can be transferred into other fields, but he can orient himself consciously in the attitudes learned in training. This is true for the self-confidence by which one masters exams. A theologian, a devotee of mountain climbing, told me that he based his self-confidence in the reverend's examination on the thought that the examiners never could have made the south wall of Marmolata in half a day or even at all. The athlete experienced in sports knows how much trouble results from not being prepared. He is aware that the material for an exam is to be learned by hard study with the same planning and disciplining effort as his sports form.

The sportsmanlike rules "not to give up" even at a threatening defeat and to abide by the rules will become his rules of life if he wants to orient himself consciously to them. There is no automatic transfer, but consciously achieved and "ignited" by pedagogical guidance sporting experiences may very well indirectly turn out to be "useful" for education in other realms.

Evidently, thus, the difference between the "authoritarian" and "democratic" way of a training-guidance is of decisive importance for general self-education.

The athlete who has been guided in a "democratic" style is then able to work out by himself a rough plan given to him and to shape the details by himself. He can arrange his energies and plan his own tactics. He knows that he is alone and has only his own capacity to count on in the competition and sometimes also during the training. He may orient himself in the self-confidence obtained in many competitions for the so-called earnestness of life so far as it occurs in similar situations. Contrary to the athlete whose training is fixed by detailed regulations for each movement he has experiences from sports in freedom to develop his own plans and the capacity for independent formation of attitudes.

One main motive of the sports activities of the athlete is the desire to prove true to his own responsibility and to confirm his own judgment and that of others as regards excellence and esteem. This aim can be fulfilled wholly only with a "democratic" training style, for the athlete under "authoritarian" training has delegated his responsibility and freedom. In the formation of the personality through sports, training in the "democratic" style is more fruitful than the "authoritarian" form, particularly because "democratic" training leadership, which is open to discussion, is the only kind that corresponds with the values of our pluralistic democratic society.

"Authoritarian" forms of coaching for trained and intelligent senior athletes capable of self-criticism are patriarchal relies which often serve only as self-justification for the manager or coach trying to prove his own indispensability. The "authoritarian" style of coaching satisfies neither our democratic ideals nor our understanding of the dignity of humanity. There are limitations on the use of the "democratic" training style because of the inexperience, youth, or the combination of the crew. These limitations are necessary, but they should be considered temporary. It should always be planned to remove them step by step as soon as possible and gradually to give the athletes the desired independence.

In any case, it should be clear by now that achievement orientation and rationalization in training is not necessarily linked with compulsion, authoritarianism, and mere stupid obedience, as some new social critics of sport inferred. If it is possible, under a "democratic", participatory style of coaching, to perform at top level without noticing any back-lash even in such an allegedly and really "hard" sport as rowing this certainly will be true for other sports, too. Sporting training usually is not, and need not be, repressive compulsory work of a schematized repetitive character reminding one of assembly-line work.

Instead, it can and should even be somehow a school for "democratic" behavior.

However, sports can only be a real school for democracy if the training follows "democratic" ideals and forms.

Summary

In the last decades, both rowing crews coached in an "authoritarian" style and other top crews guided in a "democratic" style accomplished top athletic success and won medals in international championships. With respect to the mere level of performance, hitherto neither of these styles really proved to be the more effective one. Both display advantages as well as disadvantages and different scopes of applicability. Whereas the "authoritarian" style seems to be simpler and easy to procure and to have a larger range of applicability, the "democratic" method certainly involves or engenders a greater degree of internal identification and commitment on the side of intelligent athletes. The greater participatory engagement presumably is the reason for less decrease in achievement motivation with increasing stress of training and racing load. Because of this higher-grade identification it is hypothesized that, under a "democratic" style of coaching athletes, teams, and crews may be able to mobilize psychic reserves not accessible otherwise, in particular not "on command". This hypothesis has not been systematically and scientifically tested thus far, but it comprises many reliable coaching experiences.

[1]Lippitt, R., White, R. K., "An Experimental Study of Leadership and Group Life." In: Swanson, G., Newcomb, T., Hartley, E. (eds.), Readings in Social Psychology. New York 1952[2]. Id., "Leader Behavior and Member Reaction in Three 'Social Climates' ". In: Cartwright, D., Zander, A. (eds.): Group Dynamics. Evanston, New York 1960[2], p. 527-553. Lewin, K., Lippitt, R., "An Experimental Approach to the Study of Authocracy and Democracy. A Preliminary Note." In: Hare, P., Borgatta, E. F., Bales, R. F., Small Groups. New York 1955, p. 516-522. Fiedler, F. E., Leader Attitudes and Group Effectiveness. Urbana, Ill. 1958.

[2]Myers, A. E., Fiedler, F. E., "Theorie und Probleme der Fuehrung unter spezieller Beruecksichtigung des Mannschaftssports." In: Lüschen, G. (ed.), Kleingruppenforschung und Gruppe im Sport. Sonderhelt 10/1966 der Koelner Zeitschrift fuer Soziologie und Sozialpsychologie. Koeln-Opladen, p. 92-105.

[3]Neumann, O., Sport und Persoenlichkeit. Munich 1957.

Total or Partial Engagement?

Changes Regarding the Social and the Personal Ties
with the Sport Club

An elderly official of a sports club [7], who is of the opinion that "a candid character" and informal "education within a community," the "shaping of character," fairness, and mutual respect prevalent among members are the highest values of community life in a club, complains: "All the above-mentioned positive features which in the past were something quite obvious, are partly obliterated in this present-day sports movement, or are barely existing." Above all the very large sports associations and clubs allegedly would "dilute the ideas of the sports movement a lack of contact between and towards athletes obtaining in the most glaring forms;" according to him, "the sports clubs have, after World War II, partly lost their family-like character." "In the past.... the athletes used to sit together for a while after their training.... They used to talk about their respective families or their jobs, and in such a way each participated in the joys and troubles of the others.... and such cosy evenings spent together were responsible for the fact that people felt they belonged to one big family or community. After this feeling of belonging together had made its appearance, it attracted increasing numbers of people and finally embraced the entire club."

Training took place in a way that groups interacted. Thus, contact between members went "beyond the frames of the sections and departments." "And after all, comradeship and mutual aid and assistance is the main task of sport. How could such a task be carried out, without the cultivation of contacts?" (Interview). Such comradeship in sports gave rise to private friendship, and since all the hiking trips

Adapted from International Review of Sport Sociology I(1967) 86 - 108. This chapter is mainly based on unpublished material, coming from various independent sources in the German Federal Republic. The following includes and analyzes data concerning 3,812 cases (members of the sports clubs and non-members, Lüschen) including at least 588 interviews (mainly with club members). In addition, 103 interviews were procured by the author, though not in a systematic way, with active members of rowing clubs and a number of members of club managing committees. A larger part of this material has been analyzed and presented now in the author's Materialien zur Soziologie des Sport-vereins, Ahrensburg (Czwalina) 1972. The author wants to thank Prof. Dr. G. Wurzbacher, Prof. Dr. K. G. Specht, Prof. Dr. G. Lueschen, Dr. H. Gronau, Prof. Dr. D. Kappe and D. Brockmann for having permitted the author to use as yet unpublished club analyses and results of investigations.

and excursions organized by the club (with the exception of "fathers'"
trips) were family excursions, this helped to draw the families into the
life of the club. In such a way many families made each other's acquaintance, and friendship arose, some of which survived the World
War. Since such an enlarged circle of people who felt that they had
ties with the club exerted a very good influence on the development
of the latter, the club management supported this type of development.

But at present, elderly club members are sorry to note that the
majority of the athletes "find their way to the sports field exclusively
in order to practice sport." Afterwards, they immediately leave their
comrades and the club. The younger club members misinterpret the
tasks facing club members: "The overwhelming majority of them
thinks that the only task of the sprots club is to provide sports equipment and sports fields..." Now people "know each other only quite
superficially" in the sports club. Besides the old pre-war ties, there
exists no contact outside sports events, with the exception of a few
smaller teams to which at least one pre-war gymnast belongs. The
younger athletes (from 9 to 16) and also the older ones (11 to 17) among
those under investigation had mainly only contacts with their comrades
as far as sport is concerned. Beyond that, people limited themselves
in private meetings either to friends they had won during the pre-war
period or as far as the younger athletes were concerned, to club members or comrades from their own small training group. Occasions to
make acquaintance with the members of other groups or branches,
were lacking. The younger athletes were of the opinion that, after all,
their own teams were "most important." Already for this reason
alone contact would not embrace others beyond their own narrow group.

Only thanks to holidays spent in a tent at the sea there developed
among those athletes a lasting friendship. All the 33 under investigation were of the opinion "that things are no better as regards community spirit in the other groups." The majority held the management
responsible, because "they themselves did not do anything about it" to
shape the various branches and groups into one "community." Some
of the most active officials could not take care of this because they
were overburdened with work and could not find time for it.

Even among the various training groups and teams, belonging to
the same club department, there was barely any contact "and between
the sports branches there was no contact at all." Twelve among the
16 younger athletes and all the 17 older ones who were interviewed do
not consider the cooperation between the various branches as particularly "harmonic" and think it is worse than it used to be before the war.
They look upon the branches as completely isolated islands within the
club. The distance between them grows even more because some of
the branch managers fear that their own athletes may be lured away
from them to other branches. But if somebody out of his own initiative
decided to take part in the training of other sports in the club, he was

91

received with open arms. But the athletes themselves tend to special-
ize within the club in one branch of sport.

One of the observers [7] thinks that the reason for this whole development is the fact that the war interrupted and destroyed the traditions of the club. Many club members did not return at all or came
back very late, and these latter people returning had first of all to concentrate on building up a new existence for themselves. The young
people who newly joined the club had to shape their activity in sport
and their approach to it all by themselves, without any guidance. Sharp
conflicts between generations made their appearance when more and
more of the older people returned and joined the life of the club. Finally, the members of the pre-war group gave it up and limited themselves to continue with their own traditional sports life, when they
found out that the younger ones would not accept a different approach
and could not be taught a feeling of belonging together as members of
the entire sports club. Though this observer noticed around 1955 a
tendency to go back to the pre-war habits, another observer [8] quite
independently obtained in 1963 the same results. According to him,
the size of the club was responsible for such isolationist tendencies
and the poor arrangement of the various branches from the organiz-
tional point of view, the "disappearing idealism" among the members
and tension between the various branches as well as lack of people
ready to take an official's position. Both observers held the club
officials partly responsible for they did not care for planned cultivation of comradeship and thought they needed only concentrate on technical and organizational matters related to sport; social contacts and
the feeling of belonging together, then, would develop all by themselves. In the past, the club management tried to establish contact
with the membership rather then vice versa. Today--complained one
of those interviewed--"at least some of the club officials don't notice
the club members at all" [7]. All the younger people that were interviewed had no, or rather loose, contact with the club management.
After all, the club is very large, in 1955 it had 2,100 members. The
older ones, who were already members before the war, on the other
hand, all had contact with the members of the management. Due to
long years of club membership they all knew each other. Nevertheless,
half of them [4] were of the opinion that the management should try to
establish closer contact with the members. In the past, every member was considered valuable for the club, every active member was
looked upon as a valuable acquisition. All were treated on equal
footing. A proper attitude was considered the most important quality--
valued much higher than efficiency. But today there exists the danger
that people only are ready to spend time and energy if outstanding
athletes are concerned. Of 35 people under investigation, 15 charged
some of the members of the club management, that they approached
active workers in the sports movement not according to their attitude,
but only from the point of view of their results in competitive sport.

(Only 6 were of the opinion that rsults in athletics are of secondary significance). The outstanding athletes are put into the limelight too much--in this regard all of those interviewed were unanimous. They are surrounded with solicitous care like film stars and already told that a sports career is in store for them and thus they begin to think: "Why should I still train so hard, since I am already good enough for big tasks." In such a way they are taught, even the youngest among them, to "behave like film stars" and, as a result, "envy and jealousy" are almost encouraged--declared four among the 16 under investigation. This is the fault of "several among the club officials," who want to shine together with those "aces." Twenty-eight of the 33 interviewed people were also of the opinion that disciplinary penalties are marked by injustice, depending on the skill in sports of the given athlete. Unreliability, distrust and other distortions in the sports life are the outcome of this. All those under investigation expressed such strong dissatisfaction with this state of affairs, that the observer reached the conclusion that "this is the decisive reason that disturbs comradeship and exerts a negative influence on the entire life on the sports club." The majority of those questioned were of the opinion that "the principle of equality" should be the foundation in sports clubs. Some of the club managers have already reached such a conclusion. During the past few years favoritism has been less striking, some of the officials decided to return to the pre-war practices as regards sports education.

It is possible that the author [7] of the monograph on sports clubs purposefully presented the differences of the two groups of club members in too glaring colors (as he actually himself admits to have done). Nevertheless, an observer [17] quite independently reached similar conclusions. And also in other urban clubs--especially in cities--many members of the older generation complain about the lacking idealism of the younger [8, 18] who show no readiness to devote their spare time to honorary work for the club. Simplifying the problem, the youth is being accused that "the old sports ideals are no longer alive among them" [12], there exist no longer any "idealists" [23]. "Present-day athletes play for entertainment, but no deeper ideals exist any longer. In the past... the teams stuck together as a unit. Today the young people play games, but no longer with that deep internal joy; comradeship exists only during the game, beyond that perhaps two or three men keep together. In the past, on Saturday evenings, we used to visit the pubs and send the players home... Today they would make fun of us. Today the members of a team say: 'if we didn't win, it was just bad luck!' In the past, ambition was much stronger." (Interview in a small-town club) [12]. "Today the young people are constantly busy" (interview in a city club). The criticism of the older generation is often a cliché judgment, which is based on different experience regarding club life in the past, when people, at the time of the youth movement, lived completely in and with the club. Young people, how-every, fully recognize the norms and values to be accepted in sport: "One should, as an athlete, actually give up smoking...; not go out in the evening before a contest...; our team should stick together. We should also organize something together" (interviews [12]). Also, 39% of the questioned [13] young members of clubs considered "comradeship" as one of the "most important qualities" of a true athlete. Twenty-five percent mentioned the shaping of character and 23% fairness. Twenty-one percent expressed themselves in favor of "perserverance, effort, and regular training" and just as many of "moderation, discipline, self-control." Next come "fondness of sport" (12%), "achievements, physical education" (12%), and "the value of sport for health" (5%).

Fairness is also something valued very high and often observed with meticulous correctness. Thus, what the older generation considers as "lack of interest,... decrease of idealism and readiness to make the utmost effort," is frequently or even predominantly not a lack of aspirations for values in sport in general, but only the expression of decreased readiness to devote one's whole life exclusively to the club, to sport, to a one-sided full engagement. Being at present in a situation to make one's choice [28], in a pluralistic society one engages in many leisure pursuits, not only in sport and the sports club. There is a great variety of opportunities to choose from. The atmosphere prevalent in the sports club, as shaped by the older members of the club management, seems often boring to the young people--like the convulsive attempt to stick to the old traditional spirit. The old club songs, club emblems, flags, caps, even the glorified club history--seem to the young people as sentimental, old-fashioned relics, with the help of which the old men try to keep their youthful experiences alive. 42.8% of the members of one gymnastic and sports club were unable to guess the meaning of the four stylized "F" ("frisch, fromm, fröhlich, frei"), i.e., "fresh, pious, gay, free" being the traditional slogan of the gymnasts' movement, in the old sign of the club. The young athletes knew almost nothing of the club history: only 28.6% knew the name of the old gymnastic associations from which the present club took its origin (Deutsche Turnerschaft oder Arbeiterturnerschaft--German Gymnastic Association or Workers' Gymnastic Association [3]). Symbols and historical traditions no longer appeal to many of them. Intellectuals and artists often feel aesthetically repelled, because of the naively upright character of the texts of the club songs, the pathetic identification and collective vows. Pathetic and patriotic speechifying seems often, to many, especially the younger club members, ridiculous. The younger generations can rarely muster up enthusiasm for "the ideological aspects of the sports movement" [28].

In three large clubs with a membership of 1500 and 2000 the management and the club magazine speak all the time about "the club-family," though the young members complain about the badly arranged organizational structure of the club, the red tape of the administration and the fact that the members do not know each other [8, 9, 23]. Members were called "Turnbruder," "Turnschwester" (sports brother, sports sister) [1]. "We are here one big family" (interview in a small rowing club). "The entire 09 family" (soccer club), "The handball family." "Family" has turned into a favorite expression in club reports--the more so, "the more the previously natural feeling of belonging together actually disappears" [23]. The above mentioned large club introduced a special column in its magazine, entitled "from the...Family." This was accompanied by an article, complaining about the "insufficient feeling of belonging together" among members. The slogan about the "family" used in the club magazine is to serve to prevent the increasing estrangement of the sports branches and their members from each other. However, in the very large sports club everybody knows only a couple of members. Even if one takes the average from a representative sample of all the clubs [15], 27% of the members know only a few comrades from their own club and only 19% knew all of them (49%--"many"). Under these circumstances,it is difficult to include all the other members of that same club in the term "family."

"The club life gets more materialized, it adopts a more matter-of-fact character and occupies only part of the life of the members and they don't any longer devote their entire life and time to it" [23]. A matter-of-fact approach, inclination to make private decisions, stress on individuality lead to "a considerable limitation of the aims of the club" to a "disappearance of the spell of the club life," to "a reduction of the emotional ties." The club is no longer approached as something embracing the entire aspect of "the form of life" [2] as a true "life community," but as a purposeful organization, utilized on a voluntary basis, to satisfy private needs, to spend one's leisure time. Thus, one no longer serves an idea, one barely professes any ideology, but just as a sort of consumer uses the facilities provided by the club. The majority of the younger members rather prefer to decide personally and freely what to do in their leisure time, than to take part in the "snug, planned club activity" which seems to them "artificial" and "false" (interviews). The remarkable fluctuation and frequent changes of membership in clubs, the "sometimes rather loose participation in the life of the club," and the limitation to objective purely sportive purposes, obviously meet "that cautious attitude of distance...of the post-war youth..." [14]. The sports clubs are the only absolutely voluntary organizations which can boast of a steadily growing membership after the war. Thus, a considerable number of sports clubs adapted themselves to the expectations of many of the younger members who were only partially ready to establish ties.

The conflict between the generations as regards the social range of influence of the clubs and engagement inside the club has its historical reasons. After the disappearance of the traditional order of the

medieval classes, guilds and other ties, isolation and uncertainty
caused by industrialization and the changes in the social structure which
came in its wake, gave rise to a strong need for voluntary community
ties and the desire to lean upon someone or something [19] (Riflemen's
Guilds existed since the 14th century [23]). That is why, in the past century when sports clubs were set up, "emphasis was laid on everything
that unites, that is institutional, on becoming part of a community and
on considering one's own development as something of secondary importance" [19]. It was an "idea" that won members. People were
ready to make sacrifices. Only with the help of such readiness to serve,
such wholehearted engagement was it possible to perform the pioneer
work of founding clubs. The ability to concentrate on one realm only
and the full engagement were a necessity during the troublesome building of new social forms which had not yet been tested. For the founders
this was "the purpose of their life." Today's members no longer need
much energy and feeling for this. After 1945, in many clubs, could be
noticed a pioneer spirit similar to the foundation period. The clubs
were rebuilt with much enthusiasm and personal initiative. After they
had been resurrected in their old splendour, the pioneer spirit died
down again. Also newly founded clubs--in one case this could be observed clearly--quickly passed from the road of the exceptional with
individual effort and improvisation to that of convenient passive social
representation, which did not require much initiative any more.

Also other symptoms pointed in the past to the strong ties with the
club. The members wore their club insignia also for other occasions in
life. As active members of the club they were obliged to wear them for
"all festive occasions." It indicated not only the branch of sport in
which the given member lived. Thus, the person wearing the badge
represented his club and native town. This is true as regards the flag
of the club, often "the gift of women and virgins" (inscription on one of
the flags). The flag was considered as the symbol of "fraternal harmony." It was of special value, because the ladies of the town had made
it themselves. According to the speech made for the occasion of pre-
senting the flag to the club by one of the ladies, it was to be a stimulant
for the athletes to show themselves "worthy" to represent their native
town and proof of the fact "that in our town, too, there are women and
virgins who cherish patriotic feelings for gymnastics" (from a speech
made at the consecration of a flag in 1865 [23]). Many clubs did not
permit their members (as laid down in the rules) to join other clubs
specializing in the same type of sport. "The club honor did not permit
its members to belong simultaneously to a rival club" [23] .

Sports clubs in the past century established a club library and
reading room [9, 23]. Some organized reading circles of their members. Such monthly social meetings, including a lecture on gymnastics and a patriotic subject, combined with performance of music

and songs, were intended to promote the establishment of stronger ties with the club and to supply the young athletes with some of the knowledge that "should not be missing in patriotic education." In one of the sports clubs such subjects were dealt with as: "Treatment of Hypochondria with the Help of Gymnastic Exercises," "Care of the Body with the Help of Water, Air and Gymnastics," "Jahn and Kotzebue" and a "Historical Lecture on the Liberation and the Situation of Germany in General" [23]. Corps of gymnasts with their military exercises also served the people and the community. Then there were theatre groups, choirs of gymnasts, a small musical band, and even fire-brigades and first aid companies, made up of athletes [9]. In 1863/1864 the athletes provided "a voluntary honorary guard for the newly proclaimed sovereign" in Schleswig-Holstein.

There was a regular control of attendance at gymnastic lessons. Special penalties existed for repeated absence (in the case of the leading gymnast even for one absence). Emphasis was laid on the ties connecting the individual with the club. Consciousness of the "we" left its mark on the way of living of the individual. A decision adopted at a general meeting of the members of the club forced all of them to use the "fraternal form of addressing each other by their Christian name" [9]. Strongest possible bonds were aspired to until after World War I. That is why quite a number of old members "keep entirely to the habits of the old times" with an absolute community consciousness, and they demand the same from the others. "The individual gives everything to the community. As an individual he serves his club, as an obeying member he serves the entire community," reads a proclamation on some festive occasion of a sports club, even still in 1953. Proclamations to mark some festive occasions cultivate to this day the ideology of community spirit and the adherence to tradition.

In sports clubs abroad, for example in the North-and South American German clubs, maintenance of club traditions in the old style turns into a venerable treasure to preserve the customs and habits of the fatherland and the ties with the homeland. Minorities and often immigrants were scarcely able to quickly and fully adapt themselves to the norms of the New World sticking, instead, strongly to many old features of customs, transforming them into a sentimental nursing of culturally isolated rudiments of old habits. The public looked upon such processions and sports festivals (what could possibly be the meaning of cooks in folk costume, carrying pots with sauerkraut in a procession?) as involuntary cliché caricatures of exaggerated club spirit. In this case the club nourishes, quite distinctly, illusory wishes for a completely different way of life. Identification efforts are aimed towards a petty bourgeois world with social utopian ideals. These clubs promote escape from the present time, from reality, they offer and cultivate substitute satisfaction.

97

The ideological revolution, the dissillusionment after World War II--but in Germany also the political utilization for propaganda purposes of the total readiness to establish ties on the part of the young generation in the thirties--were to a considerable extent responsible for the fact that "the skeptical generation" is today much less ready to serve such an ideology. This generation wants a clear division line between the various fields of life. They consider sport "a purposeful leisure pursuit." In addition, people want "also some social life." But everything beyond that does not fit a sports club [9]. Intelligent young athletes who are directed toward upward social mobility are politically exceptionally well-informed and show keenest interest in these problems [13]. However, they state, "There is no place in a sports club for political aims" (interview). Besides, they should "be formulated in such a way, that a United Europe could arise" (Interview [9]).

In the past, groups of club members used to march in closed ranks along the street, with flags, wearing club uniforms and symbols, singing the club song. Such public processions have today become a rarity. It happens very seldom that the club flag is carried along streets. The office of the honorable standard bearer of the past has become "superfluous" [23]. At gymnastic festivals and similar occasions the gymnastic clubs still come marching with their flag, other clubs do it now only for special club anniversaries. This abstention is undoubtedly a reaction to the exaggerated cult of the flag, to the enforced identification with "community symbols" during the Nazi period. The club as well as the individual are afraid of attaching any emotional significance to the club symbols and to make a public manifestation of this. Club badges are worn more rarely. The traditional forms of greeting connected with a given club are practically not used in private life. The ending of letters "mit rudersportkameradschaftlichem Gruss" (with comradely greetings of the rowing sportsmen) arouses a smile of many among those who receive such a letter. Such slogans as "Gut Heil!" (Hail!) of the gymnasts, "All Heil!" of the cyclists, "Kraft Heil!" of the weight lifters, the "Frei Heil!" of some workers sports clubs or the more general "Frei Sport!" are only used as group greetings before a contest. The short greeting "Heil!" is connected with rather unpleasant associations, seemingly pointing to the so-called "German greeting," especially abroad. An American report on the Ratzeburg regatta of racing-eights between the American Olympic champion of 1964 and the Ratzeburg eight indicated wrongly that the crowd had been shouting just as during the Third Reich "Sieg Heil! Sieg Heil--Heil!" ("Victory--Hail!").

Aversion of demonstrative, noisy collective identification, prevents many athletes--above all the younger ones--to join even the harmless, but equalizing "Hipp-hipp-hurra!" (Interview). Slogans like the gymnasts' "Frisch, fromm, fröhlich, frei!" and the singing of club hymns encounter the same skepticism. The club hymn is being sung only for quite special occasions. Only very few clubs still have a club song book and even if they own one, they seldom use it. "Eine grosse Schar der Jünger unseres alten Meisters Jahn wirket jetzt und wird auch immer stets hier folgen seiner Bahn" (A large number of disciples of our old master Jahn act according to his teachings and will always follow his example")--this is from a song of a gymnastic club [23]. "Der Flagge treu, auch in der Not (Hipp, hipp, hipp, hipp, hurra), so woll'n wirs halten für und für, getreu den Farben unserer Zier, Treu der Flagge hier und dort, treu dem Deutschen Rudersport" ("Faithful to the flag, even in difficult times, Hipp-hipp, hipp-hipp, hurra! We shall always keep to that promise, faithful to our colors, faithful to the flag here and there, faithful to the German Rowing Sport")--this is, again, from a song of a rowing club. There are few young athletes who would agree with these verses about glorifying devotedness to one's club and faithfulness to the flag. The majority spare themselves the effort to make any evaluation and just join the singing thoughtlessly, if they can't avoid it.

"In the past, attachment to the club meant devotedness to the given community, today exist just objective ties" [49]. Today personal liberty is valued higher than a state where one is completely imbedded in a community. The majority of the young people let themselves be only partially attracted. The great variety of leisure pursuits in a pluralistic society and the above described process of disenchantment lead to a utilitarian and consumer attitude of which the majority of the older pioneer generation does not give their approval, which they can't understand. "In the past, people felt much more that they belonged together, there was less arrogance; one was aware of living together, social club life was much stronger." In the past, "people were much fonder of their club, much more devoted," today they "think rather of themselves" (interview with an elderly person [20]).

Instead of subordinating to the institution of the club people rather utilize it for their individual requirements, and thus the members "take advantage of the liberty the structure of the club always gave them. In such a way, due to the new development... the club has come closer to its legal structure," the principle of taking care of and providing occasions for the fulfillment of individual interests [19]. During the times of the club ideology the club was a community of the type sociologists call, after Tönnies "Gemeinschaft," ("community") only today has it become an organization of the type "Gesellschaft." ("association", "organization").

Due to financial reasons there exists, in many places, a tendency to set up very large sports clubs. In a medium-sized town an outsider tried to bring about such an integration. First he was not successful, but eventually "people began to think seriously about it." The observer [23] was of the opinion that in the impersonal relationship with members via an organized and organizing centre the personal feeling of security gets lost. One turns into a student attending an adult education course in a sort of people's university; indeed, this kind of university already organizes gymnastics courses. As soon as people who are not members of the club get opportunities to receive instruction from paid trainers on the premises of the club and with its equipment, the club loses its traditional character. The observer [39] is of the opinion "that the club life in the traditional style" will soon be replaced by a bureaucratic large organization or a private, intimate club, "or it will change back to the previous forms of taking care of its members." Initial stages of the local large organization have already been established. Twenty-one sports clubs are already registered in the Committee of Physical Culture of the Town Council (of a medium-sized town). This committee works out an annual plan for the use of the sports facilities and a preliminary fund, it collects statistical data and conducts a sports medicine advisory centre. In this regard, the various clubs cooperate [23].

It is possible that the description of this entire development is purposefully sometimes exaggerated and things are accepted as a completed fact which really are still subject to all sorts of changes and transformations. Maybe, it is being approached only from the point of view of the intellectual. But, the above-mentioned interviews show that, according to the opinions of the members also, this description is correct, at least regarding one main feature of this development. Maybe, it is a little rash to consider the ideological approach to the gymnastic club, as a community with strong bonds, as something belonging to "an obsolete 19th century mode of life." But all the analyses of club life leave no doubt that there is a tendency to transform it into a utilitarian, only partly binding organization. This does not mean that there exist no social contacts or that they are disappearing; it is only that they are no longer obligatory.

There can be also noted remarkable differences among the various groups. Side by side with the "old men" also ladies and some of the youth groups seem to establish stronger ties with the club than outstanding athletes and students. Some of the "old men" [27] of a small town soccer club said about themselves "they keep the club flag flying." In two gymnastic clubs (a city-club and a village club) the ladies' section was called "the pillar of the whole club." They kept it together, due to their "devoted attitude," their "inventive spirit"--"but above all because the members of this section are still 'wholeheartedly' devoted to the club life" [1, 9]. In one club, in a medium-sized town [23], one section made up of school youth has organized a small music band, playing regularly at all the festive occasions organized by the club. Attempts are made to attract the young people, not only through sport, but also with the help of film shows, slides, exchange of stamps, hiking excursions, Santa Claus evenings and masquerades for children. Special festivities are organized to mark the occasion of promotion to older youth groups. Best wishes are extended to the school youth "that they may stay within the large... family... of their club, which has already given them so much, and that they may remain faithful, first as athletes and later as coaches"(from a club paper). The leader of a youth sports section would like to teach his young athletes to live according to "Jahn's principles," "to believe in God and humanity... nation and fatherland... comradeship and adjustment, fidelity and readiness to help" (club paper). Regarding the older youth such efforts remained almost without success. Summing up, the leader of the youth sports section reached the conclusion that the club does not yet possess such "young athletes" as he is dreaming of. Most of the adolescents have not yet "thought" about the conception of "young athletes;" they are only interested in the use of the sports facilities and equipment belonging to the club. According to him, it is a pity that the award for years of devoted work in coaching and training them, is that "they are now practicing their sports activity in other clubs or organizations (outside the German Gymnastic Association)." According to the ideals of this leader of the youth sports section a group of 14-year-old girls was conducted in an arbitrary "heavy-handed" and "convulsive" way. They wrote their group diary which reveals how rigidly they were forced to follow this artificial plan. They were constantly reminded and admonished what community life means, taught to be punctual, decent, ladylike; in the form of slogans they were taught some sort of artificial freedom and "frankness." The group soon dissolved when "the carefree young ladies turned into very busy ladies" (club paper). In the meantime (1959) in the club there took shape all by itself and unnoticed a durable youth group which later joined the municipal youth organization [23]. Also in one of the village gymnastic and sports clubs [1] a group of older members wanted to revive the old club tradition and ideals. Though the interviewer found out that "the ideas of Jahn, the father of gymnastics," actually were some sort of "leitmotiv" ('guideline') for them, they were nevertheless unable to define what these ideas actually meant: "It was more... some sort of a password." But how did they want to convey these ideas to the young people?

The main purpose was still "to lead the young people, uprooted by the war, back to the right path," "to get them off the streets," "away from the dangers of a mass society," "to encourage them to lead a respectable life" and "in a playful way to prepare them for the seriousness of life,""to make them try out public education in a practical way," "to provide young people through the intermediary of sport with the necessary incentives for physical development"--as well as all "the virtues... which can be taught so well with the help of sport" (interview). Not only exercise lessons serve these general aims, but also successful holidays in tents and hiking tours, in which often more than 100 young people (also non-members) participated. The youth circles of a big-city gymnastics club "have become known among all young sportsmen... because of their social evenings, evenings of songs, various games, music, discussions, folk dances, hiking tours and excursions... They emphasize most strongly the principle of gymnastics as a whole, in contradistinction to those specializing in artistic gymnastics, etc., and the older members connect great hopes with them, since it seems to them that these young people are the perpetuators of the old spirit of gymnastic clubs..." [18]. It seems that young members of gymnastic clubs, remaining under the influence of the older club generation show some more readiness to adhere to the community ideology and the "Turnverein" ideology (the "ideals of the gymnastic club members"), than young people belonging to sports clubs. But grown-up outstanding gymnasts are usually concerned, too, exclusively about the achievements in sport and the utilitarian purposes of the club. No wonder therefore that there developed such fierce tensions between the top-class gymnasts and the above-mentioned youth circles. Spokesmen for the gymnastic section of the village club, who against the will of the young gymnasts wanted to isolate the old "Turnverein" (gymnastic club) as a separate unit, had the aspiration "to supply the youth, side by side with physical education, also with the old ideals, which they should try to follow. Both tasks are closely related and bring great services to the German people and the fatherland" (interview) [1]--Traditional patriotism--just remember the proud role played by the "Turnercorps" (Corps of Gymnasts) in the Schleswig-Holstein Wars and during the 1848 revolution [9, 23]--and the demand for all-embracing engagement in the community of gymnasts led in this sports association--as well as in many others--to sharp clashes with the younger members of other sports sections who were in favor of purely objective limitation to sports purposes. After World War II sharp ideological discussion took place in connection with the re-establishment of the sports clubs and associations [1, 12]. Many representatives of the old national and all-embracing ideals of the gymnasts distrusted the liberalistic and individualistic ideas of those who considered sport as a private pleasure, without any obligations and tried in this sense to introduce new order. One of the reasons of this distrust on the part of the adherents to tradition was the fact that they felt that the occupying authorities were in a way "patronizing" them in this process of democratization [12]. The ideological strife between the gymnasts and the sporting movement in the narrower sense from the twenties exists in many hearts of the old gymnasts to this day, as shown by the statement made by a youth instructor who did not want his young people to take part in other sports sections [1, 23]. One of the gymnastic clubs which has also other sections, makes it to this day "obligatory" for all its active members, to take part twice a week in gymnastic exercises [27].

More than half of the inhabitants of a village who were questionnaired, declared that the club life does not at all disturb family life.
Only one-tenth was of the opinion that there were disadvantages, while
one-fourth saw a positive influence: "My wife is also interested in
soccer; when there are any contests my wife goes, too, from time to
time, as a spectator to watch the game" [21]. It seems that several
members of one family belong to gymnastics or tennis clubs. Many
of them think that the club life helps to improve family life. Sometimes
people call these sports branches "family sports" [18,27]. But also in
other clubs several family members can be found, one not typical
small-town rowing club had 12.2% of housewives among its members,
whose husbands were as a rule also members. In this case the percentage of several members from one family was on an average even higher than in the tennis clubs (11.2 housewives, some of them the only
member of the given family). Five of the married tennis players interviewed declared that, though their family life is limited due to the time-
consuming sports activity, there has never been any quarrel about it.
None of the wives was against this sports activity, and three of them
were very much in favor of it. In addition to this the ladies themselves
took part in small social entertainments organized by the teams or the
club as well as in travels abroad [25]. Due to the concentration of the
club life to the families of the members and to the "club family" one
consciously creates a more intimate atmosphere. The club does not
present its internal life so pointedly to the public, as was the case before. By trying to make the family members feel that they, too, belong
to the club, the club does not pursue, exclusively, purposes serving
only the club. What prompts the club management are also gratitude,
joy, feelings of sympathy, the desire to establish ties of friendship.
Active members receive wedding gifts from the club. Young athletes
line up double row in front of the church "dressed up in fencing dress
with raised weapons, to let the couple pass," if one of the partners
of the newlyweds happens to be a fencer; should it be a rower, they
wear the rowing dress and a slanting roof is made of the oars. "Rid-
ers accompanied a young couple to be married in a coach to church
and escorted them on horseback" [23]. Later, the club paper welcomes
the newly born infants, according to the sports branch of the parents
as "the little handball player Bernhard," "the little javelin thrower
Rolf Josef" and "the youngest gymnast" [23]. Rowing clubs used to send
its members on their birthdays printed cards with best wishes signed
by one of the members of the board. Another one prints in the column
"From Our Big Family;" "Best wishes for the following persons, cele-
brating their birthdays," in proper alphabetical order follow the names
of those who celebrate their birthday in the given month. When it is a
special anniversary (25, 50 years) the members of the board come
with gifts and words of appreciation for fidelity to the club and readiness to make a contribution on the part of the given member. The

members of the board are festively dressed up in the club jackets, caps and wear the club insignia. A school youth section organized a procession with Chinese lanterns to mark the 50th birthday of the leader of their sports section and they sang the song of gymnasts [23]. At funerals of active and merited members the chairman of the club management delivers a speech at the grave and lays a wreath on the grave on behalf of the club. A delegation of young athletes carry the club flag, which has a black mourning band. The club arranges for an obituary to appear in the local newspaper and in the club magazine. Some gymnastic clubs resolved to take care of the graves of their former members, if there remained no family [23].

Many clubs try to make the families of their members practice sports, too. They organize "sport sections for everybody" for both sexes and all age groups [27], training for housewives, for mother and child, gymnastic exercises for married women at the time when their husbands have their training--even some soccer and boxing clubs provide gymnastic lessons and games for the ladies, thus trying to win them over and make them indulgent when they take their husbands away from them. Also sports clubs exclusively for men no longer reveal antifeminist traits. The introduction of exercise lessons for whole families, gymnastics for housewives, games for adults, brought some clubs a 20%-30% increase in their membership during one year alone [4]. In some clubs which officially did not provide such possibilities, there were set up informal "cavalier-teams" as they were called in one club. One member of this group declared: "though some make fun of us, because we always take our women with us when practicing sport or make them join us later...I would not want to miss this cordial attitude that developed among the families...We have no quarrels with our women. We also try to give our wives some entertainment and get them away from the everyday chores and we combine sport with entertainment in such a way, that both parts are satisfied...[7].

The efforts that are made to enliven club life, to recruit new members, by purposefully broadening the entertainment character in the clubs or the attempts to integrate entire families into the club, arouse the response only of certain groups. Younger men, especially intellectuals most probably show greater readiness to practice sport, if one offers them "the sports field with the open door: "to be used freely by everybody" combined with some instruction, something that does not involve the necessity to join the club, without even asking them to do so. The high percentage of private people practicing sport (27% [15]), who do not wish to join any club, shows that this is true. But so far clubs, as a rule, are not very ready to accept such a state of affairs. In a village sports club (1962) only a single one of those questioned (5.6% of the total) knew something about the so-called "Zweiter Weg" ("second road" program trying to provide more sports opportunities for everyone) of the German Sports Federation (Deutscher Sportbund).

104

The "Golden Plan" of the German Olympic Society (planning local and municipal sports facilities) was also something unknown. When explanations were given people from clubs opposed most violently any plan which would place the club sports facilities at the disposal of non-members: "We have built it up with such effort and sacrifices and now everybody is to use it? No!" "We are not a public utility undertaking" (but the rules say just the opposite!). "Who will pay us for the damage?" Some were of the opinion: "Well, if they supply the money to keep the field in order, then we may agree. Maybe in such a case one or the other of those people may ultimately join the club" [1].

If a club sticks to a traditional or even patriotic ideology, it is bound to repel wide circles not only of the young people and intellectuals who, to some extent, are ready to join a club, but there arises even the danger that the club loses the ability to adapt itself to the pluralistic society and becomes isolated. A multitude of social contacts constitute no special obstacle for the all-embracing ties of club membership. If, however, a club cannot give up enforcement of tradition and conformity in regard to such members that want only partially to engage in sport, in a certain branch and without being personally involved very much, then it will lose potential members. An open, more flexible membership policy--permission to establish only partial ties with the club, to use club sports facilities--can help to increase the membership. If the club wants to take into consideration the pluralistic approach to values by society, it should not establish itself as a judge regarding values and aims outside sports, it should not demand a collective "we" consciousness and sacrifices at the alter of the "club-idea." The club may offer opportunities, but should not demand pledges of fealty of vassal. It should not only guarantee the individual the free possibility to leave the club but also unhampered freedom to develop in the club according to his liking. The individual actually is quite free to decide how far he wants to take part in club life. However, in some clubs a powerful social control can be noticed, as soon as somebody tries to act not in conformity with the others, if he voices independent opinions, refuses to pay special contributions or donations--or simply refuses to join the official "hipp-hipp hurra to the German sport" or to use the sanctioned address "Comrade." He who shows stronger inclinations to depart from club norms, is criticized and looked at askance. More than one feels repelled by the club atmosphere. Club norms and enforcement of conformity limits freedom.

The "inner discipline" of the club [23] is protected to this day by sanctions, or even "club penalties"--such as warning prohibition to take part in sports events, partial prohibition to attend club meetings and to use sport facilities, up to exclusion. A fine or such penalties, as were in use in the past, as transfer from active athletes to passive ones or prohibition to dance at club parties turned out to be not very effective.

105

Though at present club uniforms are no longer in use for all the clubs of the "Turnerbund" (Gymnastics Association), many clubs, nevertheless require special club jackets or blazers with the club insignia worn on the chest, even as far as young people are concerned [22]. Attention, like in the past, is paid to uniformity and cleanliness of the sports clothes, especially at contests. What a revolution--even in the sports press--when fifteen years ago the so-called "Naturburschen" (natural boys) of the Ratzeburg rowing club, who had only just become full-fledged athletes in their sports branch, appeared at the regattas in long tights and faded training jackets! For physiological reasons the tights were the proper thing to wear and today they are used everywhere. Money shortage of this school youth and students--and also a slightly demonstrative rebellion against the venerable club staff and their rigid traditionalism--were the reason for those ill-reputed "ragged" jackets. In turn, these traditionalist reactions led to the athletes' reaction to demonstratively cherish the "ragged" training suits as a sort of talisman.

In the past, "it was known who was a member of a given club. Bad conduct of a member was a stain for the club" [23]. Complaints were sent to the gymnastics clubs if any of their members did not behave properly in a restaurant. The clubs obliged the "culprits" to apologize and in serious cases excluded them, making an announcement of this fact in the local paper. Or they just threatened to do this. The club controlled the private life of its members. Today it uses sanctions only if a member gets into conflict with the law (almost all the rules make the provision that only people with a stainless reputation may be accepted as members) or if a member acts in a way that is not in conformity with the aims of the club. Thus "the external discipline" of the club " still plays a role...whenever the club as such makes a public appearance" [23].

Identification and Club Spirit

He who establishes only partial ties with the club, does not identify himself entirely with the club. Actually the readiness to identification and the establishment of ties goes through various successive stages. How many identify themselves passively with the athletic successes of the club, with the representative team, something that is done by non-members, too, who live in the same place, but do not wish to participate actively in the work of the club? One is quite willing to project success onto one's own person, as long as that does not cost anything. If this is followed by a period of defeats of the thus adored team, one quickly moves to the camp of critics, who declare "didn't I tell you before?" Transferred club prestige is, accordign to Arendt's criterion, a bourgeois commodity; on sale, but the customer decides about the price.

Protection against the "outside world" is to this day one of the functions of the club which it performs for many people. One should not underestimate its role in determining the attitude and giving psychic stability to mobile young people [13, 16] and in favor of the continuity of the traditional experiences to the older generation. A human being "throws off the burden" of chaotic or alienating experiences in isolation, by institutionalizing the satisfaction of his needs, establishing in this regard permanent order (Gehlen, Hofstätter). Somebody once called the "compensation" of "concealed inferiority complexes," the "protection of psychic equilibrium" one of the unavowed main purposes of any sports club [24]. In these sporting environment and reference groups one may still reflect one's autostereotype, and find support for one's own opinions as well as confirmation for one's own vanities. Isn't it a "mental feast" "to have others around, after comparison with whom, one can have such a wonderful opinion of oneself" (Tönnies)? One obtains a confirmation of one's own value--if not to own achievements--then, by being at the disposal of a collective management, serving a club idea. What does it matter if one has to share this confirmation with others? What does it matter that one has to limit the great variety of one's needs and notions to certain fields, to arrange them into simple patterns, to surrender to the coalitionist compulsion and to the collective? One acquired greater self-assurance, by leaning against others and their echo and the club ideology. Just as in the case of the phenomenon of the spectator in sport [11] it is not yet clear, from the socio-psychological point of view, how the member projects his wishes onto the community of the club, how the individual identifies himself with the club and why this identification is such a matter of course, almost automatic, such an absolute success, that one can appeal to this stereotype, without having the slightest doubts as to the outcome. Just as is the case today with the national stereotypes, so group identifications in the club are at present usually being criticized by critical youngsters and intellectuals. Not only the spectator with his local patriotism, but also the club member takes the prestige of success from "vicarious experiences" (Diem). The club member is satisfied with being represented by the proper actors. One of the authors simply defined sports clubs as "forms of a sports enterprise" which "help to make representatives of local groups join in activity." [19]. And on the other hand, the successful athletes get the confirmation of their own value to a considerable extent through the strong response and evaluation given to their achievements by the other members. This is a kind of internal "gentlemen's agreement" of the club-- some sort of "balance of prestige-giving." Though one does not yet know much about the procedure of projection and identification, there is no doubt as to the fact that the common notions about the club of all the members, as a similar autostereotype, determine their tasks, roles and also their behavior in the club. Community gives rise to a "we" consciousness, to a corporative spirit. We want to give an example of how this club spirit continues to act: In the fifties a former chairman of the Sports Club "Holstein" from Kiel went to Moscow to the soccer match between the Soviet Union and Federal Republic of Germany. When the Russian athletes and sports leaders learned who he was, they wanted "to know whether the famous 'Holstein-spirit' was still alive in the club." They had heard much from their predecessors in sports about the club spirit; in the twenties that club had played some matches in Moscow. The visitor, deeply moved by this experience, was permitted to give his reply over the Moscow radio [7].

Some people approached the "club spirit" as the characteristic feature and the factor which determines the attitude of a sports club in general [26]. They were, of course, also of the opinion that an all-round, ideologically binding "form of life" is also one of the features of the club. Undoubtedly, such an approach seems to be justified as regards the opinions and behavior of many of the members, in particular the older ones as was seen above. Passionate expressions of activity in a state of affect testify to the fact that there are many club fanatics and club egoists. Though it may be true that the epoch of only partial engagement has started as regards the active participation of the members in club work, but the notions many of them have are lagging behind, still belong to the "ideological epoch" [19]. How does this "club spirit" act? From the socio-psychological point of view it must be stated, the greater the dissimilarity of the group members, the more in danger is the cohesion of the group. The "club spirit," the consciousness of belonging together, the "we"-group picture unify, make the members to some extent "equal." The external club symbols (flags, badges, etc.) support this procedure. In such a way the members stand out distinctly against outside groups, against non-members. The social distance between members and non-members increases--and one of the most strongly confirmed hypotheses of sociology says that when social distance toward outside increases in such a way, contacts inside the group grow stronger. Even labels as the mere club name or nickname attached to individual members tend to unify and make people neglect differences between members but exaggerate differences between them and outsiders. The same psychological distortions are the result of national, race, or tribe clichés, such as "the German," "the Negro," etc. Such clichés always lead to the subjective consciousness of order, but they decrease diversity, information. Order and security, thanks to uniformity and leaning on equals, winning of prestige and gaining of self-confidence with the help of projection of desires and backfeeding of achievements conducted by athletic deputies and vicariously experienced by all members as if they were those of the group as a whole, together with identifying participation--all these are socio-psychological functions which the sports club undoubtedly performs. Engagement in the club may, in part, perhaps provide opportunities to divert local patriotic aggressive tendencies to harmless solutions and to scapegoats outside the club (as emphasized by Lorenz who specialized in research on aggressive behavior;

which, however, has still to encounter severe methodological difficulties and is apparently too generally based on a metaphysics of aggression). But, as already mentioned, these effects and procedures are rather named and not described nor explained. A socio-psychological analysis of the process is missing. No fundamental work has so far been written on the social psychology of the club or association, though this is a most interesting subject from the scientific point of view. The above-mentioned mechanisms of projection and identification are important to understand club life. Of course, nobody maintains that they exhaust the club life and its socio-psychological aspects. Also, personal and friendly contacts in a club are often a decisive matter for the club members and are frequently established. One cannot fully explain them with these identification mechanisms, which actually go only as far as to the non-personal ideological "we" consciousness of the formal club fellowship. The older generation (over 45) wins 16 percent of their personal friends and acquaintances from the club; with the younger ones a mere 9% was found [17]. This is probably a symptom of only partial readiness to establish ties. However, to state less social significance of the club life showing even a tendency to decrease still more than hitherto, cannot, according to the opinion of some sociologists, be soundly argued for [17]. That is why--and the examples quoted in this article regarding social life in the club also testify to this fact--v. Wiese is wrong, thinking that a sports club pursues in a typical way only its "immanent end in itself." The majority of the sports clubs have not the slightest intention to approach their athletes exclusively from the point of view of means to achieve the goals of the club and "to get out of each one of them as much as possible" [26], to turn their athletes into some modern variety of robot or of people "in bondage." There exists, of course, individual cases where results in the service of the club prestige are considered of such importance that the individual--especially active athletes--is only valued as a record breaker and that the activity of the officials and athletic managers is given an exaggerated evaluation. The above-mentioned upper league soccer club seems not to be too far from this extreme type. Specialized clubs that pay attention exclusively to achievements in sports activity are most strongly inclined to such an evaluation, the more so, the more exactly athletic successes in sports can be measured and the more difficult it is to obtain outstanding results in the given sports branch.

Summary

Prior to World War II, as in the pioneer time a century ago when gymnasts' and sports clubs were founded, the whole person was, so to speak, existentially tied to the respective club. Club life, then, was interpreted as a comprehensive "community of life." The members used to serve this encompassing community devoting much time, energy, orientation, and attention to it. In turn, they felt somehow sheltered and secured in the club. Today, by contrast, the club is, at least in the opinion and according to the interests of many younger members, in particular, athletes, much more restricted and reduced towards its sporting objective in the narrower sense. The club is used as an organization on purpose to gratify one's individual needs of leisure, sporting success, etc. Within the "pluralistic society" one does not any longer totally engage, commit, and tie up oneself in the club. One now only identifies partially with the club. The traditional club symbols, forms of greetings, and festive speeches displaying patriotic and pathetic slogans are not any longer apt to emotionally affect members. Instead, they sometimes appear to be ridiculous. However, the older leading officials and elderly members as well as some ladies' and youngsters' gymnastic groups are still sticking to the club ideals of old, the latter being educated towards a total identification with the traditional lifestyle in the club. In addition, the clubs nowadays try to be attractive by offering a more comprehensive "weekend culture" for the whole family of the members and new opportunities for everybody's sport, housewives' gymnastics, children's lessons, etc. The slogan of "club family" is not only meant to demonstrate, but also to, again engender emotional unity and club spirit compensating somehow for the inability to survey large mass clubs and the partial interests. The total identification as well as the traditional collective club spirit is increasingly criticized by younger members, especially by athletes concentrating on their athletic objectives. There arose heavy generation conflicts between older members and this "skeptical generation." The discrepancies, in part, arose from misinterpretations or partially from value differences. As long as one of these groups tries to impress its conceptions onto the other, the conflicts cannot be conveniently solved in a smooth manner.

[1]Brockmann, D., "Trends der Wertsetzung und Wertverwirklichung." Eine Untersuchung eines ländlichen Sportvereins. Soziol. Seminar der Universität. Kiel 1962 (typescript).

[1a]Brockmann, D., "Sport as an Integrative Factor in the Country-side." In: International Review of Sport Sociology IV (1969): 151-175.

[2]Conze, W., "Der Verein als Lebensform des 19. Jahrhunderts." In: Die Innere Mission, 1960, p. 226 ff.

[3]Dahmen, U., "Der Turn - und Sportverein im Wandel." Akademie für Wirtschaft und Politik. Hamburg 1964 (typescript).

[4]Daume, W., "Der Verein als Träger der deutschen Turn - und Sportbewegung." In: Berliner Sport, 1962, No. 11-12, p. 7 ff.

[5]Geyer, H., "Die Chance des Individuums im Sport." In: Olympisches Feuer, 1957, No. 3, p. 3.

[6]Harnecker, D., Schmidbauer, H., "Zwei Rudervereine in einer Norddentschen Großstadt. Empirisch-Soziologische Untersuchung und Gegenüberstellung." Akademie für Wirtschaft und Politik. Hamburg 1964 (typescript).

[7]Höfer, H., "Die bindenken Kräfte eines Sportvereins und die Sportauffassung der aktiven Vereinsmitglieder gestern und heute." Akademie für Wirtschaft und Politik, Hamburg, Kiel 1955 (typescript).

[8]Kurio, "Strukturanalyse eines großstädtischen Oberliga-Vereins." Soziologisches Seminar der Universität. Kiel 1963 (typescript).

[9]Kurio, "Strukturanalyse eines großstädischen Turnvereins." Soziologisches Seminar der Universität. Kiel 1963 (typescript).

[10]Lenk, H., "Konflikt und Leistung in Spitzensportmannschaften--Soziometrishce Strukturen von Wettkampfachtern im Rudern." In: Soziale Welt, 1964, p. 307 ff.

[11]Lenk, H., Werte--Ziele--Wirklichkeit der modernen Olympischen Spiele. Schorndorf bei Stuttgart 1964.

[11a]Lenk, H., Materialien zut Soziologie des Sportvereins. Ahrensburg/Germany, 1972.

(12)Lorenz, P., "Strukturwandel eines kleinstädtischen Sportvereins."
Soziol. Seminar der Universität. Kiel 1963 (typescript).

(13)Lüschen, G., "Die deutsche Sportjugend in ihrer Struktur und
ihre sozialen Verhaltungsweisen." 1960 (typescript).

(14)Lüschen, G., "Die gesellschaftliche Funktion des modernen
Sports." In: Krankengymnastik, 1964, No. 8, p. 1 ff.

(15)Lüschen, G., "Sport and Sportvereine. Materialbericht aus der
'Untersuchung Freizeit der Arbeiterschaft und ihre Beziehung zum
Sport'" (typescript).

(16)Lüschen, G., "Soziale Schichtung und soziale Mobilität bei jungen
Sportlern." In: Kölner Zeitschrift für Soziologie und Sozialpsychologie, 1963, p. 74 ff.

(17)Mackensen, R., Papalekas, J. C., Pfeil, E., Schütte, W.,
Burckhardt, L., Daseinsformen der Großstadt. Typische Formen
sozialer Existenz in Stadtmitte; Vorstadt und Gürtel der industriellen
Großstadt. Tübingen, 1959.

(18)Meyer, F., "Unterschiedliche Strukturen und Motivationen in zwei
verschiedenen Abteilungen eines Sportvereins." Akademie für Wirtschaft und Politik. Hamburg 1954 (typescript).

(19)v. Oppen, D., Das personale Zeitalter. Formen und Grundlagen
gesellschaftlichen Lebens im 20. Jahrhundert. Stuttgart--Gelnhausen
1960.

(20)v. Oppen, D., Familien in ihrer Umwelt--Äussere Bindungen von
Familien im Prozess der industriellen Verstädterung einer Zechenge-
meinde. Köln--Opladen 1958.

(21)Pflaum, R., "Die Vereine als Produkt und Gegengewicht sozialer
Differenzierung." In: Das Dorf im Spannungsfeld sozialer Entwick-
lung--Untersuchung an 45 Dörfern und Weilern einer westdeutschen
ländlichen Gameinde. Stuttgart 1954.

(22)Richter, R., "Ein Ruderclub und seine Beziehungen zur Fluktua-
tion seiner jugendlichen Mitglieder." Akademie für Wirtschaft und
Politik. Hamburg 1963 (typescript).

(23)Schmidt, H., "Das Vereinsleben der Stadt Weinheim an der
Bergstrauss." Volkskundliche Untersuchung zum Kulturellen Leben
einer Mittelstadt. Diss. Tübingen 1961 (typescript).

[24]Seybold, A., "Gameinschaft und Persönlichkeit--die Polarität des Bildungszieles in der Leibeserziehung." Diss. Erlangen 1945 (typescript).

[25]Straubinger, K., "Der Vertragsspieler im Spitzenverein--Konflikt zwischen Sport, Beruf, Familien - und Privatleben." Akademie für Wirtschaft und Politik. Hamburg 1961 (typescript).

[26]Wiemann, G., "Die Zwischenmenschlichen Beziehungen und die sozialen Gebilde des Sports." Dipl. Thesis Deutsch Sporthochschule. Cologne 1953 (typescript).

[27]Wosnik, L., "Gruppenbildung im Sport--Eine Untersuchung über die Anteilnahme der gesellschaftlichen Schichten an verschiedenen Sportarten." Cologne 1957 (typescript).

[28]Wurzbacher, G., "Der Verein in der freien Gesellschaft." In: Berliner Sport, 1962, No. 11-12, p. 2 ff.

[29]Wurzbacher, G., Pflaum, R., Das Dorf im Spannungsfeld sozialer Entwicklung--Untersuchung an 45 Dörfern und Weilern einer west-deutschen ländlichen Gameinde. Stuttgart 1954.

Trees, Tournaments, and Sociometric Graphs

Applicability of Mathematical Theory of Graphs
in Sport Sociology

Recently, the theory of graphs has been widely used--and it is being increasingly applied--in social sciences, particularly in the field of organization. Graph theoretical methods are and could be usefully applied in social psychology and sociology as well.[1] Sport sociology may also profit from this mathematical theory. We shall instantiate this statement by some examples.

Definition of "Graph" and some Basic Notions.

In mathematics, by a graph we mean a set of objects (points, nodes, or vertices) together with a two-place relation between the elements (points) of the set.[2] If the two points (elements) are in the relation concerned, they are on the same line of the graph. (Sometimes, in graphs such lines are referred to as arcs, while as edges in mathematics.)

Example: Let us assume that the points A_1, A_2, A_3, A_4, A_5, A_6 of a graph represent teams of a certain basketball league and that the lines stand for the following two-place relation between the two points, that A_1 won against A_2. Thus, the graph of a basketball round-robin tournament of the teams can be presented as a diagram (note, as in figure 1, that directed relations could be mapped with the help of arrows).

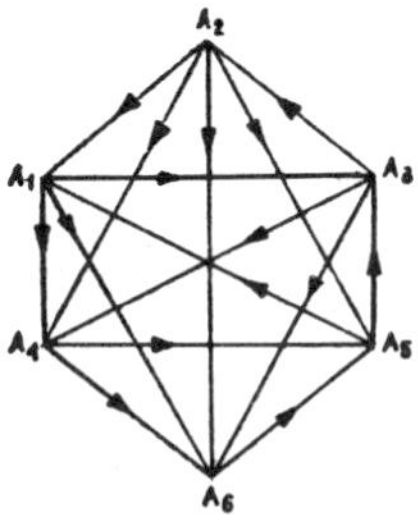

Figure 1.

Directed graphs can be presented with the help of such diagrams if the number of points is limited (finite) (and if the number of lines between the points is limited [finite], too). Since this condition is being

Adapted and revised from International Review of Sport Sociology VI (1971) 175-204. A German version was presented at the workshop of the International Committee for Sociology of Sport 1969 at Magglingen/ Switzerland and published in the author's Leistungsmotivation and Mannschaftsdynamik. Schorndorf (Hofmann)/Germany 1970, 118-145.

fulfilled by all applications in sociology, it also can be accepted as part of the definition. Harary et al., for example, understand the notion of directed graphs as one of limited (finite) graphs only. Thus, to him, directed graphs mean nothing but limited graphs, i.e. only a subset of all graphs following a more general mathematical definition.

Attention should also be drawn to two other limiting conditions required by the definition: It is required for the definition of a relation that there be no two same directed lines (parallel lines) between any two points of the graph. Therefore, configurations of this type

are unacceptable, while diagrams of this type   are possible.

Sometimes it is postulated that an object (point) is not in relation with itself, i.e., that there is no line starting and ending at the same

point.   Configurations of this type are also excluded by Harary et al. That means the relation has to be irreflexive: 'aRa' does not appear. As was the case with finiteness, there is no universal agreement on that matter. Some of the authors do, also, count as graphs

networks consisting of loops   (e.g. Flament). Since only irreflexive relations usually obtain in sport sociology, we can restrict ourselves to finite relations of reflexive type.

A directed graph (or "digraph"), therefore is a set, structured by a finite, irreflexive two-place relation defined on it; or in short, a directed graph (digraph) is a finite, irreflexive (two-place) relation.

In general, lines are directed. It is possible, however, to have undirected lines, as was the case with the quoted example of a tie game. In such cases, respectively, the graphs (with directed and undirected lines) are referred to as mixed graphs. They may be treated separately as graphs with several relations--multigraphs.[3]

Graphs which are constructed of undirected lines only are referred to as symmetric graphs. The latter may be treated as special cases of directed graphs, as each of the undirected lines could be replaced by a combination of arrows in both directions.

A graph is considered to be a complete one, if every point on the graph is connected by an immediate line with all the other points of the graph. The above example of a graph representing a basketball round-robin tournament is complete (and asymmetric).

It seems necessary to mention some other basic notions. Being fully aware of the chaos which has been dominating the basic terminology of graph theory up till now,[4] in this paper Harary's classification and terminology are applied.

Thus, by a <u>sequence</u> we mean a run of lines (including the points on them) which have one common direction. If in a sequence no points or lines are doubly contained, it is called a <u>path.</u> A succession of connected lines, not necessarily of one common direction, is defined as <u>semi-sequence</u>, or <u>semi-path</u>, respectively. Closed paths form <u>cycles,</u> whereas closed semi-paths are <u>semi-cycles.</u>

Examples:

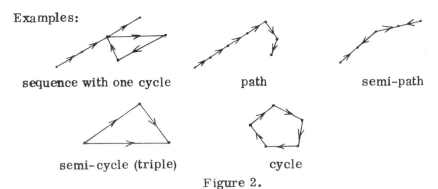

sequence with one cycle   path   semi-path

semi-cycle (triple)   cycle

Figure 2.

Further notions are explained in the course of the presentation of the paper.

In our opinion, it is worth mentioning the fact that all graphs may be presented as matrices. To each graph there is a corresponding <u>adjacency matrix</u> (a_{ik}); in line "i" and column "k", it indicates that point A_i and A_k are immediately connected by a directed line. If it is so, we find a 1 in the meeting cell a_{ik}, if it is not, the cell contains zero: 0.

This is the adjacency matrix for the basketball round presented by figure 1.

		A_1	A_2	A_3	A_4	A_5	A_6
	A_1	0	0	1	1	0	1
	A_2	1	0	0	1	1	1
	A_3	0	1	0	1	0	1
$(a_{ik}) =$	A_4	0	0	0	0	1	1
	A_5	1	0	1	0	0	0
	A_6	0	0	0	0	1	0

From an adjacency matrix, it is possible to derive further matrices.

For example, the reachability matrix (r_{ik}) supplies us with information in the i-th line and the k-th column whether point A_k can be reached from point A_i on a path. If it is so, $r_{ik} = 1$, if not: r_{ik} equals 0.

The distance matrix (d_{ik}) supplies us with information about the distance between A_i and A_k, i.e. the length (number of lines) of a shortest path between A_i and A_k. If the point cannot be reached the sign of infinity is used (∞).

The n-th power of an adjacency matrix indicates, in its cell (i,k), the number of sequences of the length n which connect points A_i and A_k.[5]

Powered matrices can be used to discover cliques; by counting the diagonal elements of the third power of the adjacent matrix one can tell the number of triple links on a returning path which leads to the respective starting point, i.e. the number of triple cliques to which the given point belongs. More comprehensive cliques are composed of these triples.[6] There is no doubt that this method is of great importance to sport sociology.

Generally speaking, the theory of graphs can be treated as the theory of these special matrices of square form. The theory of matrices is gaining extreme usefulness, especially in cases of larger group structures, for matrices then can be evaluated by computers.

In the case of the easily surveyable internal social structures of sports teams and their governing organizations, the application of this method is useful only in some instances, e.g. the assignation of opponents in a league consisting of 20 or more teams. Thus, though the matrix method is more exact, we shall and may restrict ourselves to drawing diagrams and to elaborating the most valuable data by surveying and analyzing by reading.

Applicability of Graph Theoretical Methods Within Sports Organizations.

Let us begin with some remarks concerning application of graph theoretical methods in organization sociology of sport, methods which are successfully used in sociology of organization and sociology of communication, especially in analysis of networks.

Sports organizations are formal organizations in the normal sociological sense of the term. To be classified as formal,[7] an overall structure of a group or association and/or the members of the organization have to be intending or hoping to achieve some definite ends or goals. Besides that, they are differentiated as to division of status and role, and are marked by some or other hierarchic dependence. The fact that they are mostly concerned with honorary or non-profit positions and officials has no influence upon application of organizational-sociological methods.

Division of sports organizations is often presented by charts or diagrams of formal organizational structure, where the head organizations are in directed instructional and/or communicative relations with their subordinate organizations, e.g. special federations of particular sports which in turn are similarly divided into their own branches. In accordance with graph theory, this type of hierarchy can be presented by a <u>tree</u> (sometimes called "arborescence") from the highest organizational unit (e.g., the over-all federation), i.e., by a graph which does not contain any semi-cycles, and all points of which (beginning from the top) can be reached following a single path, exactly.

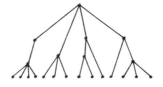

Figure 3.

Organizations of this type are marked by a clear division of competence and uniformity (consistency and compatibility) of status of the subordinated organizations and their officials. On the other hand, every line of the given tree is a path between its two terminal points. Omission of any line would result in a disconnected graph and would cause failures in passage of instructions and communications in the given system. Disturbance and disruption of communication would surely occur in the respective partial graph of communication structure. Therefore, trees are for structural reasons especially susceptible to a lack or omission of any linking point or channel (line), in other words, every non-marginal point within the system supports the so-called <u>connectedness</u> of the graph and prevents the graph from falling into disconnected pieces. Therefore, every non-marginal point in the graph is a <u>cut point.</u>

However, it is essential to differentiate formal organization from real structures of influential and communicative channels. In the latter, trees are not likely to prevail, for reasons avoiding disturbance.

Actually, relations between organizations and role-occupants of sports organizations are not marked by a unique competence of instructions flowing in one direction only. As compared with formal authority, pure role-behavior, and responsibility in such instances, personal influence and personal authority are of far greater importance here than within industrial organizations. In most cases the superior sport organization is only able to suggest or recommend the instructions, while there are no explicit possibilities of applying strong formal sanctions. Neither influence and competence, nor authority to issue instructions, nor communication channels are clearly and precisely defined as in the case of governmental and industrial organizations. In addition to that, a person may be a functionary holding official positions in a number of subordinated organizations (accumulations of functions) on the same or a different hierarchic level. If, for instance, person "a" who holds a certain position is superior to person "b", who in turn is superior to person "c", and if the person "c", who holds a certain position in another suborganization, is superior to person "a" in that respect, they are caught up in cycles of influence. Despite such influences reaching beyond the limits of (subordinated) organizations, in cases like this one, where formal division between people and positions has not very definitely developed, some incompatibilities concerning the passage and preference of instructions are sure to be present. We are facing the famous paradox of non-transitive "pecking-orders" (like the one of hens and cocks).

The optimum of organization of instructions is that the structure be a transitive graph, i.e. whenever person "a" is superior to person "b", who is in turn superior to person "c", then "c" is subordinated to "a", according to the relevant respect. Organizational graphs containing semi-cycles or cycles are likely to be subjected to conflicts, misunderstandings, tension, and disturbance.

For these reasons, factual structures of influences in sports organizations probably consist of a greater number of semi-cycles than comparable industrial and professional organizations. This may be due to the fact that organizations performing their activities during leisure-time are dependent on readily done voluntary cooperation. Therefore, they are unlikely to develop as negatively sanctioned structure of orders and instructions as are found in governmental and industrial organizations. The real structure of influences of a given organization which carries its activities during leisure is not, from the formal point of view, as clearly differentiated as in other organizations, and has fewer tree-like features. This, in turn, means that we are sure to have more vagueness as far as the range of competence of activities goes, more incompatibilities as to issuing of instructions, more ambiguity in authority structure, status assignment, and the regulations concerned within the organization itself, and more disturbance in communication.

For the same reasons such organizations are not likely to demonstrate evidence of having a semi-lattice structure of influence. [8] The uniqueness and commonness of the "supremum" (the least upper bound) of two elements is not generally guaranteed, neither is the identitivity axiom of semi-lattice structure.

Attempts to formalize (by graph theory) French's theory of power influence and power subgroups or cliques undertaken by Harary, the famous research studies on communication, networks and relative centrality of members (Bavelas and others), and studies on status problems by Kemeny-Snell and Harary by means of graph theory can be employed in sports organizations as well as in other ones.

We are not going to discuss thoroughly the results of these detailed studies carried out by means of graph theory. We shall only mention some literature on this subject. [9] In this work, however, the reader's attention should be drawn to the applicability of graph theory for solving socio-organizational problems of sports organizations.

Tournaments

Let us turn to our basketball round-robin tournament presented in Figure 1. In this type of tournament[10] each team[11] plays with all other teams. That means, as was mentioned above, that the digraph of the round-robin tournament is <u>complete</u>. Since in one round each team plays with each partner team only once, and only one of these teams can win, the digraph is <u>asymmetric,</u> which means that if A_i won over A_k, in the same round, A_k cannot have won over A_i.

These features are sufficient to characterize such graphs of round matches by structural properties. Because of evident reasons in graph theory, complete asymmetric graphs are called <u>tournaments</u>.

The theory of tournaments has an exceptional significance in sport sociology. That is confirmed, already, by our (fictitious) example of Figure 1.

The purely mathematical definition of tournaments only regards the relations "having won" and "being defeated." Ties or drawn games cannot be handled by employing graph theory and the theory of tournaments in their pure form.

In this case <u>mixed graphs</u> should be employed; they are not purely asymmetric, any more. Undirected lines stand for a drawn game here. Drawn games in basketball happen very rarely, so many tournaments of basketball round-robin matches will be pure. In English football (soccer), on the other hand, there are many drawn games.

Some theorems of pure tournament theory can be transferred to the respective mixed graphs which we will call <u>mixed tournaments</u>.

Unfortunately, the theory of mixed tournaments has hardly been developed at all. In general, there are the following possibilities: 1) to treat such mixed graphs as <u>multigraphs,</u> i.e. as graphs with two various relations—a directed and an undirected one—or, 2) to substitute the undirected line by two lines going in opposite directions and thus examine the received complete graphs. In both cases only the subgraph which is determined by all points and the remaining unisensory lines will be an asymmetric one. If, in fact, there were drawn games, this graph will not be complete. When drawn games are taken into consideration, changes in the theory are necessarily required.

In order not to complicate the problem we will not pay attention to such changes at first. We shall examine some phenomena of pure tournaments. As for some theorems, special attention will be drawn to the possibility of their transfer to mixed tournament.

Each tournament, at most, has one pure sending point (called "transmitter") (showing only out-arrows), i.e. at most one winning team which won against all the others. For if one team wins against all the remaining ones, they, in the form of terminal points, are at least on one line directed to these points, so they are not pure sending points (transmitters). Such a transmitter (total winner) is, of course, a source point or source of the graph (so it is a point-basis consisting of one point--i.e., the smallest set of points from which paths lead to every point of the graph). This theorem also refers to mixed graphs, of course (in the interpretation as it was given above under point 2).

In graph theory a principle of directional duality is valid, which means that from one valid theorem a corresponding valid theorem can be obtained if each notion it includes will be substituted by the respective converse or dual notion (obtained by reversal of direction of every line).

Due to that principle, the dual theorem can be deduced from the above one, referring to pure and mixed tournaments, too: each tournament contains at most one pure receiving point ("receiver") (with entering lines only)--so, at most, one total loser.

In a tournament with p points (teams or individual players) the total winner has a score (the number of won games $\approx$ the number of lines outgoing from the point) which is p-1. The number of the entering lines of the total loser is also p-1. If there is no total winner. there exists at least one point with the highest score of the graph which, of course, will be less than p-1. Thus, A_2 of the basketball tournament presented on figure 1 has the score 4 (whereas p=6).

An interesting theorem of tournament theory indicates that the distance from a certain point A^{12} with the highest score of the tournament to any other point is 1 or 2. [13]

A conclusion can be drawn from the above: in round-robin matches displaying a character of pure tournaments, each team with the highest score, which is <p-1, (i.e., a team which is the leader of the score list without being a total winner), was defeated by a team which was in turn defeated by another team that was weaker than the leading team. This can be expressed more simply: each team, not winning totally, is in a triple cycle with a defeat (put plainly in a "triple of loss" or "defeat triple"):

This result implies that tournaments without a total winner are not transitive, i.e. they cannot only include transitive triple semicycles like   . So, it is concluded that a tournament without a total winner cannot represent a strict (complete) order (or chain) with a structure of the following type:

Figure 4.

since a transitive tournament per se is a complete strict order.

Measures can be constructed, from which it appears how much a nontransitive tournament is deviant from the resp. complete order.

$$1 - \frac{\text{the number of cyclic triples}}{\text{the maximum number of possible cyclic triples}} \quad \text{is}$$

just such a measure (Kendall-Smith[14]). Another measure (Berge) of vicinity of a tournament to transivity is constituted by the quotient of number t of transitive triples and of all possible triples, i.e. $t/\binom{p}{3}$). Exactly in complete orders this measure is evaluated as 1 (necessarily here $p > 3 \rightarrow t > 0$).

Morrison, Harary and their collaborators calculated the probability of occurrence of cyclic triples obtaining the result 1/4. From that statistically anticipated value follows that in tournaments one can most probably expect 3/4 of all triples to be transitive, i.e., that also non-transitive triples "show a rather high degree of consistency," that not being surprising (Harary). Thus, even the conqueror of all favorites can, on the average, in one-fourth of the cases, break the expected preestimated rank order of winning games. That is why the distribution of won and lost games will reveal a relative transitive distribution. In other words: single won games of the weaker teams do not influence very much the statistical distribution of transitive and cyclic triples, though they may exert a deciding influence on the position of the respective single team (for example, the leading one).

In our basketball round of figure 1 the sequence of scores is as follows: 1, 2, 2, 3, 3, 4. The value of deviation from transitivity (Berge) is 0.7. In the given tournament of basketball there are 14 transitive and $\binom{6}{3} - 14 = 6$ cyclic triples, The non-total winner A_2 is participating in 2 cyclic triples, namely in A_2, A_1, A_3, A_2 and in A_2, A_5, A_3, A_2. The tournament is non-transitive.

Non-total tournament winners not only lie within a "defeat triple" (or "triple of loss"), but under certain circumstances they may constitute final (or terminal) points of a "defeat path," leading from each other point to them, which means that by single comparisons each team is "better" than the winner, so to speak, since each team defeated another team which in turn defeated another team, etc., up to a team that won against the winner.

After a season, there will be sports journalists who will find such hidden "defeat paths" of the winner, in order to diminish the spectacular siginficance of his winning position. There will be officials of sports clubs who would strive to present their team, which finally appeared to be weak, as indirectly "better."

That is why Ore calls this phenomenon "the sportswriter's paradox."[15] If sports journalists and club officials would know anything about graph theory, they would not interpret such a path as a concealed particular weakness of the winner, neither as a "proper supremacy" of their team, but as an ordinary mathematical consequence of tournament structure, and as a mere consequence of the fact that the winner is non-total. Further, the condition must be met with that an existing team which never by chance won, certainly can be neither the beginning nor an intermediate point ("carrier") of a defeat path for the winner. This is evident. Besides, a chosen starting point of the "defeat path" for the winner cannot belong to an outclassed group, i.e., to a team which did not gain a win over any team from outside.

The following theorem is valid: From each point which does not belong to an outclassed group there is a path through all the points of the tournament,[16] that is, also through the point of the winner, if it is not the starting point itself. This theorem is a more rigorous version than that one saying that every tournament has a complete path (leading through all points). Both theorems are valid not only for tournaments, but, in general, for all complete directed graphs. They are also valid, of course, for complete mixed graphs if each undirected line is treated as two lines of opposite direction.

Therefore, sports journalists and club officials will be disappointed, since also, in mixed football (or soccer) tournaments (with many drawn games), this sport writer's paradox does appear. One has only to recognize a drawn game as a confirmation that both teams are "really" of the same quality. It should also be taken into account that during the given tournament not only drawn games take place. For the worst, a club official has to console himself with a conviction that his team, though not "better" than the winning team, is but "really of the same quality." That case occurs when there is no "defeat path" from that team to the winner, but when there is only a connection between them exclusively consisting of paths of undirected lines (drawn games).

When there is no outclassed group in a tournament (or in the complete digraph, respectively) the theorem can be made more rigorous: a complete digraph without an outclassed group includes a complete closed sequence[17] (and even possesses a complete cycle). This theorem, also, clearly refers to mixed tournaments (according to interpretation 2). Every team, consequently, is really "better" or "worse" than itself.

The mentioned closed structure implies that each point is reachable from any other point on a path, and vice versa--this one from each other one; in other words, the graph is <u>strongly connected</u>.[18] (With respect to the complete cycle A_2, A_1, A_4, A_6, A_5, A_3, A_2, the basketball round-robin tournament from figure 1 is strongly connected.)

Since strongly connected (complete) graphs cannot represent a strict order, it is obvious that no complete digraph without an outclassed group is a strict order; or, in other words, every strict (complete) order (i.e. every transitive tournament) includes at least one outclassed group which, after all, then consists exactly of one element: the one and only total loser.

Strict, complete orders (as do complete digraphs) include, however, a complete path; besides, they are characterized by the existence of only one complete path. Therefore, it is possible here to strictly arrange them in accordance with the "win" path of the "defeat path" and so to attach to them a graded level assignment. This level assignment, however, is not always possible in tournaments because of the fact that tournaments usually contain cycles (i.e. they are non-transitive and so they do not constitute a complete strict order).

In order to distinguish the transitive and the strongly connected tournaments, additional criteria have been worked out.[19] They are based on the sequence of scores (Harary and collaborators).

A tournament is <u>transitive</u> if for every $k \leq p$ the following is valid:

$$\sum_{i=1}^{k} s_i = \binom{k}{2}$$

A tournament is <u>strongly connected</u> if always:

$$\sum_{i=1}^{k} s_i > \binom{k}{2}$$

For each tournament, by the way, $\displaystyle\sum_{i=1}^{k} s_i \geq \binom{k}{2}$ is valid.

Nevertheless, not every tournament is transitive or strongly connected. The following tournament can be the proof:

Figure 5.

In this case,[20] $s_1 > \binom{1}{2} = 0$; $s_1 + s_2 > \binom{2}{2} = 1$, but not $s_1 + s_2 + s_3 > \binom{3}{2} = 3$, $s_1 + s_2 + s_3 = 3$, however.

For score sequences of tournaments the following restrictive condition is necessary:

$$\sum_{i=1}^{p} s_i = \binom{p}{2}.$$

Only a series of numbers that satisfies this condition (due to Landau) can represent a score sequence of a tournament.

Now, we would like to present a sufficient condition, which is simple in usage. It can help in deciding whether a tournament is a strongly connected one: If the difference between each two scores is $< \binom{p}{2}$, the tournament is strongly connected (Harary and collaborators). Since the greatest difference between each two scores in the basketball round-robin tournament from figure 1 is $3 = \binom{3}{2}$, and that graph, as was mentioned above, is strongly connected, it appears that the condition is not necessary, but only sufficient.

It is worth mentioning finally that there also exists a measure of deviation of a mixed tournament from a respective pure tournament. It is the number of undirected lines ($\approx$ the number of drawn games) of a mixed tournament, which may serve as such a measure. If this number is divided by the total number of lines, a relative measure is obtained. In pure tournaments the number is 0; in complete digraphs with only undirected lines exclusively, the measure 1 is easily evaluated (this is the maximum of relative deviation). The more similar the mixed tournament is to the pure one, the more distinct will those features already be which are necessary (but not sufficient) for the respective pure tournament.

It is urgent to further develop the theory of mixed tournaments, since just these graphs are of particular importance to sport sociology. They are, by the way, necessary to all comparisons of pairs, where everyone is ranked with each other, equal ranking or equal evaluation being possible (as for example in the case of "pecking orders"), and also in deciding the problems connected with a combination of various individual ranking orders into a common one.[21] It was possible to transfer a number of theorems from the theory of pure tournaments to mixed tournaments, in part by the application of respective changes. It has been demonstrated that some of these theorems are not trivial. On the contrary, they show that specific definite configurations do not reveal particular, empirical features, but that these are a logical consequence of the model itself, i.e., of the structure of tournaments.

Sociometric Digraphs

Graph theory may be successfully employed in sociometric studies on groups and teams.

Although the matrix method has been employed in sociometry for 20 years (beginning with Katz, Festinger, Luce, Perry)[22], graph theory has not been widely utilized until Harary's and Norman's studies.[23] Only Luce's studies on groups and cliques, in a sense related to the analysis of the connectedness of graphs and subgraphs, are somewhat similar to the studies carried out by means of graph theory.

In sociological studies on sport, graph theory has at first been employed in sociometric studies on high performance eight oar crews in rowing.[24] Some special graphs, i.e., semi-lattices,[25] reveal a characteristic closedness of structure; if a sociogram had a semi-lattice structure, this fact was clear evidence, from the sociological point of view, of a meaningful emphasis on the choice criterion which led to the formation of the respective sociogram. When the sociogram of positive choices (selection according to performance ability of strength, preference in the choice of sports and dormitory colleagues, election of team resp. crew captains) revealed a semi-lattice structure that confirmed the fact that, in this case, this criterion of sociogram choice dominated the integration of the crew and the internal sociometric relations.

In cases under examination (with one exception), a semi-lattice structure of a sociogram of rejections between one another indicated, at the same time, the prevalence or even eruption of violent conflicts and tensions. Several sociograms of the same team did not show such structural compactness (closedness) at the same time (except one case, when both the sociogram of rejections and the diagram of election of captain revealed semi-lattice character; but this was due to sufficiently different criteria of choice, so that no contradiction in sociological

126

accentuation conditioned by structure would arise).[26] In one case the semi-lattice structure of the sociogram of achievement preference (choice according to performance ability) was lost, whereas exactly at the same time a group conflict was arising between two emotionally contrasting and competing cliques when this tension began to prevail over the chiefly performance-oriented choices, which dominated the social preference structure a year before.

In another example,[27] that type of the graph structure, referred to as a lattice, which is far more specific and rarely appears in sociology, logically represented the system of values and aims of the Olympic games, as far as it supplied the participants with immanence of orientation, i.e. norms which are adhered to in the given social system. This kind of lattice structure, stretching between the main value (the "Olympic idea" and pedagogical values) and a basic aim (idea of participation), gives the system of values and aims a comparatively strong compactness of structure and internal consistency. Though, at the same time, it causes a certain fixation of tradition and ideology, and leads to a certain obsoleteness of organizational structure and norms.

Besides, as to the author's knowledge, up to now no attempts whatsoever were undertaken to employ the structural notions based on graph theory in sport sociology. Veit's sociometric analyses of ball passages, carried out among teams of indoor German handball and junior soccer teams are somewhat related to the methods of graph thoery.[28] Matrix methods and measures of relative centrality, since earlier employed in special studies on communication networks (Bavelas and others), were put to a good use by Veit in his studies on the structure of ball passages between the respective roles of players. Besides the usually employed, statistically analyzed transfer quotas between the respective roles of players[29] and the team members which are analyzed in sociometric manner, too, the structural aspect has become a significant factor of Veit's analysis. Indeed, communication networks are particularly apt cases of employing graph theory, and they have been, from the point of view of this theory, comparatively well-examined. The transfer of structural analysis and graph theoretical methods to the analysis of the ball passages also proves the applicability of graph theory in such studies, and its efficiency. There exists a close, though not complete structural similarity between the transmission of information and the ball passage[30].

The usefulness of transferring graph theoretical methods from the study of communication networks to the group dynamics and game dynamics of ball teams can be proven by the fact that in actual analyses of games, very often, all-around "leaders" (Spielmacher), permanent cliques of addressed and addressing persons (Abspielcliquen), regarding the ball passages, are constituted; this corresponds with the arising of communication cliques (so-called: communes) around "opinion leaders" or discussion leaders.

Communication experiments with the free choice of channels can be also treated as a kind of sociometric experiment which leads to the arising of a sociogram of preference choices of communication partners. So, there is nothing unusual about the fact that in both cases simliar methods of analysis by means of graph theory can be employed. Some phenomena that are observed in the studies on communication networks can be transferred to the socoimetric analysis of group structures, including the structures which appear in sport sociology.

For instance, Harary's work[31] on applying methods of graph theory in the formalization of French's theory on social influence in "face-to-face" groups, is, undoubtedly, important for the socio-psychological development and realization of decisions, for the propagation of tactical conceptions and new methods of training. If the channels of influence are arranged in a strongly connected digraph, the coach, together with his team, will finally work out a common average opinion in discussion which will be acceptable to everybody, if a "democratic" style of coaching[32] allows any discussions at all. Power subgroups play an important role in French's theory. As regards structure, they correspond exactly with strongly connected components of the respective digraph. If, in the power subgroups, there is a tendency toward the emergence of common opinion, so, at the end, such opinion will become common to the whole group. The same is true when the adjacency matrix of a graph has double stochastic form, i.e., if the graph has the form of a Markoff-chain.

On the basis of this type of analysis of influence in sports teams, in which processes of social decision exist, new characteristics of the player's role can possibly be found. A question arises whether in big team games the "leader" (Spielmacher) often is the chief of such a power clique, or whether his role is only of practical meaning for the game when he is representing the only connecting point (cut-point) between the power cliques, or on the other hand, whether he is distinguished within the whole group or subgroup by a particularly high relative centrality (Bavelas), whether his position in the structure of influence agrees with his position in the entanglement of average ball passages. Or is it just vice versa—is his relative status (Harary), which represents exactly the opposite value of relative centrality,[33] typically high? Such, or similar, questions may also be put concerning other players' roles, and may be analyzed by means of graph theory, as far as structural properties are relevant.

It is obvious that characteristic differences between typical networks of action or structures of influence according to the type of sports team should appear. The questions, how far that type of structure depends upon the kind of cooperation particular for that sport, or on the quantitative composition of a team, can be answered only after carrying out differentiated analyses. Up to now, the colloquial rough classifications between artificial teams (summing up of points referring to individual achievements, e.g., team horse-riding), mechanical summing up of a physical effort (rowing crews), individually differentiated coordination towards collective social action (ball games), obviously are not sufficient to explain typical structural differences of the mentioned kind and of the psycho-social team dynamics. One can observe, indeed, a certain similarity in the sociometric arrangements of members around the leading persons and in the constituting of cliques in teams of very different disciplines, like German handball[34] (Veit) and rowing[35] (Lenk). Generally, the special kind of cooperation in this or another sports discipline seems to have less influence on typical features of the structure of sociometric graphs than is commonly supposed. The other way around are results of comparisons of the analysis of actual patterns of action or cooperation: analysis of ball passages and tactial cooperation in German handball are absolutely incongruent and incomparable with metrical orientations, as regards the beat rhythm and the tactical coordination concerning changes in speed rate etc., in rowing.

Cliques

Special results of sociological studies on cliques which have been conducted up to the present will not be discussed in detail here.[36] The author's intention is only to indicate the way of applying graph theory to to clique analysis.

Beginning with the already mentioned studies which were conducted by Katz, Festinger and Luce (see note 6) in the analysis of cliques and similar groups, the mathematical method of matrix analysis was applied--even in sport sociology, too. The matrix method and its modifications are graph theoretical methods: analyses of adjacency matrices, distance and reachability matrices, are only another mathematically isomorphic representation of graph theoretical analyses in the narrower sense. Particularly, the powered matrices of the adjacency matrix have been applied to clique analysis.

It was possible to use here differently strict notions of cliques. Thus, for example, according to Festinger and Luce,[37] every strongly connected complete subgraph is a clique, i.e., each member of a clique has to be directly in the specific, preferential, communicational or other clique-promoting relation with all other members of the clique. This is a very limited and special notion of "clique." Of course, cliques of this strict type are very rarely realized in social groups; so, this notion cannot be considered very promising.

Therefore, it was suggested instead to call such cliques "complete cliques" and, in principle, to work on subgroups which perhaps lack a few direct connections to form a complete clique. These cliques (or "almost"-cliques: Luce) appear more often and are much more typical than complete cliques; therefore, they should not be neglected. From the viewpoint of matrix calculation, this means that instead of the main elements of the diagonal of the cubicly-powered matrix of the symmetric partial matrix of the adjacency matrix, one has now to calculate the main elements of the diagonal of the cubicly-powered matrix of the full adjacency matrix itself in order to fix the number of tricliques to which the group members belong, and from which major cliques are formed. The small additional calculation work is worth the trouble, since in this way much more clique-resembling structures can be recognized and analyzed.

Moreover, due to this method, the stages of formation and disappearance or dissolving of complete cliques can be much better examined. That has been confirmed by the example of the 1962 World Champion eight oar crew in rowing which was completely dominated by a complete clique constituted according to performance criteria[38]. This clique still existed, to be sure, in the next year, but it was not a complete clique any longer--but only an "almost"-clique. Simultaneously a new "almost"-clique of outsiders was formed in the emotional sociogram of preferences and it was strongly emotionally contrasted to the mentioned dominating clique. The performance criterion was not the one and only dominating factor any more (semi-lattice structure of the preference sociogram had been lost in accordance with that). However, serious conflicts between leaders and tensions between cliques occurred. This phenomenon could be and was foreseen earlier because of the definite symmetric dualism in the sociogram of election of captain and because of the distinct separation of the dominating clique from the "others."[39] If these studies had been based exclusively on the analysis of complete cliques, this process could not have been presented and analyzed in so differentiated a manner and "clique conflicts" could not have been explained so easily.

Harary[40] proposes another, weaker, definition of "clique." According to him each strongly connected component of the graph is a clique (i.e. each maximum strongly connected subgraph in which each point is reachable from any other point on a path). In the same place, Harary also describes additional possibilities of regarding unilaterally connected components as cliques (i.e., maximum subgraphs in which, of each two points, at least one of them can be reached from the other). The last two definitions, however, seem to be too weak to be treated as significant for cliques, socially authentic and real. That may be the case already in view of the more strict notion: if every strong component is a clique, every graph contains cliques. Even if by definition the trivial strong components which consist of only one element are excluded, and even if one excludes dual cliques by definition, too, we still face the phenomenon of cliques that originated purely structurally (from structural reasons alone). In a sociogram

130

with a fixed number of votes from one voter there would occur at
least as many cliques as votes are cast by each of the voters.

Let us dwell for a moment on the number of votes amounting to
1: each voter has to make exactly one preferential selection. A sociogram results which, in this case, is a <u>functional digraph</u>,[41] i.e.
a graph in which from each point only one line goes out (each point
has "<u>outdegree</u>" 1).

Functional graphs always have, because of purely structural reasons, the form of (at least) one cycle on which trees adhere which
are directed toward the cycle, for example:

Figure 6.

The proof is easily done.[42] Every functional digraph contains at
least one cycle--and exactly one cycle, if the graph is (weakly) connected at all, i.e., if it is not split up into disconnected parts.

Functional digraphs contain cliques (i.e. non-trivial strongly connected components) because of purely structural reasons.

Sociograms which consist exactly of two votes of each voter can
be treated as a combination of two functional digraphs. They contain
at least two cycles (two cliques). When the amount of votes is enlarged, the number of cycles grows accordingly.

Apparently, purely functional digraphs do not occur very often
in empirical sociograms of sports teams. Among all rowing eights
which were examined by means of sociometric method, only one completely pure, connected functional digraph could be found, namely, an
election diagram of the crew captain which consisted of one dominating cycle of two elements and of one tree towards each point of the
cycle.

If single, non-voting persons are not taken into account,[43] it is
obvious that the remaining digraph is a functional one, if it does not
contain a loop, which appears by giving one's vote to oneself (that
happens quite often).

Besides, the division of election sociograms of the team captain into two disconnected, weak components is typical, each of which parts represents a functional subgraph with one cycle. (The particular case mentioned, which happens very often, can be included here: it is when someone elects oneself as the captain resp. as the person most suitable for this role. The loop of this particular type of election can be, in a trivial way, included in the category of cycle).[44]

This structure explicitly expresses a definite tendency of high performance rowing eight oar crews towards a "dual of leadership" as it happened both in the 1962 and the 1966 World Champion eight oar crews; in one instance (1962) two independent, completely isomorphic in structure, functional subgraphs appeared (symmetric leaders' dualism or leadership "dual").[45]

The statement saying that a sociogram with an equal number of votes of the voters or a communication network with points of equal out-degrees contains cycles is not of great empirical value, since it does not contain empirical content or information, if the notion of weak cliques is understood according to Harary. Such cliques, namely, appear as a necessary consequence of structure resp. of putting the question. Cliques which appear as the unavoidable consequence of structure are not interesting from the empirical point of view.

Having the above given reasons in mind, it seems more sensible to use a notion of cliques which is not so strict or strong, for example the notion of "almost"-cliques. Continuing the analysis it is possible to recognize complete cliques, for example, by applying Harary's method based on successive finding of members which belong only to one clique (unicliqual members), eliminating them and repeating the whole procedure up to the moment when, even after division into subgroups, such members are not be to found any more.

Complete cliques are, after all, always balanced if the sociogram is not inconsistent, i.e., when it is not the case that one person simultaneously elects and rejects someone. In the case of "almost"-cliques, however, the degree of balance and the smallest number of line values which are to be changed to the opposite, as well as the least number of lines which are to be omitted, in order to generate a balanced graph, is to be regarded as empirically interesting. Also the greater possibility of empirically differentiating may suggest carrying out, first of all, studies on the "almost"-clique.

Balanced and Unbalanced Graphs

The analysis of cliques resulted in referring to the notion of balanced graphs.

In order to be able to introduce this notion, the graph must contain positively and negatively evaluated lines: e.g. positive preferential

132

choices and negative rejection votes included in sociograms (being a combination of both of these types of votes). The respective graph then, is an algebraic graph (a bigraph, i.e., a graph with two relations to which the respective plus or minus signs will be attributed.)

A graph is balanced exactly when all its semi-cycles (closed sequences of lines or sequences without taking into account the direction of the composing lines) contain an even number of lines with a negative value including 0, which is considered to be an even number.

For instance, this notion has been employed by Cartwright and Harary in their work on formalization of Heider's theory about compatibility of intersubjective attitudes, also by Flament who interpreted the structural type-creating relation between father, mother, mother's brother, and son, [46] thus using graph theory for problems of cultural anthropology.

Since sociometry distinguishes between positive, preferential choices and rejections (negative choices), the notion of balanced and unbalanced graph can be directly applied to sociograms.

It has already been mentioned that all complete cliques (in consistent sociograms) are balanced subgraphs. If the "almost"-cliques are not in a state of balance already, there is, according to Harary, a tendency to change some attitudes in such a direction that balanced subgraphs of cliques are developing.

But what about the whole of the team, regarding this problem?

It is characteristic that all eight oar crews in rowing hitherto studied by means of sociometric methods, displayed unbalanced sociograms, exclusively. That is valid concerning the choice of boat-partners, the preference according to achievement criteria, and the choice of the person(s) to share room with in sports voyages.[47] This result, that all sociograms of high performance eight oar crews were unbalanced, cannot have arisen by chance. [48]

Here is an explanatory hypothesis which agrees completely with Heider's theory. The high performance teams concerned always had to sustain permanent competition abound with stress both outside and inside the crews: everyone stood in awe of his position in the first class crew. In skiff or double sculls he had again and again to qualify in races and in training and to be on guard against his crew colleagues, spare men, and athletes from the second class team ready to take his place. This permanent pressure of competition urging to new levels of achievement, physically wearing down and psychically unnerving, the tremendous amount of time and energy envisaging the permanent risk of accidental defeats, permanent over-nervousness because of continued alternation of professional work, of regatta tours, of training and training camps, of boat-races--all of that together with an overloaded contact within the group--everything leads, especially at the beginning of the second half of the season, to a typical nervousness of the team which manifests itself in the relations of the members one to each other, to the coach and persons from outside (officials, etc.). "The threshold value of aggression" (Lorenz) is lowered, so to speak. Then, it is easily understandable that the respective sociograms are unbalanced. That is valid even for crews with a relatively small number of conflicts. Factors which evoke aggression and conflicts create, also in these teams, a hidden conflict situation or, at least, a situation pregnant with conflicts.

If a risen psychic aggression energy cannot be in any way directed or deflected to any outside object, conflicts within a team arise relatively easily, often because of insignificant reasons. (Among the eight oar crew which, during the 1964 Olympics, won the silver medal, a quarrel broke out and members almost came to blows, when they only wanted to justly distribute a box of bottles with apple juice which they had got as a present.) Such conflicts are not at all necessarily succeeded by a considerable debasement of strength of performance. They are absolutely compatible with full development and putting into action of the supreme amount of achievement ability.[49] In addition, such conflicts and tensions seem to be unavoidable in such extreme psychic situations of competition. They obviously can only be regulated, for instance, by directing them outside or by partly relieving oneself of them and controlling them in open discussions: verbal quarrels are the least harmful form of relieving tensions.

These conflicts being frequently inevitable, conscious stimulating of aggression in order to extend performance ability cannot be a subject of discussion here, as some harmonistic-ideological specialists of physical education erroneously tried to insinuate again and again. Aggressions of such type are only accompanying phenomena, and teams must learn to coexist with them as well as with open or hidden conflicts. These aggression states and emotions cannot be dismissed once and for all. The coach also should not be panicked at arising conflicts, but has to work out methods to relieve and control them.

Since in high performance sports teams preferential choices and rejections are influenced, in great part, by the assessment of achievement abilities,[50] and since even emotional evaluations and preferences (choice of partners to share room with) are prevailingly based on that, unbalanced sociometric graphs cannot, by means of quickly adaptive changes in attitudes, reach the state of balance. The sociograms remain unbalanced in most cases. In addition, according to Heider's theory, growing "psychic tensions" are the result of the above. Teams with permanently unbalanced sociograms are entangled, so to say, in a vicious circle promoting internal conflicts and stimulating aggression which they can evade only by some "out-valve" or by means of a scapegoat outside (coxswain, coach, sports officials, etc.) which will make it possible to drain off the aggressive psychic energy.

It would be interesting to examine, whether ball teams, for example junior, school or old-boy ones, as they were studied by Veit, also permanently reveal unbalanced graphs. Be it not so, the explanatory hypothesis presented here would become very significant, since the signs of extreme stress which prevail in high performance teams of of a sports discipline like rowing, where intensive training, permanent eminent concentration of the will, strength combined with endurance is needed, certainly do not appear so intensively in amateurish ball teams and in teams of lower performance standards, where elements of play itself prevail over the record-seeking ambition. Unfortunately, comparisons in this direction could not be conducted, since Veit's work supplies us only with synthetic estimation and summaries of sociogram analyses and sociomatrices and not with the detailed description of these data.

The empirical findings that sociograms of high performance teams in endurance sports are unbalanced may be explained, indeed, on the basis of the above mentioned general hypothesis. However, the notion of balanced graph can also be employed in elaborating further differentiations between teams all of which are having unbalanced sociograms, namely, by means of measuring the different degrees of approach to the respective "next" balanced graph. If the number of balanced semi-cycles of the graph is divided by the total number of its semi-cycles, such a relative measure is obtained. A relative conflictless[51] rowing eight crew displayed a respectively (in spite of its unbalanced total graph) higher degree of sociometric balance than the teams persecuted by open conflicts:[52] the sociogram was much closer to the "state of balance."

Because of a considerably higher average number of complete (and consequently balanced) or "almost-complete" cliques (with balanced semi-cycles prevailing) among ball teams[53], the degree of balance of the majority of ball teams should be higher than in rowing eight crews where at the outmost two cliques stand in opposition to each other.

Final Remarks

The studies presented in this paper might have demonstrated that methods of graph theory can be, to the advantage of the exactness and conceptualization of structural properties and factors, successfully applied to sport sociology. A sport sociologist (as well as sociologists in general) cannot dispense with this instrument anymore, if he does not want to deprive himself of possibilities of giving his models and theory a precise formulation. But not only a better means of presentation is at stake here; in fact, certain connections, properties and statements, generally understood as empirical ones, turn out to be structural-mathematical consequences of the model itself that can be revealed as statements of such a logic-mathematical character only by the employment of graph theory. The above mentioned theorem that sociograms with a strictly defined number of votes necessarily contain cliques (cycles, strongly connected components), if all the members actually participate in voting, constitutes an example of a non-trivial statement gained by the application of graph theory. Another significant, non-trivial result reveals that each group can, at the outmost, include two members the presence of which weakens the structural connectedness of the group (Harary, Norman, Cartwright).[54] Both the results are, in fact, of the greatest importance to sociograms concerning teams and to investigations of cliques in sport sociology.

There is another argument, confirming the usefulness of wider employment of graph theory in sociology of sport. In three very distinct branches of this scientific discipline the following structures and methods of the same theory of graphs can be successfully applied: in the analysis of sports organizations, in investigations of round-robin matches, and in studies on the group dynamics of teams, In the above mentioned branches, various graph structures are prevailing in application, indeed: trees, partial orders and/or quasi-orders, semi-lattices in studies of organizations; pure and mixed tournaments and, also, more generally, complete digraphs in investigating round-robin matches; and finally, functional digraphs, strongly connected components, and complete symmetric subgraphs (cliques) as well as balanced or unbalanced algebraic digraphs, and analysis of powered matrices in in sociometry of teams. However, a uniform mathematical theory of graph structure and relations (exactly: of double-place "relatives" in the the mathematical sense, i.e., sets with double-place relations defined on them) is the basis for all instances mentioned.

Although some mathematical problems and questions of graph theory concerning the employment of this theory in sociology are still open,[55] a sociologist should take advantage of theorems of graph theory in constructing his own sociological theories. The theorems of graph theory have been fruitfully applied hitherto and promise to promote a significant theoretical progress in standardization, preciseness, and specification of theories.

Sociologists must be aware, however, of the fact that graph theory only by itself is not sufficient to construct empirical hypotheses or to derive them from structural properties. The attachment or "mapping" of relations and points to objects and connections which appear in social reality cannot be a subject of purely structural and theoretic studies, only.

Mathematical models themselves cannot substitute for the creative ideas of a theoretician himself, though they might be fruitful and even indispensable for elaborating a relatively precise formulation of these ideas or for a formalization, after all. This statement refers to sport sociology as well as to any other empirical sociology.

FOOTNOTES

(1)Harary, E., Norman, R. Z., Graph Theory as a Mathematical Model in Social Science, Ann Arbor 1953. Flament, C., Applications of Graph Theory to Group Structure, Englewood Cliffs 1963. Harary, F., Norman, R. Z., Cartwright, D., Structural Models. An Introduction to the Theory of Directed Graphs, New York-London-Sidney (1965), 1966. Busacker, R. G., Saaty, T. L., Finite Graphs and Networks. An Introduction with Applications, New York a.o. 1965. Harary, F., "Graph Theory and Group Structure", in: Luce, R. D., Bush, R. R., Galanter, E., Readings in Mathematical Psychology, New York-London-Sidney, 1965, Vol. II, p. 225-241. Lenk, H., Graphen und Gruppen. "Anwendungsmöglichkeiten der mathematischen Graphentheorie in Soziologie und Sozialpsychologie" in: Soziale Welt XX (1969), p. 407-427. Also see: Roy, B., Algèbre moderne et théorie des graphes orientées vers les sciences économiques et sociales, Vol. I (Notions et résults fondamentaux, Paris 1969). II (Applications et problemes spécifiques, Paris).

(2)The R relation is a two-place one, if everytime it can--and can only--obtain exclusively between two objects: aRb--more exactly: if by means of substitution of exactly two constant designations (names) of the object for the two variables in 'xRy' a full closed, true or false, statement appears containing no object variables any longer. In general, 'aRb' does not mean the same as 'bRa,' i.e., the relation is not always symmetric. Therefore, the terms "directed relations" and "directed graphs," ("digraphs") are used.

(3)The most important multigraphs are so-called algebraic graphs, where a positive relation can be distinguished from a negative one. They may be also understood as evaluated graphs in which the evaluation of line is done by +,-=signs.

(4)See: Lenk, Graphen und Gruppen, l. c.

(5)The n-th power of a square matrix with r lines is calculated in the following way:

$$\left(a_{st}^{(n)}\right) = \left(a_{st}\right)^n = \left(\sum_{i_1,i_2,i_3,\ldots,i_{n-1}}^{r} a_{si_1} \cdot a_{i_1i_2} \cdot a_{i_2i_3} \cdots a_{i_{n-1}t}\right)$$

[6]Katz, L., "On Matrix Analysis of Sociometric Data", In: Sociometry 1947, p. 233 ff. Festinger, L., "The Analysis of Sociograms Using Matrix Algebra", In: Human Relations 1949, p. 153 ff. Luce, R. D., Perry, A. D., "A Method of Matrix Analysis of Group Structure", In: Psychometrika 1949, p. 95 f. Luce, R. D., "Connectivity and Generalized Cliques in Socio-metric Group Structure", In: Psychometrika 1950, p. 169 ff. Comp. also: Harary, Norman, Cartwright, Structural Models op. cit., p. 111 f. Lenk, H., "Konflikt und Leistung in Spitze sportmannschaften--Soziometrische Strukturen von Wettkamp-fachtern im Rudern", In: Sozalie Welt 1964, (p. 307-343), p. 310 f.

[7]Mayntz, R., Soziologie der Organisation. Reinbek near Hamburg 1963, pp. 36, 40 ff.

[8]A supremum semi-lattice is an ordered set structured by a partial or complete order (i.e., a transitive, identitive, and most often not reflexive and not symmetric relation) in which for each two elements there is exactly one common least upper bound (neighbor in the sense of the relation).

The relation R is transitive, if 'aRb' and 'bRc' are always implying 'aRc'. Reflexive are such relations for which always 'aRa' is valid; irreflexive are those relations in which this statement does not apply to any a (so, there are relations which are neither reflexive or irreflexive). Likewise, not to be a symmetric relation ('aRb' implies 'bRa' always) is not the same as being asymmetric (never 'aRb' and 'bRa'). Identitive is a relation, where with 'aRb' and 'bRa' there is always a=b.

[9]Harary, Norman, Cartwright, Structural Models, op. cit., containing a bibliography. The above mentioned pioneer papers are the following: Bavelas, A., "Communication Patterns in Task-oriented Groups", In: Cartwright, D., Zander, A., (eds.) Group Dynamics, Evanston 1960, p. 669-682. Harary, F., "A Criterion for Unanimity in French's Theory of Social Power," In: Cartwright, C. (ed.), Studies in Social Power, Ann Arbor 1959, p. 168-182. Kemeny, J. G., Snell, J. L., Mathematical Models in the Social Sciences, New York 1962. Harary, F., "Status and Contrastus," In: Sociometry 1959, p. 23-43. For a survey see also: Lenk, Graphen and Gruppen, l.c.

[10]Double round-robin tournaments (each team plays with every other one twice) may be simply considered as two single round-robin tournaments; here the score sequences of both rounds are

summed up. Many theorems concerning tournaments can be
transferred from the field of pure tournament theory to double
tournaments, without any additional conditions.

(11)There also exist, of course, tournaments played between individual sportsmen (e.g., in tennis). The theory also refers to
them.

(12)Proof: The distance between A and the teams defeated by A
is of course, 1. It has to be proved that the distance to the other
teams is 2. They defeated A; U may be taken as one of them. Assuming that there is not any point among the teams defeated by A
from which the distance to U would be 1 (so that d (A, U) = 2), U
would have defeated all teams defeated by A and also A itself.
This amounts to a contradiction with: the assumption saying that
A has the highest score of the graph, completing the (indirect)
proof of the theorem.

(13)This theorem, after all, holds for every complete directed
graph, without any changes, though not for mixed tournaments.
If the fictitious distance 0 is introduced for a drawn game between teams, some of the respective distances in the case of
mixed tournaments can only be reduced by 1 as against pure
tournaments. Therefore for mixed tournaments the theorem is
valid, that the distance from a point of highest score to every
other point is 0, 1, or 2.

(14)According to Harary, Norman, Cartwright, op. cit., p. 299,
p. 300 ff. Since the number of transitive triples can be calucla-
ted as $\sum_{i=1}^{p} \binom{s}{2}i$ from the (for instance growing) sequence of
scores, s_i, of all points, and, since the total number of triples
is $\binom{p}{3}$, the number of cyclic triples is: $\binom{p}{3} - \sum_{i=1}^{p} \binom{s}{2}i$. The
maximum of cyclic triples is $\frac{p^3-p}{24}$, p being an odd integer, and
respectively, $\frac{p^3-4p}{24}$, p being an even integer.

(15)Ore, O., Graphs and Their Uses, New York 1963, p. 75 ff.

(16)Proof (the stronger proof at the same time is a proof that
every complete digraph--and also every tournament--has a
complete path at all): Since the starting point A does not belong
to any outclassed group, there is a path going out from A_1. If
all paths going out from A_1 ceased before they reached all the
other points of the graph, the points reached by these paths going out from A_1 would constitute an outclassed group. (Other-

140

wise, there would exist a line leading from one of these points to a point situated outside of this subset. In this case, the path from A_1 to that point could be extended by means of this line.) Thus, A_1 would belong to an outclassed group, which would contradict the assumption.

(This new proof is much simpler and shorter than all others hitherto carried out. By the way, those arguments up till now, by means of the complete induction concerning the number of points in graphs or by means of a successive construction firstly proved the more general theorem: every tournament contains a complete path; and, then, by variation of the assumptions and by further argument, proved the stronger special version of the theorem.)

[17] Proof: A complete path may lead from the starting point A_1 with the least score to the final point A_e; but from A_e a line has to go out, otherwise A_e would be outclassed. So, the graph contains cycles. We assume that the line $A_e A_1$ is not in the graph (otherwise everything would already be proved). By directional dualization the above mentioned theorem implies that the distance of the point with the smallest score from any other one is, at the very most, 2. In this instance the distance from A_e is exactly 2, which means that there is at least one complete closed sequence, and that was to be demonstrated. (This new argument is simpler than the previous ones.)

Since the path of length 2 from A_e to A_1 has to go through one point of the complete path leading from A_1 to A_e, we are not confronted here with a cycle. The complete sequence consists exactly of two partial cycles, not having lines in common, though having one common intersection point on the path leading from A_e to A_1.

However, this theorem can be sharpened in such sense that every complete digraph contains a complete cycle. Yet it is of no importance to tournaments of teams, whether one of the complete closed sequences is a complete cycle, i.e., whether these sequences can be constructed without repetition of points, or not.

[18] The existence of complete cycles is naturally necessary for the strong connectedness of complete digraphs (first of all for asymmetric ones; since, however, the other complete digraphs also contain all the lines of a respective tournament, this theorem is valid in general).

[19] To mixed tournaments these criteria do not apply, clearly.

[20] The example of Harary, Norman, Cartwright, Structural Models, p. 309, as above. Here, the mentioned criteria are worked out, too (p. 251, 307 ff., 315).

(21)Ibid., p. 313, see also Lenk, Graphen and Gruppen, as above.

(22)See also note 6.

(23)Harary, Norman, Graph Theory as a Mathematical Model in Social Science, as above.

(24) Lenk, Konflikt und Leistung in Spitzensportmannschaften, as above.

(25)Compare note 8.

(26)See: Lenk, Graphen und Gruppen, as above. [In such instances connecting lines running in both of the opposite directions (double lines) must be counted only once in order to keep the identity. F. Or some other regulations have to be proposed, e.g. analysis of the sociograms as multigraphs or investigation of the so-called indifference relation induced by the to-and-fro choices of the concerned graph etc.]

"Rejections" are called the answers to the question: "Together with whom do you only reluctantly row in one crew?" The word "rejection" is too sharp in general, though real conflicts and tensions often take place. Nevertheless, any other accurate and short term has not been found.

(27) Lenk, H., Werte, Ziele Wirklichkeit der modernen Olympischen Spiele, Schorndorf near Stuttgart 1964, 1972^2, p. 299 ff.

(28)Veit, H., Untersuchungen und Ueberlegungen zur Dynamik von Hallenhandballmannschaften Lehrte 1964 (manuscript). Veit, H., Analyse des Ballverlaufs in spontanen Hallenhandballmannschaften, 1964 (manuscript). See also: Veit, H., Sozialpsychologische Untersuchungen von Ballspielmannschaften, Lehrte 1965–1966 (duplicated), paragraph 6. See also Veit, H., Untersuchungen zur Gruppendynamik von Ballspielmannschaften Ein empirischer Beitrag zur Kleingruppenforschung. Schorndorf/Germany (Hofmann) 1971.

(29)Klein, M., Christansen, G., Gruppenkomposition, Gruppenstruktur und Effektivität von Basketballmannschaften. Published in: Lüschen, G. (ed.), Kleingruppenforschung und Gruppe im Sport. Sonderheft No. 10/1966 of the "Koelner Zeitschrift für Soziologie und Sozialpsychologie," Cologne-Opladen, pp. 181–199.

(30)This analogy, of course, is valid only within certain limits: information can be passed on, nevertheless all the informants keep it for themselves. There is no analogy of this phenomenon in the ball passage.

[31] Harary, F., Ein Kriterium für Einmütigkeit in Frenchs Theorie der sozialen Macht. Published in: Mayntz R. (ed.) Formalisierte Modelle in der Soziologie, Neuwied-Berlin 1967, p. 121 ff. (For the English original see note 9).

[32] Lenk, H., "Autoritär" oder "demokratisch" geleitetes Training? Published in: Rudersport 1965, p. 221 ff. and in Gymnasion, 1965, No. 3, pp. 13-21. Lenk, H., "Zur Sozialpsychologie der Trainingsmannschaften," In: Adam, K.; Lenk, H.; Nowacki, P.; Rulffs, M.; Schroeder, W.: Rudertraining. Francfort, (in press).

[33] The relative centrality C_{rel} of a point is obtained from the distance matrix as a quotient of the sum of all distances and of the distances of all points from the given point.

$$C_{rel} = \frac{\text{total sum of all distances}}{\text{sum of the matrix line referring to the given point}} = \frac{1}{S}$$

S_{rel} refers to the relative status.

[34] Veit, H., Sozialpsychologische Untersuchungen von Ballspielmannschaften, op. cit. What is usually called "clique," Veit calls here "nucleus" (Kern). Veit, Über Untersuchungen zur Gruppendynamik von Ballspielmannschaften, 1967-68 (manuscript). Veit, "Die Bedeutung sozialpsychologischer Untersuchungen von Sportmannschaften für die Praxis," In: Die Leibeserziehung, 1968, pp. 80-87. See also note 28.

[35] Lenk, H., Konflikt und Leistung, as above.

[36] Veit, H., Sozialpsychologische Untersuchungen von Ballspielmannschaften, op. cit. Veit, Untersuchungen zur Gruppendynamik von Ballspielmannschaften, op. cit. Lenk, "Konflikt and Leistung in spitzensportmannschaften," as above. See also: Lenk, "Zur Socialpsychologie der Trainingsmannschaften," as above. The author differentiated between club cliques and leadership cliques and, accordingly, attributed various conflicts inside the teams which, as a typical phenomenon, result from too strong separation or emphasis of a clique.

[37] Compare note 6.

[38] Lenk, H., "Konflikt und Leistung in Spitzenmannschaften," as above.

[39] Lenk, H., "Soziogramm eines Vereinsachters." Published in: Lehrbeilage of Rudersport, 1963, No. 11, p. 5 f.

[40] Harary: Graph Theory and Group Structure, as above, p. 299. See also Harary, F., "A Procedure for Clique Detection in Using the Group Matrix." Published in: Sociometry, 1959, pp. 139-147.

[41] A functional digraph is an irreflexive function, i.e. a (two-place) relation with a unique second-place relatum, no element being in the relation with itself.

[42] Proof: We assume that the digraph is functional and as a whole (weakly) connected. Since each point has out-degree a pure receiving point ("receiver") cannot exist (it would have out-degree 0). From that directly follows that the digraph contains at least one cycle, since the terminal point of each maximum path has an outgoing line which must return to one point of the path. If that one were a new point (not lying on the path) the path would not be a maximum one. If the digraph is connected, it cannot contain two cycles, since one connection point of the two cycles, or one point on the semi-path joining both of the cycles, would have out-degree 2. If the functional digraph includes two or more cycles, it is composed of two or more disconnected component parts, each one having one cycle. Then, the total proof concerns each component part, separately.

Non-cyclic parts of the connected functional digraph are trees, each of them being directed towards one point of the cycle. Each maximum path, not lying on the cycle, has a terminal point with out-degree 1. The outgoing line cannot include a point which lies outside the path as well as outside the cycle; were it so, the path would not be a maximum one. The line cannot be directed back to the path, either, since then the path itself would contain one cycle more.

[43] A subgraph containing non-isolated persons, who do not vote, is not functional any more. Example: the 1966 World Champion eight. Lenk, "Zur Sozialpsychologie der Trainingsmannschaften," op. cit.

[44] This structure, according to Harary, is not a graph, since it is not irreflexive, but a finite relations with loop.

[45] Lenk, "Konflikt und Leistung," as above. Lenk, "Zur Sozial-psychologie der Trainingsmannschaften," as above.

[46] Cartwright, D., Harary, F., "Structural Balance: a Generalization of Heider's Theory." Published in: Psychol. Rev., 1956, pp. 277-293. Berger, J.; Cohen, B. P.; Snell, J. L.; Zelditch, M., "Eine Formalisierung von Heiders Gleichgewichtstheorie." Published in: Mayntz, R. (ed.), Formalisierte Modelle in der Soziologie. Neuwied-Berlin 1967, pp. 101-119. Flament, "Application of Graph Theory to Group Structure," as above, p. 124 ff.

[47] Lenk, H., "Konflikt und Leistung," as above. As for the 1966 World Champion eight, compare Lenk, "Zur Sozialpsychologie der Trainingsmannschaften," as above.

[48] Probability of obtaining an unbalanced graph grows, however, more rapidly than the number of the team members. Nevertheless, also in rowing fours up till now only graphs of unbalanced structures were found. On the other hand, with the increase of the number of participants the number of cliques also increases, even, as it seems to be, very considerably. While a rowing eight is on the limit of the average highest number of team members (amounting to 7, as established by means of socio-psychological studies), where a group does not have to disjoin into subgroups, the ball teams with 11 players clearly lie beyond this limit. Therefore, according to Veit, in ball teams much more cliques are found (often three or four). Veit, Sozialpsychologische Untersuchungen von Ballspielmannschaften, op. cit., and Veit, Untersuchungen zur Gruppendynamik von Ballspielmannschaften, op. cit.

[49] Lenk, "Konflikt und Leistung in Spitzenmannschaften," as above.

[50] Lenk, "Konflikt und Leistung," as above.

[51] Eight oar crews in: Lenk, "Konflikt and Leistung," as above.

[52] The 1962 World Champion eight oar crew: the 1963 Champion eight of Europe, and the 1960 Olympic Champion eight crew.

[53] Compare note 48.

[54] Harary, F., "Graph Theory and Group Structure," as above, p. 233.

[55] Lenk, "Graphen and Gruppen," as above.

Epistemological Problems and the Personality and Social Systems in Social Psychology of Sport

(with Gunther Luschen, University of Illinois)

If we understand social psychology to be an area where sociology and psychology overlap, or more precisely where we try to explain interaction on the basis of psychological and sociological propositions and concepts, we have singled out a field that should be quite challenging not only in theory and method but in the fundamental questions it raises for both sociology and psychology. Actually, the discipline is not that well integrated and is constituted by such disparate approaches as reinforcement theory, field theory, role theory, small group theory, game theory and psychoanalysis. Many sociologists have abandoned the field altogether. Nor have the proponents of these sub-fields made much effort to consolidate, integrate or reconcile their methodologies. Epistemological questions have been notably absent and only now have arguments from the philosophy of science point of view reemerged to revive the critical and potentially fruitful methodological discussions of earlier theorists (Allport; Lewin; Mead; Simmel) and their more recent followers (Homans; Malewski).

After considering epistemological problems dealing with the generality of theory and explanations, behavioristic vs. action approaches, operational and model structural implications, we want to argue for a better understanding of social system variables besides those of the personality system and of system theory in general. In our discussion we use examples from the area of sport because it composes a complex system, that is not too difficult to observe at the same time that it shows in relative clarity all of the different levels of an action system. It has, furthermore, many features of an almost experimental design in a natural field. In so far it is a model area to allow due consideration for our demand that social psychology rediscover the method of field studies. This will help to reverse the trend characterized by a general neglect of theory that has resulted from behavioral dogmatism and the expedience of research pragmatism mostly based on two-variable linear models. This is not to say that we disfavor rigorous research design and data analysis—to the contrary. We just want it to be done in the context of broader theoretical concerns and in clear recognition of the pitfalls of operationalism and the merits of action theory.

Paper presented May 15, 1973, at the NASPA-conference on Social Psychology, Allerton House, University of Illinois at Urbana. The paper was written together with Gunther Luschen under equal co-authorship. I thank him for his kind permission to publish the paper in this book. I would also like to thank Donald Dixon for many helpful criticisms.

Some Remarks on Theories--Universal and Quasi Explanations

Hypotheses in social psychology, notably in small group research, are frequently cited as the most clear-cut examples of proper social laws (i.e., general conditional statements). They are claimed to have a kind of nomological connection beyond chance associaton of phenomena. They may take on a form like this: for all x; if x is P then x is also Z, where P and Q are constant predicates. The following is a typical example: for all pairs of individuals within social groups, if individuals x and y are members of the same group and are not in a formal authority relationship to one another, then the observable increase in the (relative) frequency of interactions between them will result in an increase of positive sentiment for one another (cf. Homans, 1950), and we may conject from the results of that analysis, unless a certain limit of contact because of overload is passed.

No statement of a social law is allowed to contain constants or proper names referring to individuals, to specific time-space-regions or historical epoches, or to some kind of unique collective phenomenon such as "Christianity." Homans (1950) in the above tried to formulate truly universal laws of group behavior. His statements of the interrelationship between activity, sentiment and interaction are meant to be valid no matter what the socio-cultural background of the group under study. However, in his later work, Homans introduced a number of qualifications (e.g., the principle of distributive justice) in order to explain the observable phenomena of group behavior (1961). Thus, as Malewski (1964) argues, there is a real dilemma with universal theories in the social sciences since a higher level of generality decreases the chance for empirical confirmation; and conditional statements point to the fact of the non-universal applicability of social science theories.

It is a truism in the social sciences, that only very few instances of truly universal social and social psychological laws can be quoted. If one restricts oneself to statements that can be explained by proper social laws, most theories of the social sciences, including remarkable sections of social psychology would have to be eliminated.

Here is an example of findings pertaining to a theory to explain the emergence of sport and high achievements in sport, i.e., success at the Olympics, that would have to be discarded: Among high-achieving athletes such as medal winners at the Olympics, it was found that there is an over-representation of Protestants (Lüschen, 1967). Following Max Weber this finding suggests that the ethics of Protestantism parallel the value system of sport, thus bringing specific people to sport, and among athletes, tending to reinforce their motivation to excel, especially for individual sports. Thus, Protestants stressing individual achievement appear in higher ratios in sport as well as in

147

economics and science. Thus, Protestantism "explains" the participation of top athletes and the emergence of sport as such. Seppänen
confirmed this result and linked it to the inner-worldly orientation of
the Protestant who tries to control the world, although he predicts that
Marxism, in this regard, figures even stronger (1972). These interpretations employ or use proper names, that is to say they refer to
socio-historical constants rather than to universal species concepts.
"Protestantism," "Marxism" obviously are proper names.

Lüschen in the attempt to reach a universal interpretation for
the emergence of sport referred in this context to the value of achievement to explain the emergence of sport and the participation of top
athletes among specific groups and in certain areas of the world. Although the achievement value interpretation aims at an universal explanation, one may question whether or not a reference to cultural-
historical factors is still implicit. At least in the application of the
theory to specific articulations of behavior, e.g., a Western concept
of individualistic, competitive achievement and emphasis on measurement, this is very likely so. Using such constants as "Protestantism"
"Marxism," "Western" in otherwise lawlike statements, by definition,
results in quasi-laws. Using quasi-laws in explanatory arguments provide quasi-explanations and quasi-theories. This is discouraging only
at first sight. Nothing is wrong with quasi-explanations, although one
should be aware of their character. Physics in earlier times often
used quasi-explanations: Galileo's law of the freely falling body as
well as Kepler's laws of planetary motion are instances of quasi-laws,
the one referring to the individual constant "the earth" the other to
"the sun." Quasi-explanations using those quasi-laws were as exact
as any kind of explanation that used proper universal laws. Even today some people think that the use of universal natural constants in
quantum and relativity theory produces actually quasi-explanations.
Why then should social psychology be worried about using quasi-laws?
Quasi-laws (and consequently, quasi-theories) might be unavoidable
in order to get really interesting results beyond some genuinely law-
like truisms.

Quasi-explanations can give us the same degree of exactness and
predictive usage as explanations using universal laws. An explanation
based on the finding that upper-middle-class groups, who take the upper
class as their reference group, tend to develop a relatively high degree of n-achievement might be as useful, interesting, and important
for explanatory and predictive purposes no matter whether it holds only for the present industrial society or for all industrial societies on
this planet or elsewhere. No empirical evidence is available beyond
the known industrial epoch at this time in history. The aim of maxi-
mizing empirical content clearly recommends restricting the scope of
a hypothesis to the well-known historical phenomena, i.e., to interpret the statement as a quasi-law. This is not to deny that attempts
to generalize such a quasi-law to other kinds of "industrial societies",

now figuring as a species term, might be fruitful in the search for universal laws. Under special conditions--lawlikeness, other theoretical presuppositions being fixed--this also increases the degree of falsification. If this further generalization is falsified, the restricted validity of the quasi-law might nevertheless be preserved and its usefulness for quasi-explanation maintained in the historic "industrial society," now again taken as proper name.

Behavioristic and/or Action Explanations

Quasi-laws have another advantage: they are well-suited to include system regularities composed of social norms and cultural conditions as explanatory units. In that way it might be possible to provide a solution to the old problem of whether one should use only movement behavior terms for explanations of human action or whether one could also use so-called action terms as theoretical constructs referring to belief systems, social systems, cultural values, action dispositions or "internal states." Whether the activity of a man throwing a javelin is to be described as a sport or a war action clearly depends on the socio-cultural context of this activity. In isolation the same movement might be interpreted very differently from its meaning and significance to the individual, to the socio-cultural system at large or to the subsystems of sport and track. Also the same kind of action might be attributed to different movements: whether an athlete, e.g., uses his left or right arm for throwing the javelin does not matter for the acceptability and judgment of the action as a successful realization of throwing the javelin in an Olympic contest. Whether some kind of movement is analyzed as being one and the same action is dependent on the theoretical point of departure. A biomechanist might well find some interesting differences where the social psychologist does or need not.

In order to interpret a movement pattern as an action, it does not suffice to observe the very outward behavior pattern and analyze it in terms of a stimulus-response model. Not only might it be necessary to introduce a historical and sociological interpretation in order to assign some meaning to the observed data, not only can cultural phenomena such as the achievement value imprint itself on the action, but it might be revealing or even necessary to combine, in the very same explanatory hypothesis, behavioral and action terms, the latter ones of which interpreting it with reference to a specific socio-cultural setting. In the above example the analyst might explain a characteristic change in the movement pattern of throwing a javelin through not only a biomechanical analysis but also the innovative throwers adherence to the cultural values of achievement and innovativeness plus a conditional statement specifying the state of the sport discipline and its code of rules.

149

The discussion at this point is more general than the previous on quasi-explanations and quasi-laws. It may well be that general-action terms can be used without relying on a cultural-historical interpretation of a social system, thus making it universal. This is very rarely the case. You cannot always do away with the cultural context of a social system. Culture and its tradition, or the cultural system after Parsons, exert strong controls over the subsystems of the action system. Thus, one would have to even go beyond the consideration of the personality and social system in social psychology. Norms on the social system level are influenced to a certain degree by the cultural values at large. In assessing the Fosbury flop within the institution of sport, an explanatory analysis has to make reference to rather abstract phenomena, such as an achievement, risk-oriented culture like the American and its Western tradition. The point we want to make is that the analyst might be compelled, in his attempt to get a sufficient explanation, to resort to a kind of general lawlike (or quasi-lawlike) hypothesis comprising both behavioral and action terms. "Action," after Max Weber incorporates "gemeinter Sinn" and means interpreted behavior. To quote a famous example from epistemological literature: "the rising of Jones' arm" is purely behavioral (movement or physical) language, whereas "the raising of Jones' arm" is in action language. Epistemological analysis of the social sciences lately revealed that there is no necessity in a single comprehensive analysis of action-behavior to only rely on one of the two kinds of vocabularies, be it behavioristic or actionistic (Mischel, 1969 and others).

In restricting one's analysis to behavioral aspects, one might eliminate important features of the respective phenomenon under study from the realm of explainable traits, which is a kind of dogmatic, self-restriction; and science would never get at a reasonable comprehensive explanation of statements concerning very complex and interdisciplinary social phenomena. This also applies to the introduction of variables from a sociological framework into socio-psychological and even psychological analysis. We shall come back to this below. To be sure, all of this is not to deny that it may be heuristically useful or try to use, as far as possible, pure behavioral language for explanatory purposes. But whenever this restricted language does not take the explanation further or misleadingly neglects important social and cultural features, one has to broaden one's epistemological perspective. In the social sciences, this is soon to be encountered.

To epitomize the last passages, one might deem it preferable to extend the meaning of the term "explanation," or "quasi-explanation" respectively, by defining: An event e has been (quasi-) explained under the description D if a statement E about the occurrence of that event is deduced (a) from a well-confirmed (quasi-) law in the apodosis of which a behavioral description B is contained, (b) from a true description D using the general term A of some of the respective relevent situational and boundary conditions in action-terms obtained prior to the occurrence of the event, and (c) from a well-confirmed (quasi-) law-like general statement that for all respective phenomena in question, x, whenever x is B, x is also A. For a different statement on similar lines, one may consult Sher (1973). This definition covers both proper explanation by laws and quasi-explanation. It excludes mere trend-extrapolations and arguments using isolated ad-hoc empirical generalizations without (quasi-) explanations. For lawful or quasi-lawful predictions the same conditions may be maintained, notwith-standing the fact that some more or less reliable predictions might be possible and unavoidable by using some other unorthodox, predictive methods. This is to be found in some applied social sciences, e.g., in model simulating, expertises, etc.

Furthermore, the definition of explanation might be modified in such a way as to apply to statistical reasoning as well, taking into account that statistical hypotheses can also comprise behavioral as well as action terms. There is a kind of epistemological quarrel whether it is apt to label that kind of argument statistical explanation. Since it is not possible logically, to derive statistical statements from singular events, but only to increase its a posteriori probability weight in a statistical relevant manner (cf. Salmon, 1971) as compared with the a priori probability weight, we prefer the label of "statistical reasoning." Statistical arguments do not provide strictly deductive explanations about events, but attribute credibility and probability weights.

The Problem of Operationalism in Social Psychology

Operationalism denotes another important epistemological problem area, which is not free from implicit ideologies. There is an obvious tendency in current social psychology to restrict scientific thinking to operationalized or operationalizable concepts. We might add that such tendencies are particularly strong in applied social sciences, where the term "scientific" is often falsely interchanged with "measurable." To provide operational definitions of all concepts seems to be a methodological must. Thus, a strict empiricist-operationalist will argue: Only what is accounted for in measurable conceptualizations and only as far as it is operationalized can a concept be scientific or is at least scientifically applicable. Very often, however, the surplus meaning of such concepts will be dispensed with. Soon it is alleged "intelligence is what the IQ-Test measures," because we don't know how to handle the eventual surplus meaning of intelligence in an operational way.

One of the best known examples in social psychology, achievement motivation, is reshaped into a technical concept n-ach, which is deemed to be precisely defined by a test method, the TAT-Test. It is important to note that McClelland (1961) not only analyzed test papers written by probationers, but also stories from prime-readers, fairy tales of old, the shape of lines on vases in order to evaluate the degree of n-achievement of a certain group of people or society at a definite period in history. The reason for those different operational explications of the concept n-ach was as simple as the fact, that you can not test persons of antiquity by submitting them to the TAT. Instead you have to look for measuring techniques and measures to replace the actual test.

Operationally speaking, everything seemed to be alright; but, epistemologically pure operationalism is outdated and, in fact, refuted, regardless of the necessity of applying an empirical test to theories as a whole. First of all, the ideology of identifiable pure observation statements, the neopositivist ideology of independent data, has been rejected for quite a while. It is not possible to draw a clear-cut line between theoretical statements on the one hand and pure observational statements (encompassing no theoretical or structural content) on the other. Nor is it possible to deduce or constitute whole theories from such observation statements. Observation statements are unavoidably theory-impregnated, as Ryle, Putnam, Lakatos and others pointed out. Hempel (1970) changed his earlier views and no longer talks about observation statements, but (with regard to a specific theory) of pre-theoretical statements in contrast to theoretical ones. Clearly, in order to be able to perform tests at all, one has to rely on some (pretheoretical, currently unproblematic) statements. One has to draw a line somewhere. But where it is drawn depends on the historical development of the respective science and the succession of theories within its domain. In part it is conventional.

In fact, operationalism itself incorporates the position that each statement is theory-impregnated (at least by theoretical precursors) in so far as concepts are imprinted with a theory of measurement, the make-up of measuring procedures and their connection with the general theory. But if one takes this for granted, the immediate consequence would be that different measuring techniques would necessarily result in different concepts. The operationist physicist would be obliged to work with very many different concepts of temperature ranging from the one established by thermometer measuring, which is not applicable on the surface of sun, to those applying radiation evaluation in terms of intensity, color of light, etc. One can easily imagine how impractical a radical operationalistic point of view would be. To repeat again, one would have to work with very many different, in principle infinitely many, concepts of temperature and one would be compelled to establish interconnecting nomological hypotheses between those different concepts. It is much more preferable to use a single theoretical concept of temperature and to assign several different measuring techniques to statements about temperature, although each single measuring device (and consequently all of the potential ones together) only provides an incomplete interpretation of the respective theoretical concept; it will refer only to a certain restricted domain of applicability. In view of this position, theoretical concepts cannot be specified completely nor can they be given a full meaning by means of assigning

152

measuring techniques to them. They can, in principle, only be partially interpreted. One might very well argue whether such an interpretation, using incomplete theoretical constructs is necessary or even preferable at all. However, there are more conclusive arguments against strict operationalism.

Before turning to those arguments, let us draw the conclusion for the paradigmatic case of achievement-motivation. Having already mentioned that several very different measuring techniques have unavoidably been used to evaluate n-achievement, we immediately see now it is not possible to interpret n-achievement as a single concept at all, even, from an operationalistic point of view. N-achievement in McClelland's and Atkinson's theory is construed as a theoretical concept. If we consider the claim that this theoretical concept should scientifically stand for and explicate the common language phenomena of achievement motivation in a more precise sense, then obviously this approach is incompatible with a strict operationalism. This is true, and does not even account for the fact that epistemologically speaking there are other methodological shortcomings in the application of that concept (concerning, e.g., metrizability and linearity assumptions).

Let us now turn to another argument against the feasibility of full-fledged operationalism. Most predicates to be ascribed by psychological tests are disposition terms. The logical difficulties of dispositional predicates have long bothered philosophers of science. It is not possible here to resume nor even to epitomize this extended epistemological discussion (cf. Carnap, 1936, 1937, 1954; Stegmüller, 1969 p. 120, 1970 p. 213). It might be sufficient to mention some results relevant for the discussion of operationalism. Firstly, it is not possible to explicitly define disposition predicates; one would be obliged to assign the disposition in question to every element (person) which has, at least in principle, never been, or will never be submitted to the very test-conditions. This is true for logical reasons; an implication with a principally false protasis is always true and might be used to infer the disposition in question to whoever is never tested, whenever the dispositional predicate is defined as a conditional test statement. Thus, let us sketch the more complex introduction of a disposition term from our previous example: If, under standardized test conditions S, a person is submitted to the specified TAT-test and the resultant relative frequency of occurrences of achievement issues is that, and that (T&R), then the person is assigned the respective value as a measure of his n-achievement-motivation (A). We might symbolize the statement by:

$$A_X \left[S(x) \rightarrow \Big(T(x) \; \& \; R(x) \rightarrow A(x) \Big) \right],$$

x being a variable referring here to persons or similarly to groups, societies or tests, etc. A sentence of this structure is called a sufficient reduction statement for the introduction of the disposition term

A in question, here: n-achievement-motivation. The implication sign in the apodosis might be replaced by an equivalence sign, this representing a stronger contention. Since several different techniques are deemed apt for assigning n-achievement-values, one also has at least another sufficient reduction statement:

$$A_x \left[S^*(x) \rightarrow \Big(\ T^*(x) \ \& \ R^*(x) \rightarrow A^*(x) \Big) \right] \ .$$

"A*" designates the same disposition as "A," just before, The operationalist, however, would be obliged to distinguish between A* and A, in any case, whether or not they are numerically equal in any comparable respect. Furthermore, he has to introduce the additional empirical law:

$$A_x \ \Big(A(x) \longleftrightarrow A^*(x) \Big).$$

There are not only sufficient, but also necessary reduction sentences of the form:

$$A_x \left[A(x) \rightarrow \Big(S^{**}(x) \rightarrow R^{**}(x) \Big) \right] \qquad .$$

That is, it is deemed that if a person shows this n-achievement-motivation under certain conditions, he will necessarily reveal some other traits, too. If he, e.g., turns out to be n-achievement-motivated to a certain high degree, this would clearly imply that he is not, at the same time and under the same standard conditions, highly motivated to avoid failure. Taken together, then, the first sufficient and this necessary reduction statement logically imply:

$$A_x \left[S(x) \ \& \ T(x) \ \& \ R(x) \rightarrow \Big(S^{**}(x) \rightarrow R^{**}(x) \Big) \right] \ .$$

This is an empirical generalization which is logically implied by the apparently definitional reduction statements. This is to say that the introduction of reduction statements cannot be a purely definitional matter, but, instead, that introduction of concepts and the design of empirical nomological hypotheses are inextricably interlaced with one another. Therefore, one is obliged to contend that dispositional concepts have structural empirical content from the very beginning of their introduction, if as often, more than one reduction statement including sufficient and necessary ones are needed. That is to say: disposition terms have to be constructed as <u>theoretical concepts</u>, which cannot solely be defined by reducing them to pure observational concepts. As discussed earlier, these do not even exist besides theoretical constructions. If the analyst would resort to operationalization anyway, he would be obliged to hypothetically assume such an empirical content by an equivalence law of the above mentioned form.

Furthermore, he would preclude the possibility of revising any normally performed test ascription ex post facto; after all, he may learn only after the test that the subject had been in a very depressive mood distorting the result. Revision or critical refutation of the test

154

result would clearly mean that he does not, indeed, use the disposition concept in question as an operational concept, but as a theoretical one. This, however, obviously is in contradiction to his operationalism proper. Using dispositions as theoretical concepts is evidently incompatible with strict operationalism, the representative of which, in turn, has to contend that each such concept is to be defined only in terms of observational terms and measuring devices. There are other reasons why disposition concepts should be rather constructed as theoretical concepts.

Other attempts to rescue operationalism have equally failed on principal and practical grounds (Stegmüller, 1971, pp. 221 pp. 226). Besides, there is another complex problem, whether scientific theories can, in principle, dispense with theoretical terms (Ramsey); practically, and also with regard to the theory of measurement, they cannot avoid theorizing. (cf. Stegmüller, 1971).

Thus strict operationalists' reduction of empirical science of all kinds and especially of the social sciences including social psychology does not work. One has to use creative theorizing again. "Thinking is again allowed, after all" -- Herrmann, President of the German Psychological Association, concluded his presidential address on epistemological problems of psychology in 1972, and McGuire (1973) made a similar pledge to social psychology. Social psychologists must be aware of how far and when they use and are obliged to use theoretical concepts. This is important especially in connection with concepts of attitudes, motivations and motives--all of which are disposition concepts. All of those have to be handled as theoretical concepts. They can neither be dealt with in purely behavioristic or operationistic terms nor can they be interpreted as some kind of real force within the organism as a kind of "ghost in the machine," although some people dealing with sports science apparently even nowadays seem to prefer such a naive interpretation.

Other researcheer keep silent about those problems or do not even notice them. As a typical example, one of the most explicit analyses on achievement motivation of high performance swimmers by Gabler (1972) does not even mention these epistemological problems.

Test and Model Structural Implications

The range and kind of possible social psychological results might be restricted (not only due to methodological and epistemological problems). Also presuppositions and distortions of specific measuring techniques and models including specific conceptual predeterminations have an affect. Take an example from group dynamics. For convenience, it may be assumed that mathematical graph theoretical concepts are used to represent the argumentations and results, e.g., in the technique of sociometry. Sociograms, as well as the respective

155

sociomatrices might be analyzed as digraphs, i.e., directed graphs. The point (or vertices) of the digraph represent persons or position holders, while the lines (edges) of the digraph stand for directed social relationships, sociometric choices of (regular) social interactions within the groups.

An interesting case in question is the occurrence of cliques, more precisely to be exemplified by non-complete cliques. Such cliques are, graph theoretically speaking, maximally strong connected subgraphs; every point of the subgraph can be reached by using the directed lines of the graph in unisense-direction starting from each other point of the subgraph. A sociogram of preference choices indicated by a fixed number of choices of every member might then be interpreted as a superposition of functional graphs with the same elements. Functional graphs, by definition, not only admit to, but also require that each point has the out-degree 1, i.e., that each respective member exactly releases 1 preference judgment. For simplicity let us take a sociogram with an overall out-degree of 1; everybody has only one vote to submit. Sociograms with the fixed number of choices being "n", then are easily reconstructed as a superposition of n simple functional graphs.

Now the interesting result is that sociometric graphs with a fixed number of choices, n, necessarily contain n cliques of the mentioned kind, some of which might overlap, since functional graphs necessarily comprise cycles. These necessarily have the form of a cycle with trees directed to a point of the cycle attached to it: For instance, in the case n=I (functional graphs), a structure like the following one occurs:

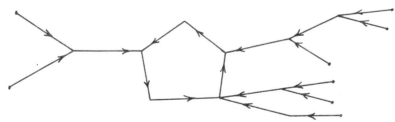

The mathematical proof is given elsewhere (Lenk, 1970, p. 139; 1971). The import of this result is that clique structures of the mentioned kind are not an empirical result, but a consequence of the designed and applied model in the sociometric test. The occurrence of such cliques is a logical consequence of the structure of the experimental set-up, an analytical statement which necessarily follows from the assumed and applied model. Only the specification of who is involved in which cliques would require empirical information.

More familiar examples of such specific test or model <u>structural</u> <u>implications</u> are to be found, when suggestive questions occur in interviews, when an attitude toward a subject is only engendered or exaggerated by the very form of questionnaires, or as a kind of operationistic fallacy, when a complex social relationship is reduced to only one specific narrow type of response, usch as interpersonal sympathy being measured by a hypothetical preference choice of a roommate.

Another kind of structural implication is provided by the famous sportswriter's paradox (<u>Ore</u> 1963, p. 75). Round-Robin-Tournaments in sport can be represented by asymmetric digraphs, also called "tournaments," this time being a mathematical term. After the season there are journalists or fans who pretend that their own very average team should be looked upon in a specific sense as the best team, superior to the champion, since it has beaten another team, which in turn has been victorious over another and so forth--until a beaten team in that sequence is found that itself beat the champion team.

Ore has shown, and there is an even simpler proof elsewhere (<u>Lenk,</u> 1971, p. 186), that if there is no total winner succeeding in all games, and if a particular fan's team is not a member of an outclassed group of teams which won no game against outsiders of that group of teams, then, by structural implication, there is such a sequence of loss, a "defeat path," of the above mentioned kind. Had the fans gotten some insight into structural analysis of this kind, they would not hail the excellence of "their" team as a specific "alleged" insight. They would know that such sequences of loss (or "defeat paths") necessarily exist for a champion (being not a total winner) and that the alleged hidden superiority would be valid for all teams which are not members of an outclassed group.

Again we have a structural implication introduced by the very set-up. However, this time it is not by the experimental set-up in a test, but by the very make-up of the rules of the games tournament itself. The model structural implication and the respective restrictions are built into the structure of the games organization and its institutional rules. Thus, here is an example how a kind of "real" social structure imprints itself onto empirical situational conditions which seem to have come about by chance, while they are actually the result of a logical derivation from the bulit-in representational model, a structrual implication from the made-up model and its institutional rules. The very social system and the behavioral outcome are structured to an unforeseen degree. Such cases are often to be found in social science. They are rather typical in the area of sport and may be analyzed and exemplified there with relative case. They also very aptly demonstrate that social psychology cannot derive its insights solely from the personality characteristics of individuals.

Personality and Social System

Our last remark that social psychology cannot derive its insights from personality characteristics alone are prompted by a situation where variables reflecting paradigms of the individual personality have dominated the field. Simple two-variable, unilinear S-R-designs are the characteristic of the majority of research attempts depicting a state of the discipline that puts all its emphasis on rigid testing and little on theory and interpretation. In line with our last example we want to redirect social psychology to a stronger consideration of the potential insights of sociology, or for that matter, a renewed effort from the side of sociology toward more exchange with social psychology proper. However, we want our argument to go further than that. Social psychology as exemplified in the above encounter on behavioristic vs. action explanations has to open up to the insights provided by systems theory in order to overcome a situation that is marred by a vast accumulation of knowledge of not altogether meaningful problems. According to McGuire, we should improve our methodology and "cope with the dirty data of the real world" (1973). In recognizing the system quality of the object of study we will be forced to account for a greater complexity by among others multiple analysis and field research and by acknowledging that the majority of interactions in social psychology are cybernetic in nature and are not all open to testing.

While in the following we are going to refer both to the personality and social system level, this is not intended to bar any other levels of analysis. An open-systems approach will, of course, have to account for the cultural system and the organic system as well, to name the two most obvious. Paramount at this time appears, however, a better understanding of the meaning of the social system vs. the personality system. Although there is awareness of commodities of the social system in social psychology, there is also evidence to reduce explanations beyond the level of psychology, or the personality system, to that of physiology. In part this is just another result of an operationalistic orientation, S-R-approaches and the search for so-called "efficient causes" in explaining the structure of interpersonal relations and processes. To be sure, there are physiological factors that are powerful explanatory variables in social psychology such as need for food as interpersonal behavioral determinant. In general, however, the field of social psychology should make every effort to develop its theories first of all on the basis of psychological and sociological propositions and concepts, and variables relating to the personality and social system. The social system is at times explicitly referred to in research although all too often in a way, that gives it only residual quality (cf. Watson, 1971).

The limited understanding of the distinction between personality and social system is mainly due to (1) the use of common sense concepts for easy operationalization, the abstention from conceptual differentiation and (2) the operationalist's and behaviorist's belief in the power and validity of test results, that as sensual positivism, emulates a kind of physicalistic reductionism. Epistemologically speaking, strict neopositivism is long outdated, even according to some of its earlier adherents (e.g. Carnap). And G.W. Allport has long assailed such approach for psychology (1960).

With regard to the distinction of personality and social system variables it should be stated that this distinction is not only for analytical purposes in the heads of certain social psychologists. Besides the bias introduced by the model, the example of the sportswriter's paradox illustrates the power that social systems or social structures have in determining the actions of individuals. Homans (1964) in sociology leads with his demand "Bringing Man Back in" to a thorough confusion, which does not at all help the understanding of the structure of social and personality systems in the analysis. Of course, men (or better, the respective reconstructed sociological units) are part of the social system, but only in reference to the social system level, not as whole persons. And the same analytical distinction can be made for the personality system. Social systems have a reality component very much independent of the personalities of individuals and their psychological make-up. When we want to understand the structure of a unit at a specific time, it helps very little for the analysis of units such as groups to look at their historical creation by men. Also, in this way, Homans leads social psychology away from a better conceptual understanding of its very own methodological approach.

F.H. Allport (1961) has in his concern over the group concept and "the lack of critical attention to the designations used for societal realities," or our notion of the social system level, exemplified our problem when he describes the action of a team in a football game. He refers to the considerable amount of difficulty for the analysis of groups with regard to instability and uncertainty of concepts of collective entity, which are individually as well as socially determined. While he would probably take issue with our understanding of the social system, the conceptual distinction of individuals and groups is very much at the core of his argument.

To be more specific, in an earlier attempt at conceptual clarification in social psychology, one of the authors tried to analyze the concept of cooperation in its general use as actually consisting of at least two (Lüschen 1970) or better three (1972) separate concepts--association, cooperation and attraction. All three describe forms of mutual interpersonal relations and should be conceived as responses to the social system level (association), the personality system level (cooperation, attraction), whereby cooperation as sharing of rewards is still in part determined by socio-cultural constellations, while attraction is strictly to be seen as a relationship on the level of personality system.

Lewin in one of his theoretical papers and in his conceptual practice in field theory, specifically group dynamics, already opened the way for accomodating in social psychology by an implicit concept both personality and social system concerns, when he pleaded for the use of constructs and introduced terms like locomotion, cohesiveness or when he redefined frustration in analytical terms (1951, orig. 1944). To be sure, Lewin was at this time more concerned with overcoming the behavioral psychology of stimulus-response theorists. And while he defines field theory strictly as a psychological discipline, he makes ample reference to consider the "life-space" of an individual in the analysis, under which he mentions physical as well as social surroundings.

Group cohesiveness is a construct very much in use in small group research and also in the study of sport groups (cf. Martens and Peterson, 1971). It may be operationally defined as the sum of forces that keep members in a group. The mean rating on a number of responses is taken as a measure of cohesiveness, which is then related as an independent explanatory variable to, e.g., efficiency in groups. This variable is somewhat cumbersome, since it is not all the time defined in a unique and precise way; furthermore, despite its fair validity it is not a very reliable predictor, an experience that has been made with other system variables and specifically those of field-theory as well. A closer observation of the situational context, or of the social system level would probably control for much of the noise (information theoretically understood) in the variable. Instead of using it operationally as some single, unique factor one should research its meaning under different situational definitions and with different response indicators. Problems like those of cohesiveness indicate a built-in characteristic of such constructs, which in the long run will lead to considerable insight into situational or social system influences on an outcome variable such as the efficiency of teams of different organizational structures and tasks. Field-theoretical concepts may thus be a critical guard against operationalism and dogmatic behaviorism, a quality for which they were set up very much by Lewin in the first place.

Implications of Personality and Social System Constructs for Research

A crucial aspect is, of course, all the time the partial operationalization of concepts and, specifically, constructs. Social system level variables not only pose theoretical problems for social psychology, but are quite cumbersome in research. Tests and questionnaires are most times constructed in a way that they refer to responses of individuals. Also observational data leave their strongest imprint on

160

individualistic item scores. Social system variables often have to
be inferred from individual response data, specifically in social psychology, while, e.g., the sociology of organizations can use other
sources of data such as documents or formal rules. The difficulty of
investigating the social system level in interaction patterns should,
however, be blamed on inadequacy of measuring techniques rather
than lead to the conclusion that the social system level is of no rele-
vance, has no controlling influence or that its use will result in teleo-
logical arguments.

One of the best examples of social system influences on individual behavior in a group context is to be found in W.F. Whyte's parti-
cipant-observation study "Street Corner Society" (1943). In bowling
two individuals were, over time, by consistent pressure from the
group made to perform exactly on a level corresponding to their social rank in the group, although their individual skill and capability
in bowling was in reverse to their rank in the group. Insights like
these cannot easily be provided by ordinary tests, but need the involve-
ment in the field end of social systems factors by the investigator
over long periods of time. Moreover, the process of gradual adjustment of individual behavior to the group structure could hardly have
been so well understood, were it not for the fact of the participant observation method in the field. Of course, one undertakes such research with the understanding that replication is difficult and leaves
oneself open to the criticisms of rigid objectivist methodologists.
In the ongoing debate social psychology should not hesitate to sacri-
fice rigidity of a very specific design for theoretically more meaningful field research, and creative argumentation.

Experimental research set-ups and their structure can with regard to the personality and social system, be very misleading if results
are taken at face-validity. A very instructive example comes out of the
lab experiment by G. Roberts (1969). He investigated risk-taking disposition and its determination by personality factors and social situational factors in a motor task. The study produced significant results
for the personality variable, but nothing of significance (only mild
trends) for the social situational variables (competition, cooperation,
aloneness, audience). This result did not lead to the conclusion that
the personality system is all that counts, but rather to interpretations
explaining the little difference that the social system variables made:
The experimentally-created social situation had to be learned at this
very moment, while the personality variable had not been created in
the laboratory, but was well-internalized into the respondents' personalities. Also the situation might socially not have created a very
meaningful task. To be sure, validity tests were employed as usual
asking the respondents whether they understood the situation. But
there is certainly a big difference from indicating understanding to
letting the situation control one's behavior. The interpretation is certainly justified that an artificially created lab situation is not a very

161

meaningful way to test the complexity and magnitude of social systems, just after one has severely interferred with and interrupted a normal social situation. And for the present problem, e.g., values on the cultural system level have been found to produce a variance in risk-taking as well (Baron, 1971). Such influences are, of course, neglected altogether despite some earlier attempts in group dynamics to account for leadership styles and their outcomes in different countries. And while one might argue that the cultural system should not be of immediate concern to the social psychologist, a neglect of the social system deprives social psychology of possible (quasi-) explanatory variables in its immediate field. Our interpretation above suggests that laboratories have built-in problems for the social psychologist. Many heuristic results have had their origin in laboratories, including that classic study on the social psychology of sport by Tripplet (1898). But there is ample evidence to suggest, that a return toward more field research, experiment or non-experimental, qualitative as well as quantitative, will make social psychology theoretically more meaningful to both psychology and sociology. It is, in particular, the field of sport and games, which would open up a Pandora's Box for all sorts of insights. After all, in sports there are many controlled situations in a natural setting of quasi-experimental character (cf. Lenk, 1970). And although social systems at large, such as societies, as well as cultural system variables, are not absent, their influence is fairly well controlled in the situation of a competitive game restricted by time and space. At least we know the quasi-character of explanations coming from such settings and can make an attempt to clarify their dispositions, while the purely lab-restricted social psychologist produces theories that often are considered universal, while they are in fact quasi-theories and may often be less interesting for theoretical generalizations than those of the field theorist or the observer of a group of children on the playground. To avoid misunderstanding, it has to be stressed again that laboratory work is indispensable for getting and confirming research hypotheses, but it should not be the major method. A social psychologist who would only rely on lab situations might be very much led astray by neglecting influential factors of the social system, which is best understood in a field setting.

Summary and Conclusion

Social psychology appears at this time little integrated and of comparatively low-level theoretical scope because it often focuses against the background of one-sided operationalism and dogmatic behavioristic positions, on limited concepts that pose no problem for standardized research procedures. Since social psychology relies heavily on complex disposition concepts and because such disposition predicates have to be constructed as theoretical concepts, social psychology must say farewell to strict observationistic-operationalism. This does not deny the necessity of empirical confirmation of theories. A theoretical approach using laws (or quasi-laws) to connect action and behavior

162

terms would encompass a type of theorizing, which would be more integrated and theoretically more meaningful to social psychology and adjacent fields. One step in this direction would combine the employment of theoretical constructs with more careful conceptual differentiation and investigation that takes into consideration social systems (and their structural impact) as well as personality systems. In this way, the often hidden quasi-theoretical character of social-psychological theories and the frequent socio-cultural impregnation of their subject matter would be better exposed and test as well as model structural implications would be revealed more easily. This should allow insights beyond the mere employment of test results.

Specifically, the area of sport with its rich and fairly well controlled social and personality system levels is an area that cannot only gain from more field research, but exemplify for social psychology in general, the usefulness of theoretical constructs in a system context that will avoid the pitfalls of strict behaviorism and operationalism. Finally, it should be stated that the production of quasi-theories is quite appropriate despite the fact that one may still search for general theories. Quasi-theories can help in this attempt. Their clear exposure makes such attempts also more likely to occur. But one may also state, that quasi-theories are very useful for prediction and social practice despite the fact that they allow for considerable variance in the phenomena under study.

REFERENCES

[1] Allport, F. H., "The contemporary appraisal of an old problem." Contemporary Psychology 6 (1961) 195-196.

[2] Allport, G. W., Personality and Social Encounter. Beacon, Boston, 1960.

[3] Baron, R. S., et al., "Group consensus and cultural values as determinants of risk taking." Journal of Personality and Social Psychology 20 (1971) 446-455.

[4] Bertalanffy, L. V., General System Theory. Braziller, New York, 1968.

[5] Bickman, L. and Henchy, T. (eds.), Beyond the Laboratory: Field Research in Social Psychology. McGraw-Hill, New York, 1972.

[6] Borger, R. and Cioffi, F. (eds.), Explanation in the Behavioral Sciences. Cambridge University Press, Cambridge, 1970.

[7] Bridgman, P. W., The Logic of Modern Physics. MacMillan, New York, 1928.

[8] Carnap, R., Testability and Meaning. Yale University Press, New Haven 1954 (Orig. 1936-1937).

[9] Deutsch, M. and Krauss, R. M., Theories in Social Psychology. Basic Books, London and New York, 1965.

[10] Gabler, H., Leistungsmotivation in Hochleistungssport. Hofmann, Schorndorf, 1972.

[11] Goffman, E., Encounters. Bobbs-Merrill, Indianapolis, 1961.

[12] Hempel, C. G., "On the 'Standard Conception' of scientific theories." In M. Radner and S. Winokur, (eds.), Minnesota Studies in the Philosophy of Science IV, University of Minnesota Press, Minneapolis, 1970, pp. 142-163.

[13] Homans, G. C., The Human Group. Harcourt, Brace & World, New York, 1950.

[14] Homans, G. C., Social Behavior: Its Elementary Forms. Harcourt, Brace and World, New York, 1961.

[15] Homans, G. C., "Bringing man back in." American Sociological Review 29 (1964) 809-818.

[16] Lenk, H., Leistungsmotivation und Mannschaftsdynamik, Hofmann, Schorndorf/Stuttgart, 1970.

[17] Lenk, H., "Trees, tournaments and sociometric graphs." International Review of Sport Sociology 6 (1971) 175-204.

[18] Lenk, H., Erklärung, Prognose, Planung, Rombach, Freiburg, 1972.

[19] Lewin, K., Field Theory in Social Science. Harper & Row, New York, 1951.

[20] Lüschen, G. (ed.), Kleingruppenforschung und Gruppe in Sport, Westdeutscher Verlag, Köln, Opladen, 1966 (Sonderheft 10 der Kölner Zeitschrift für Soziologie und Sozialpsychologie.)

[21] Lüschen, G., "Small group research and the group in sport," in G. Kenyon, Sociology of Sport. Athletic Institute, Chicago, 1969, pp. 57-66.

[22] Lüschen, G., "Association, cooperation and contest." Journal of Conflict Resolution 14 (1970) 21-34.

[23] Lüschen, G., "The interdependence of sport and culture," in G. Lüschen (ed.), The Cross-Cultural Analysis of Sport and Games. Stipes, Champaign, Ill., 1970, pp. 85-99 (orig. 1967).

[24] Lüschen, G., "Psychologischer Reduktionismus und die informellen Beziehungen in Wettkampf," in G. Albrecht et al., Soziologie. Westdeutscher Verlag Opladen 1973, pp. 753-759.

[25] Luhmann, N., "Einfache Sozialsysteme," Zeitschrift für Soziologie, 1 (1972) 51-65.

[26] Malewski, A., Verhalten und Interaktion (orig. Polish 1964). Mohr, Tübingen, 1967.

[27] Martens, R. and Petersen, J., "Group cohesiveness as a determinant of success and member satisfaction in team performance." International Review of Sport Sociology 6 (1971) 49-62.

[28] McClelland, D. C., The Achieving Society. VanNostrand, New York, 1961.

(29)McGuire, W., "The Yin and Yan of Social Psychology: 7 Koan," Journal of Personality and Social Psychology, 26 (1973) 446-456.

(30)Mischel, R. (ed.), Human Action, Conceptual and Empirical Issues. Academic Press, New York and London, 1969.

(31)Ore, O., Graphs and their Uses. Random House--Singer, New York, 1963.

(32)Piaget, J., Structuralism. Basic Books, New York, 1970.

(33)Roberts, G., "The effect of risk taking disposition, presence of other, cooperation and competition of risk taking and perform-ance." Ph.D. Thesis, University of Illinois, Urbana, 1969.

(34)Salmon, W. C., Statistical Explanation and Statistical Rele-vance. University of Pittsburgh Press, Pittsburgh, 1971.

(35)Seppänen, P., "Die Rolle des Leistungssports in den Gesell-schaften der Welt." Sportwissenschaft 2 (1972) 133-155.

(36)Sher, C., "Causal explanation and the vocabulary of action." Mind 82 (1973) 22-30.

(37)Simmel, C., Soziologie. Duncker und Humblot, Berlin, 1958.

(38)Stegmüller, W., Probleme und Resultate der Wissenschafts-theorie und Analytischen Philosophie. Springer, Berlin, Heidel-berg und New York, 1969 I, 1970 II.

(39)Stone, G., Begriffliche Probleme in der Kleingruppenfor-schung, in G. Lüschen (ed.), Kleingruppenforschung und Gruppe im Sport. Westdeutscher Verlag, Opladen 1966, pp. 44-65.

(40)Tripplett, N., "The dynamogenic factors in pacemaking and competition." American Journal of Psychology (1898) 507-533.

(41)Watson, D., "Reinforcement theory of personality and social system." Journal of Personality and Social Psychology 20 (1971) 180-185.

(42)Whyte, W. F., Street Corner Society. University of Chicago Press, Chicago, 1943.

Against the New Socio-Philosophical
Criticism of Athletics and Achievement

To date, no comprehensive philosophy of achievement behavior has been developed. Nevertheless, the new critical generation and the so-called establishment agree about one thing: both believe that we live in an "achieving society" guided by the "performance principle" (or "the principle of achievement"). Social ranks and opportunities, advancement, remuneration, and influence have been assessed and allotted solely on the basis of personal professional performance. A society that assigns roles and ranks to its members on this principle is called an "achieving society" (McClelland).

On the above points, both sides are in agreement. However, on other issues there is a parting of minds: While the new protest generation considers all workers to be yoked under the inhuman and also unnecessary pressure or even "terror" of performance and the compulsion of productivity which ought be to eliminated as quickly as possible, the members of the Establishment resolutely plead for the preservation of the "performance principle" which, as they claim, has brought us prosperity and economic security. Anyone who preaches defeatism regarding production, performance, and achievement, is, they say, plainly asocial and irresponsible in view of the need to raise productivity for the future welfare of mankind. There is something "human, all too human" about these all-or-nothing-dichromies which are highly convenient for dividing people into supporters and opponents, into members of ingroups and outgroups: hedonists and hippies versus ascetic puritans. Performance or pleasure? The hedonists plead: "Then we prefer to choose pleasure;" the puritans reply: "We don't want any socio-economic catastrophe--therefore we are for performance."

Apparently, however, performance, as it is claimed by the critics, always also involves the pressure of productiveness and "pressure for achievement." Pleasure or the compulsion of achievement, this alternative seems to be the only one: puristic thinking in terms of alternatives on both sides--whether from the Left or the Right. Yet thinking in terms of totality is, in fact, always wrong. Reality is not that simple. This line of thought leads too easily to totalitarianism.

This kind of thinking in cliches is typical of that argument which is used ideologically for the apparently theoretical justification of one's own values as well as for the rejection of those of others.

"Performance is strongly imbued with emotions depending upon interests and social values of the person pronouncing upon it: to some people it is a concept of quality, a price tag, which even advertising uses suggestively: in the year of the last Olympic Games some service stations used the slogan "Performance decides" for advertising purposes. By advocating competition and by talking about performance the advertisement created, or attempted to create, the illusion of achievement. The other connotations of this word of many meanings, "Leistung," i.e., performance (achievement), were also--implicitly at least--suggested in one way or another. On the other hand, the social critics, who saw through this trick, rejected all ideas of competition, all merits in training to improve performance, as ideological perfidy on the part of holders of power or the ruling class to maintain their established privileges and positions. They evey regarded the reference to successful achievement as conservative ideology.

The criticism of the performance principle and the model of the "achieving society" is transferred ready-made to athletics. Particularly in the so-called late capitalist system athletics are regarded by the critics as a "national and international demonstration of the performance potential and the ideology of achievement of the political and economic system." Athletes would, they say, serve "to restore and preserve physical fitness...which, in turn, is exploited in the process of work." This criticism claims that the popular sports find their function in "canalizing aggressions (which mainly arise in the process of work) into harmless channels." That is to say they have a "bread-and-circus function." Even school sports ("as the acknowledged reservoir for the training of new sports champions, who would also be used by other people as tools of the capitalist system") are alleged to contribute "decisively to the stabilization and consolidation of this capitalist system." These assertions come from a resolution put forward by the Young Socialists of West-Germany at their Party conference some years ago. Sport not only as an "object of manipulation by the ruling class" for canalizing the frustrations arising out of everyday work, for disciplining the attitude towards achievement and for exploiting successful sportsmen in a nationalistically demonstrative manner, but also as an opportunity for profitable advertising, as a sphere of business activity and money-making, as a stabilizing mechanism of identification for the masses and as an institution for promoting willingness to perform. This extreme vision of the totally formative effect of sport in a moulded society simply adopted all the main negative propositions of the current social criticism (without analysing them carefully or revising them in the light of knowledge gained by experience) and it summarized them once again as follows: "A society which has made a point of converting the concept of achievement through the performance principle into an ideology cannot avoid applying it in sport, too. This ideologically irrational performance principle is reflected in sport in just the same way as it is in the processes of industrial work and production. The top sportsmen, as muscle-machines and symbolic reflections of the political and economic system that they represent, become mechanical medal-producers." Two years earlier a document of the Socialist German Students' Association (SDS) had already regarded "the performance in sports as an indirect encroachment of social repression" itself. All that the Young Socialists did was to repeat this sweeping judgment in more intelligible language.

Yet even an otherwise deliberate author as Günter Grass recently expressed the opinion that the "dictatorship of the performance principle" was becoming increasingly reflected in competitive sports. A substitute "arms race" was taking place in all the nations that go in for sports and especially for the Olympics. The sportsmen were not motivated solely by "personal ambition:" "It is the collective performance principle that drives them." "Athletics do not provide a release from pressures. They are the result of the pressures to which competitive societies submit themselves. They have trained crack sportsmen by means of blind compliance in order to be represented by them." Yet, "where achievement does not help to solve social problems it creates additional social problems. Achievement on principle makes excessive demands on those from whom it is extorted, devours and dissipates their strength, their health and their time, senselessly produces a surplus, mixes poison in the air and the water and creates slag piles which not even weeds can make turn green." "Misapplied social ambition" would call for excessive output also in sport. It was not only the professionally employed who were subjected to "professional coercion" and "the terror of performance," but also the crack sportsmen who "make their bodies available for the interests of others."

Are athletics to be regarded as the most conducive instantiating model of the performance principle, as the clear reflection of the achieving society," as the open embodiment of systematic coercion to compete, with all the manifestations of socio-pathological and psycho-neurotic compulsion? What the "performance principle" means, in this alleged interpretation, is compulsion to perform. The total cliché permits of no differentiation. Competitive sports are competitive terrorism. Pleasure in performance--that is unknown. One author, Rigauer, had already described the methods of training for sports as "repressive...systems of operational instructions:" "To practice competitive sports means that one must perform in order to fulfil society's expectations of (one's) performance".

But does performance in sports actually and totally come under the "performance principle" in the sense used by the social critics? Can criticism be transferred from the business sphere to competitive sports so simply without further distinction? As always, analysis is more difficult than general pro-and-contra clichés.

In the first place the talk about "the performance principle" is by no means unambiguous. Marcuse uses it in his book Eros and Civilization (p. 115) in at least three different meanings. In one place he says: "The definition of the standard of living in terms of automobiles, television sets, airplanes and tractors is that of the performance principle itself." In this first meaning he equates "performance principle" with the principle of economic competition and with the contention that the society is stratified in accordance with the economic criteria of profit and success. In the second meaning, Marcuse denotes only the "extra" or surplus, repression exerted above and beyond that required for ensuring an appropriate standard of living, i.e., the enforced, "alienated" labor, as coming under the "performance principle." Finally, in the third case Marcuse also interprets the "performance principle" for our society and for our culture as a principle of the identity of the personality, as a principle of self-presentation and self-confirmation, even self-constitution. He does not subordinate artistic achievements to the performance principle but to the "criticism of the performance principle".

What, then, is a Marcusean position which makes sense regarding achievement in sports? The relationship of sports to the "performance principle" naturally differs according to each of the three interpretations. According to the first interpretation the amateur's achievement in sports does not, in fact, belong to the performance principle, apart from few highly earning athletes or professionals who determine and enhance their status on the "performance market" partly through the sale of their mercenary "goods" called "performance." And in the second version, too, achievement in sports does not come under the performance principle if one disregards coercive measures by the directors of associations or sanctions in the form of threats that a sports scholarship would be withdrawn if an athlete does not turn up at a training course or a meet, etc. According to this interpretation, normal achievement in sports is even a part of a "libidinally" hued, or tinged, activity in Marcuse's sense: the athlete does, in fact, personally aspire to this particularly strongly and attaches intense emotional value and feelings of delight to it, even if it is to some extent a question of an abstract "delight" at success in the future and a "delight" at the performance achieved. In this interpretation achievement in sports would have to be classed, according to Marcuse's definition, precisely with what he calls "criticism of the performance principle"--an obvious absurdity as compared with the normal usage of the language. In competitive sports one would actually have a "libidinally" hued and constituted activity in a culture subordinated to the play impulse, which is what Marcuse calls for in place of the listless monotony of the assembly-line work of factories of today.

It is completely wrong to suppose that every achievement in sport is the result of pressure to perform, that every performance in sport is extorted from the athlete. Hardly anyone makes more demands upon him than the sportsman himself. This assessment and this experience of the athlete should not be ignored--not even if it is contended that this attitude towards performance was manipulated in his early childhood. The differences between the fact that the athlete aspires to high achievements in sports and strives for success on the one hand and the attitude toward compulsory labor or toward the maintenance of production norms at the assembly-line on the other simply cannot be

170

ignored. Purely sociological criticism all too often fails to take into account this crucial difference. Evaluated attitudes are, however, constitutive for these differences. Mark Twain was puzzled long ago why to gum up paper-bags was work, yet the climbing of Montblanc was sport.

In the third interpretation of the performance principle given by Marcuse, in which it is explained as a criterion of self-assertion, achievement in sports is most certainly included in the "performance principle." Everything said about "libidinally" hued and constituted activity would also be applicable here.

Before this explanation can be gone into a little more fully, however, it is necessary first to discuss (in view of the points of the general criticism of social critics of the "performance principle" in the professional field), how far this criticism applies to performance in sports. This criticism might be briefly summarized: The social-philosophical criticism of the professional "performance principle" is directed, firstly, against the compulsory character of the routine work which is extorted unilaterally from the worker contrary to his interests and abilities; secondly, against the non-attributability of the result of complex production processes, of a "performance," of an accomplished work to the person producing it; thirdly, against the lacking, but falsely claimed equality of opportunities in education and employment and, fourthly, against the inhumanity of a hypostasized perfect implementation of the "performance principle."

On the transferability of point 1 of this criticism what may be said is this: Achievement in sports is not as a rule (apart from extreme exceptions) extorted from the individuals under pressure; it corresponds to the maximum extent to the interests and abilities of the athlete.

On point 2: As a result success or performance as well as achievement in sports is still to be attributed exclusively to the individual as his own work--in contrast to the "performance on the assembly-line." Only the individual athlete can accomplish the achievement. The performance is unmistakably effected by a personal feat. National help in fostering and funding can facilitate it, but cannot be a substitute for it. Even if the rate of success of the performance decreases in comparison with that of better assisted competitors, the individual accountability for the performance is thereby not diminished, nor is its emotional content. Every attraction for the athlete himself, the effort to succeed, the pleasure in performance; and, the pride in achievement and the importance of all these for proving and confirming oneself cannot be simply argued away. They are psychic realities.

On point 3: The equality of opportunities in competitive sports is, indeed, also impeded by national and social promotional measures, but it is still more nearly achieved than in the professional "start in

171

life." This certainly applies not only to the participants from countries somewhat on an equal footing of fostering athletic improvement; this also applies to the already motivated and experienced sportsmen themselves, and not to all who could potentially take part in a competition. The points of criticism that were directed against the applicability of the performance principle in the professional sphere can, therefore, hardly be transferred to sports and achievement in sports--and, by the way, also not to professional work in general--but only to some specific forms--admittedly still deplorable ones--e.g., assembly-line work. (But there are initiatives underway to improve human conditions of factory work--and they should be supported intensively.) Not only emtoional preoccupation but also personal accountability and attributability are completely guaranteed in athletic achievement. Equality of opportunity is, within limits, relatively easier to achieve here than in any other social sphere.

The fourth point of the criticism, which was directed against the all-too-perfect implementation of the performance principle and against a total "achieving society," can likewise not be utilized as an argument against competitive sports as a social phenomenon. For the latter by no means requires a total "achieving society," even if, as a social segment, it is organized in restricted aspects in accordance with the criteria of achievement. Sports by no means requires that all other social spheres should be regulated and evaluated according to the criteria of performance nor that every single person has to be regarded only as an object of productiveness of achievements, even if an evaluation of the individual in his performance role prevails within the very disciplines relating to competitive sports.

Perhaps one could advance some more detailed arguments against the gross conception of athletics as the ideal model of the "achieving society" in general such as was advocated by Adam and v. Krockow.

Adam describes "the attitude towards achievement in sports as a model...for...the attitude to proficiency in general:" Advancement on the social scale as a result of an objective and impartial comparison of performance reconciles the initially seemingly antagonistic principles of equality and of differentiated assignment of ranks. In an ideal "achieving society," according to Adam, "all orders of precedence would be based on comparative performance." Absolute objectivity of comparison (especially of different kinds of performance) is impossible. But this objectivity can most nearly be achieved in a model manner in competitive sports (through measurement, contriving a decisive situation or counting successful attempts--less or hardly at all objectively through assessment of points and scores on the basis of subjective decisions). "The mechanism of self-affirmation" through one's own performance stabilizes, according to Adam, the "feeling of one's own value"--particularly in the overcoming of intentionally induced feelings of listlessness and obstacles in training for sports. In

172

athletics, moreover, the attitude toward achievement is trained in an exemplary manner and, in Adam's opinion, that is essential for the preservation of the species and for the balance of fortune of mankind in view of the problems of the growing population. While Adam analyzes the model of competitive sports more from a socio-pedagogic perspective, v. Krockow (1962, p. 58 ff., 52 ff.) goes in more for a sociological and socio-philosophical interpretation: "Athletics--a product of the industrial society"--v. Krockow expands this almost trivial sociological proposition to the philosophical one "that competitive sports... are the symbolically concentrated representation of the society's basic principles." It is in sport that "exactitude," "ideality," "objectivity," equality of opportunities, measurability and comparability, spectacularness and general intelligibility represent symbolically more clearly than anywhere else the principles of differentiation in performance (i.e., attribution of a social rank on the grounds of individual achievements); the same is, according to v. Krockow, true of the principle of competition and yet also of the equality of opportunities for success. "Performance, competition and equality. What makes modern sport so pregnant with symbolism and so fascinating is not at least the exactness, not to mention the ideality, with which it realizes these basic principles of the industrial society." (1972, p. 94). V. Krockow (Ibid. p. 96) even asserts: "Sport gives expression to the principles of the industrial society far better than the latter itself does:" The objectivity and also the transparency of the comparison of performances, which are nearly perfectly realized in sport, are not exhibited by anything like so completely and visibly in any of the other fields of the complex, almost unsurveyable industrial society. The achievements of the research-worker can only be assessed by experts, the celebrities of our publicity-conscious society create the illusion of achievements, often through acts of self-advertisement. Yet here--in sport--"the record jump is transmitted optically into every house, intelligible to everyone and measured three times over" (Ibid. p. 95).

Thus, we apparently have sport as the ideal-typical (purely idealized, trenchantly demonstrated) model of the so-called "achieving society." This model thesis seems attractive: It not only explains the fascination of sport and its stormy development parallel with the industrial society itself. It also enables one to understand the protest of the new social criticism, which criticizes the so-called performance principle and competitive sports jointly in a like manner. Moreover, this model thesis is compatible with the relative separation or "extraworldly demarcation" (v. Krockow) of the sphere of sport from the so-called vicissitudes of life, from the sphere of work. Model character and relative own-worldliness can very well go together.

On the other hand, this model thesis also encounters certain difficulties: What is too easily overlooked is the fact that the so-called "achieving society" is intrinsically a "success society," sometimes of sham achievements sold by means of publicity and of careers, all the more so because professional and social achievement can scarcely be attributed any longer to the individual alone: team, boom and system constitute the determinants of general social achievements. Somewhat exaggeratedly one might say: We no longer live in the idealized, publicly proclaimed "achieving society" but in a "success society:" The really personally accomplished achievement counts less in the acquiring of status than do the social effect of achievements, the success or even the semblance of achievement or of talent, or in certain cases the publicity given to alleged achievements (e.g., election successes). Publicity as a substitute for achievement? Is social success already proof of achievement? Certainly, this overall equating of publicity, success and achievement applies, if at all, primarily to representatives of the upper middle classes, to employees laden with responsibilities and promotion-seeking "performance men." For the lower classes the requirements of production are increasingly converted into standardized and routinized functions of supervision of standards, which do not allow the individual to stand out from the rest and to distinguish himself through his own efforts, for their main requirement seems to be, rather, the avoidance of acts of disruption and the adherence to average norms as far as possible without any loss due to friction. Whereas social climbers are more inclined to regard the attitude to performance from the point of view of ability to achieve social success, for members of the lower classes the required "performance orientation" seems to consist exclusively in the postulate of allocation and subordination to complex organizational processes with as little disruption as possible.

Ichheiser, as early as 1936 made a clear distinction between ability to perform and ability to succeed in his book Kritik des Erfolges (Criticism of Success). He also drew attention to the mechanism of deception whereby the Machiavellian exploitation of the ability to succeed and the concomitant, but mostly concealed violations of norms imperceptibly favor those who are already able to succeed or who are privileged, and he pointed out that this is not regarded as, let us say, a sign of plain good fortune but is considered by others (and by those concerned themselves) to be a personal achievement. The sociological requirements of the socio-psychological factors of all these variations of the "performance principle" have not yet been sufficiently examined. It is only in the most recent period that the psychological theory of attribution (Weiner and others) has been going more closely into these questions, in that it is examining the cognitive conditions under which particular types of personality attribute success to themselves as personal achievements or are more inclined to believe that they owe it to fortunate circumstances.

Are the above-mentioned deviations from the idealized "performance principle" the reason for the special fascination of athletics? Does achievement in sports still represent relatively purely, as it were, something which is no longer to be found in the assessment of professional and public achievement: The individual accountability and attributability, the "joyful" experience and "pleasure" in success, the fact that the possibility of deception and corruption does not exist as a rule, or else is subjected to strict controls and the absense of real dependence in the sense of submission to power ?

The new criticism of sport mostly relates the outlined character of sport (as a model for the ideal principles of an achieving society) exclusively or predominantly, to the so-called capitalist or late capitalist societies. This is undoubtedly a biased restriction as socialists industrial societies or, to put it better, state capitalist systems of society are even more dedicated to the raising of production norms and are inclined to make even more severe demands on the individual for the fulfillment of such norms. Naturally, that also applies to athletics in the socialist countries.

The social criticism of sport is not directed against every demand for achievement but only against the ideology of the achieving society which subordinates all other requirements to the raising of production and achievement and which is oriented to the assurance and creation of privileges of a class-conditioned kind: In particular, a striving for achievement that is motivated by the class struggle is expressly approved by the critics.

Admittedly, a total achieving society would be terrible: The competition of all against all in all activities--man preying upon man (homo homini lupus)--would make Hobbes' primordial vision come true. The "achieving society" is only a Utopian model which cannot be truly brought into existence, although in some areas, as in sport, it is one ideal orientational symbol among others and additional to other models for guidance. It can certainly only be applied to limited social spheres and also only in a restricted degree that would be ideal typical (in the sociological meaning of the word after Max Weber); in fact it applies exclusively to social spheres that are distinguished by their comparative competitiveness. It is certainly not desirable to judge a person as a whole solely by his performances in limited, social spheres, whether the latter relate to his profession or, say, to sport. Nor should all the members of a society be subjected to the necessity of achievement even in limited spheres. The "achieving society," which serves as a model in a good many respects, must not become the "compulsorily productive and achieving society," in every respect. A model like this one can only give limited guidelines for limited applicability conditions. Yet, it is true, that even our society still cannot dispense with certain constrictions of achievement for quite a long time. That, however, is another matter.

But science, art, and sport could be spheres of performance for individually differentiated possibilities of distinction, and they could be opportunities for enjoyable, libidinally motivated and hued (Marcuse) activities, which could be conducive to self-confirmation, social self-assertion and in this way to the stabilizing development of the personality. The pedagogical applications obviously are at hand. The younger Marx's anthropology of the creative, freely evolving human being, as displayed in the ideal image of the scientist and the engineer, is in every way also comparable with the ideal image of the role of the competitive athlete, whose free "self-chosen activity" and whose opportunity to fashion his performance freely and in a certain sense to reflect and unfold his personality therein ought not to be replaced by a thesis of compulsion for a perfect and excessive performance in competitive sport. That is by no means to deny that in a good many kinds of sports and disciplines which are especially subjected to public interest and public pressure one may discern tendencies of a quasi-moral public pressure on performance or the authoritarianism of a corporate dirigistic power and corresponding influences on athletes.

There is no doubt that the new criticism of sport is right in one respect: The concept of the "achieving society" as well as that of the so-called "performance principle" have hitherto been simply taken for granted and have not been more closely examined from the socio-philosophical point of view. This also leads to the partly grotesquely unworldly and excessively incisive black-and-white analysis of athletics. A hitherto non-existent philosophy of achievement would still have a lot of work to do here in respect of more precise distinctions, necessary differentiations and balanced judgments.

What becomes clear after this analysis is this: One cannot simplify the matter as the German writer Günter Grass does and just assert that the "collective performance principle" impels or compels the athletes as forcefully as it does people in the professional field and that "performance terror" and "compulsion by the object in question" ("Sachzwang") would prevent them from making their own decisions and determining their own actions. Apart from extreme cases which are not to be denied, the athlete identifies himself to a very great extent with his athletic achievements--especially those in training, which scarcely attract public attention. He finds pleasure in the fulfillment of tasks which demand of him all his energy subject to a calculated risk. He identifies himself completely with this subjectively and freely chosen attitude of his.

The thesis of compulsion can, therefore, only fall back on a thesis of manipulation: To the effect that the competitive sportsmen were, in fact, drilled through educational influences in early childhood into adopting the competitive attitude, which our culture positively prizes, and into internalizing the "achieving principle." Certainly, athletes are not more manipulated here than anyone else who has grown up in the Western industrial society. Surely almost all education tion, then, had to be regarded as manipulation--and nobody could then be called free, for everybody would be "manipulated" in every respect. Viewed empirically, manipulation could hardly be separated from education. In fact, merely relative freedom is identifiable by the fact

176

that the person who is already competent to judge responsibly subscribes to a decision, adopts it as his own, and even defends it. From the point of view of moral philosophy this must be accepted as his opinion, even if the decision to be defended should in some cases prove to be a pleasant illusion.

Obviously acute problems arise in the case of young adolescents who are not yet able to perceive and assess the problems of an excessive training for performance. Nowadays there are a good many disciplines, ranging from swimming to gymnastics, in which such an intensive regimen of training is required, even at the youthful age of 10-12 years, that manifestations of narrow-mindedness, regimentation and dependence on the authoritarian decisions of the parents or coach cannot be precluded in all cases. Nevertheless, the guiding aim in every case should be to avoid forcing even the child to act against his own will, but as often as possible to discuss critically with him (albeit in a preparatory manner) the intelligible problems of the training and gradually to develop his powers of discernment so that the child will later on be able to form his own, relatively independent opinions and to make his own decisions. A coach, too, must be prepared to point out the problems to an athlete and, in some cases, to advise him rather to choose another way of self-development if the sporting one seems to be too onerous to that boy or girl.

Quite apart from that, the achievement of the highest performance is scarcely possible if one does not completely identify oneself with the training and with the significance of this activity.

Self-determined motivation of performance (so far as it is relatively possible) is always preferable in every respect to extraneously-determined pressure to perform. Thus, the "democratic" style of coaching founded on the ideal of participatory decisions is by no means a Utopian fiction: It was already introduced and further developed in a good many kinds of team-sports quite a long time ago, especially with respect to the Olympic gold medal crews of the successful rowing coach, Karl Adam, although it ought to have been more difficult to guide a team towards this objective then, say, an athlete concerned with a single discipline. The possibility of practicing exemplarily "democratic" behavior in a small group of sportsmen shall not be gone into further here.

At any rate, it is clear that the mere system-stabilizing, compensatory function of sport and its alleged function to serve only as vehicle for the regeneration of the labor force, as well as the diverting manipulating and "de-politicizing" effect of athletics, cannot properly represent all the aspects of this complex social and psychosocial phenomenon, as the critics claim.

It is true that the star athletes are also regarded as representa-

177

tives of the nation, but this function is primarily projected onto them by public opinion. This does not, however, mean that they become just "mechanical medal-producers," "efficient muscle-machines," pampered beasts of top level performance and "reproduced symbols of the political and economic system" and nothing else. Not only are their psychic experience and the significance of sport for the development and the stabilization of their personality to be looked at in another light, but sport also acquires another meaning in its cultural-philosophical aspect: As a modern Heraclean-Promethean myth of daring, energetic action it embodies the dynamic character of the archetypal roles of the contest and of competitiveness in a symbolical manner resembling the way in which life was reflected for the ancient Greeks in some of their great classical dramas of fate. Yet this interpretation of competitive sport has still only been mentioned. It cannot be presented in detail here; an attempt has been made elsewhere (by the author in 1972) to indicate its main outlines.

The socio-philosophical discussion of sport and of the attitude towards achievement has only just begun. To extricate it from the mere polarization of thinking in black and white, of "pro and contra," is the task of a detailed analysis and criticism in the future. What is particularly noteworthy is the fact that the society, which regards itself as an "achieving society," does not possess any kind of elaborated, let alone well-founded, philosophy of the types of attitudes towards achievement. A wide field of activity remains open for bold philosophical theses and critical considerations.